Negotiating Diversity

Identity, Pluralism and Democracy

P.I.E. Peter Lang

Bruxelles Bern Berlin Frankfurt am Main New York Oxford Wien

Alain-G. Gagnon & José María Sauca (eds.)

Negotiating Diversity

Identity, Pluralism and Democracy

“Diversitas”
No. 18

Éditions scientifiques internationales
Brussels, 2014
1 avenue Maurice, B-1050 Brussels, Belgium
info@peterlang.com; www.peterlang.com

ISSN 2031-0331
ISBN 978-2-87574-171-4
D/2014/5678/58

Printed in Germany

CIP available from the British Library, GB and the Library of Congress, USA.

Bibliographic information published by "Die Deutsche Nationalbibliothek".

"Die Deutsche Nationalbibliothek" lists this publication in the "Deutsche National-bibliografie"; detailed bibliographic data is available on the Internet at <http://dnb.d-nb.de>.

Contents

Introduction

Alain-G. Gagnon & José María Sauca

This book on *Negotiating Diversity* builds on a research programme pertaining to Identity, Pluralism and Democracy that has been financed by the *Ministerio de Ciencia e Innovación de España* (DER 2009-12683) and the Canadian Social Sciences and Humanities Research Council and it is part of a larger joint initiative led by the Research Group on Plurinational Societies (Université du Québec à Montréal) and the Research Group on Democracy and Justice (Carlos III University of Madrid). Since 2007, members of our research groups have been in constant dialogue and have organized a series of scientific activities both in Madrid and Montreal. Our two research groups have teamed up in developing a scientific discourse that stresses concepts such as Culture, Identity, Diversity, Pluralism, Trust, Civil Society, Citizenship and Governance. Members of our research teams have not only shared conceptual tools but they have also taken a stand on many fronts including respect to deep diversity, strengthening democratic practices, and empowering political communities.

The last two decades have witnessed an increase of interest in the domains of identity politics, legal and constitutional pluralism as well as in the implementation of democratic practices in complex societies. This is why we decided to concentrate on those key issues to improve present-day political life.

Since the collapse of the Berlin Wall, we have experienced the emergence of new themes pertaining to cultural identity that brought to the fore not only religion, nationality, and gender but also historical trajectories, memory, migration, issues related to inclusion and exclusion and by extension citizenship. Minority and majority nations have been busy working on these fronts so as not to lose any ground, as if everything about these issues could reduced to a zero-sum game. In short, in addition to usual debates pertaining to community tensions and redistributive policies inspired by a theory of justice, there has emerged a field still to be plowed in the areas of recognition and empowerment.

Such political changes have led researchers to embark on a new journey and go beyond questions that are essentially descriptive and often times technical. Instead of examining qualitative dimensions linking political bodies, specialists have too often portrayed power relations from a quantitative perspective. Scholars have generally focused on who is best positioned to find a solution that would concern the entire country. Responses have generally favored the central state. Other times, authors have focused on the separation of powers between the executive, legislative and judiciary branches, failing to explore political dynamics between those powers or, in the cases of federal states, between orders of government.

Subsequent to an intense workshop, hosted in May 2010 by the Universidad Carlos III, we mandated conference speakers to write original contributions that took into account up-to-date materials and to cross-examine the literature. Contributions to this volume benefitted greatly from interactions with several professors involved in the conference. Many thanks to Xavier Arbos, Jesús Prieto de Pedro, Luis Rodríguez Abascal, Andrés de Francisco, Rainer Nickel, Francisco Colom, Carlos Thiebault Louis-André, José María Rosales, Maria José Fariñas and Alicia Cebada.

Colleagues took on the challenge and revisited their contributions with inspiration and drive. In addition to these original contributors, we invited Ramón Máiz (Universidade de Santiago de Compostela), Gérard Bouchard (Université du Québec à Chicoutimi) and Isabel Wences (Centro de Estudios Políticos y Constitucionales and Carlos III University of Madrid), three well-established scholars, to join this book project. These specialists study complex societies from three distinct vantage points, namely political philosophy, history, and political science, and innovate by providing an ambitious multi-dimensional approach to tackle issues of identity, pluralism and democracy.

The book is organized around four parts. In part I, Ramón Máiz and François Rocher explore political and social dynamics in plural societies and reflect on a series of normative issues that ought to be considered by political actors in the management of federal and non-federal societies. This is followed in Part II by studies conducted by Alain-G. Gagnon, José María Sauca and Jocelyn Maclure of a growing literature pertaining to governance, recognition and empowerment as it applies to countries experiencing tensions with respect to identity politics, majority/minority cultures and religion. In Part III, José Woehrling, Ascensión Elvira and Eduardo Ruiz team up in proposing an in-depth exploration of human rights, political rights and institutional pluralism in Europe and Canada with a special interest in the protection of rights and freedoms, the role of supranational bodies in upholding national and sub-national political rights as well as the evolving nature of self-determination from a human rights angle. In Part IV, Gérard Bouchard, Joxerramon Bengoetxea and Isabel Wences address a central concern in the politics of diversity by putting to test approaches founded on multiculturalism and interculturalism. Quebec, Catalonia and Scotland constitute relevant experiments for societies seeking to advance models of deep diversity in advanced liberal democracies.

In connection with this international initiative, it is worth pointing out some recent publications produced by our respective research teams that provide foundational elements to the present endeavour.

Members of the Research Group on Plurinational Societies (www.grsp.uqam.ca) have released several important studies among which is included *Multinational Democracies*[1] that provided theoretical and normative considerations for three structuring projects. In 2009, GRSP published an important volume entitled *Dominant Nationalism, Dominant Ethnicity*[2] in which contributors explain how nation-states proceed to impose their own nationalism and how minority nations resist or not or even renegotiate their place within a given state. A parallel endeavour led to the publication of *Contemporary Majority Nationalism*[3]. This book illustrates the extent to which minority nations do not have a monopoly over the incarnation of nationalism and that, often times, majority nations have advanced their own nationalist agenda through the implementation of targeted public policies. These two previous studies have led GRSP members to launch into a new project addressing trust and mistrust[4] between majority and minority nations that bring together European and Canadian scholars specializing on divided polities.

Similarly, members of the Research Group on Law and Justice (www.derechoyjusticia.net/en) have been working on pluralism in its different dimensions: cultural diversity, human rights, cosmopolitanism, religion, immigration, and gender. Their collectives works have focused on reinforcing civil society's ideals[5], on recovering historical memory[6] and on deepening trust and lawfulness[7]. As a result, researchers in the areas of

---

1 Gagnon, Alain-G. and James Tully (eds.), *Multinational Democracies*, Cambridge, Cambridge University Press, 2001.

2 Lecours, André and Geneviève Nootens (eds.), *Dominant Nationalism, Dominant Ethnicity. Identity, Federalism and Democracy*, Brussels, PIE Peter Lang, 2009.

3 Gagnon, Alain-G., André Lecours and Geneviève Nootens (eds.), *Contemporary Majority Nationalism*, Montreal, McGill-Queen's University Press, 2011.

4 Karmis, Dimitrios and François Rocher (eds.), *La dynamique confiance-méfiance dans les démocraties multinationales: le Canada en perspectives comparatives*, Québec, Les Presses de l'Université Laval, 2012.

5 Sauca, José María and Isabel Wences (eds.), *Lecturas de la sociedad civil. Un mapa contemporáneo de sus teorías*, Madrid, Trotta, 2007.

6 Pallín, José Antonio Martín and Rafael Escudero Alday (eds.), *Derecho y Memoria Histórica*, Madrid, Trotta, 2008; Alday, Rafael Escudero (ed.), *Diccionario de memoria histórica. Conceptos contra el olvido*, Madrid, Libros de la Catarata, 2011.

7 Mendieta, Manuel Villoria and Isabel Wences (eds.), *Cultura de la Legalidad: Instituciones, Procesos y Estructuras*, Madrid, Libros de la Catarata, 2009. See also

legal theories, political philosophy and international law have developed an interdisciplinary approach to diversity from different vantage points and especially exploring the impact of law on the social construction of identity.

Building on these political and juridical interpretations, this book seeks not only to synthesize and question current-day literature but to go beyond conventional approaches. It does so in three ways: first, by moving beyond the debates between communitarianism and liberalism through an in-depth interpretation of cultural and national diversity in the context of democratic multinational societies; second, by further sensitizing political and social actors in countries such as Canada and Spain, as well as the United Kingdom, Belgium and Switzerland, to the importance of both legal and constitutional implementation of diversity; and third, by advancing a theoretical stance that questions conventional wisdom and puts to the test dominant approaches in the field of comparative politics and law. Through these efforts, we will continue to advance a project based on an ongoing intellectual exchange within as well as across national settings.

As editors of this book, we are particularly grateful to all authors for their continued trust and support as well as to Olivier De Champlain and Thomas Lafontaine (UQAM) as well as Kyle Ritchie (Concordia University) who have assisted us in the last phase of the book preparation.

Eunomía. Revista en Cultura de la Legalidad (eunomia.tirant.com) edited by the *Program on Culture of Lawfulness* (www.trust-cm.net).

Part I

Divided Societies and Federalism

CHAPTER 1

The Normative Theory of Federalism and the Idea of Nation

Ramón MÁIZ

Professor, Department of Political Sciences and Public Administration, Universidade de Santiago de Compostela

"[...] not merely a nation but a teeming nation of nations"

Walt Whitman, *Leaves of Grass*, Preface

Introduction: Is a Normative Theory of Federalism Necessary Today?

The *positive theory* of federalism of an empirical and comparative orientation has flowered in recent years, to a great extent driven by neo-institutionalist perspectives and those of political economy[1]. But this has not, however, been a mere development and perfecting of traditional analyses, facilitated by the availability of new models and theoretical tools, nor of the appearance, up until recently non-existent, of reliable empirical evidence. If we compare it with the works of classic political thinkers – Althusius, Madison, Tocqueville –, or with the most recent works of economics (*Public choice theory*, *Welfare economics*, etc.), current theory on federalism introduces, with a rare unanimity, at least two ruptures of significant importance. First, it is formulated from an

1 Inman, Robert and Daniel Rubinfeld, "Rethinking federalism", *Journal of Economic Perspectives*, vol. 11, nº 4, 1997, pp. 43-64; Máiz, Ramón and Pablo Beramendi, "La segunda generación de análisis institucionales del federalismo" in Pablo Beramendi and Ramón Máiz, *Federalismo y Neoinstitucionalismo*, Zona Abierta, nº 104-105, 2003, pp. 1-16; Rodden, Jonathan, "The Dilemma of Fiscal Federalism: Grants and Fiscal performance around the World", *American Political Science Review*, vol. 46, nº 3, 2002, pp. 670-687; Colino Cámara, César, *Teoría y realidad del cambio institucional de las federaciones*. Ph.D. dissertation, Madrid, UNED, 2005; Wibbels, Erik, "Madison in Baghdad?: Decentralization and Federalism in Comparative Politics", *Annual Review of Political Science*, vol. 9, 2006, pp. 165-188.

openly positivist perspective and with an empirical orientation, indebted to the most recent social sciences, and with the intention of being on the margin of the traditional normative issues which monopolized earlier debate. Thus, the extravagant assumptions underlying initial economic analyses (complete information on voters, on the responsibility of each level of government, on the mobility of business and individuals, on the fidelity of local politicians to the preferences of the electorate, etc.) have been subject to an empirical scrutiny from which they have not come out well[2]. Secondly, it is much more circumspect, if not openly reticent in arguing that there are unlimited universal and decontextualized benefits to the federal form of organization of the state for the quality of democracy or the functioning of the economy. The prospective beneficial effects of federation (overcoming problems of aggregating preferences through local spheres of decision making and control) are not considered ubiquitous and universal, but rather dependent on the concurrence of a good number of contextual variables, such as: a greater or lesser clear distinction between levels of government, broad economic powers of regional governments, general control over the market on the part of the central government, the internalization of costs by each level of government, etc[3].

However, does the confirmation that federation is not the panacea that some of the classical thinkers dreamt of and the excellent quality of a good part of the disillusioned recent literature obviate the need for a substantive normative theory of federalism? The general thesis defended here is that this new body of positive empirical studies does not exhaust or resolve by itself the need for a substantive *normative theory*. In other words, the question of the *stability* of federal systems, specific to positive empirical theory, does not by itself provide an answer to the question regarding the *justice* of the political-territorial organization of complex societies[4]. It is still imperative to have a theory capable of providing answers to questions such as: is the federal organization of states desirable, should multinational states have a federal structure, upon what normative principles should political-territorial organization be constructed, how do we evaluate different federal designs, etc. In the end, the evaluation of the

---

2 Rodden, Jonathan and Susan Rose-Ackerman, "Does Federalism Preserve Markets?", *Virginia Law Review*, vol. 83, 1987, pp. 1521-1572; Treisman, Daniel, *The Architecture of Government: Rethinking Political Decentralization*, Cambridge, Cambridge University Press, 2007.

3 Gagnon, Alain-G., "The moral foundations of asymmetrical federalism: a normative exploration of the case of Quebec and Canada" in Alain-G. Gagnon and James Tully (eds.), *Multinational Democracies*, Cambridge, Cambridge University Press, 2001.

4 Gagnon, Alain-G., "The moral foundations of asymmetrical federalism: a normative exploration of the case of Quebec and Canada" in Alain-G. Gagnon and James Tully (eds.), *Multinational Democracies*, Cambridge, Cambridge University Press, 2001.

institutional performance of a federation or a federal mechanism depends on the normative perspective of the evaluator. Moreover "empirical study in the social sciences is meaningless if it has no normative import"[5]. And this cannot be at the mercy of mere subjective opinions, *ad hoc* normative assumptions or unchallenged pre-judgments; rather, it requires the systematic and substantive elaboration of an argument through internally consistent propositions that can be debated and tested.

To do this, however, the rigid separation between *federalism* and *federation* must be overcome[6]; in other words, between the theories, movements and ideologies that propose federal formulas and solutions; and those existing federal political systems, in debt to historically specific ideas, traditions, contexts, experiences and trajectories. In short, an autonomous argument that federation is the institutional architecture of a *just political* order is essential, or in other words, an argument for the moral political value of the federal principle[7]. In fact, today more than ever, from Canada to Iraq, from Spain to India, major issues related to peace, liberty, equality and political stability are found to be connected to the design of federations. And this design requires normative, as much as positive empirical debate, on values, institutional solutions and federal public policies.

In this sense, the reintroduction of politics and institutions, as well as the endogeneity of the latter, in the most recent federalist theory of an empirical and comparative orientation, opens up the possibility for a fruitful dialogue between both positive/empirical and normative dimensions, which can only be beneficial to both. In any case, although autonomous and substantive, a normative theory of federalism, to respond to the problems and challenges of modern democracies, cannot be distant from the developments of positive/empirical theory, nor the advances made in the comparative politics of federalism. On the contrary, endowed with a new modesty regarding its pretensions, it should be, in the strictest sense, contextualist and developed, overcoming the endemic tradition of "separate tables" within the broad discipline of political science.

In this vein, the arguments discussed in this text revolve around two basic assertions. (1) Federalism constitutes not only a specific institutional

---

5 Gerring, John and Joshua Yesnowitz, "A Normative Turn in Political Science?", *Polity*, vol. 38, nº 1, 2006, pp. 101-133.

6 King, Preston, *Federalism and Federation*, London, Croom Helm, 1982; Elazar, Daniel, *Exploring Federalism*, Tuscaloosa, Alabama University Press, 1987; Burgess, Michael, *Comparative Federalism*, London, Routledge, 2006.

7 Gagnon, Alain-G. and Charles Gibbs, "The Normative Basis of Asymmetrical Federalism" in Robert Agranoff (ed.), *Accommodating Diversity: Asymmetry in Federal States*, Baden-Baden, Nomos, 1999, p. 76.

formula based on political decentralization and accommodation, but an authentic political philosophy, a normative model of democracy based on the covenant and the pact, *clearly differentiated from liberalism and communitarianism and in debt to the republican tradition*; and (2) federalism has, however, historically developed into two well differentiated traditions: one, monist, derived from the North American experience of the federal construction of a nation-state, which has been predominant (national federalism); and the other pluralist, minoritarian, focused on reconciling different and overlapping local, regional and national identities (plurinational federalism)[8].

However, to take into account the synthesis of self-government and shared government, of unity and diversity, of the federation as a conceptual design of a state of states; as well as, in contrast to the premises of the nation-state, the coexistence of different nations within one state, requires at least two tasks. These are (1) the reformulation in a democratic-republican key of the classic, organic and pre-political concept of the nation; and (2) the construction of a normative theory of federal democracy.

1. The Veil of Ignorance and the Federal Principle of Autonomy (Self-Government)

Surprisingly, the canonical theory of liberalism is absolutely silent regarding the normative questions raised by the federal principle. As Norman recently pointed out, "our 'mentors' – philosophers like Rawls, Nozick, and Dworkin – were silent on the mysteries of federalism"[9]. In effect, as is well-known, Rawls thought that the institutional details of a just society should only be addressed subsequent to when the parties in the original position have established the principles of justice, in other words, when the veil of ignorance is partially lifted and the basic details of

8 Caminal, Miquel, *El federalismo pluralista*. Barcelona, Paidós, 2002; Hueglin, Thomas, "Federalism at the Crossroads: Old meanings, New Significance", *Canadian Journal of Political Science*, vol. 36, nº 2, 2003; Karmis, Dimitrios and Wayne Norman, *Theories of Federalism: A Reader*, London, Palgrave, 2005; Máiz, Ramón, "Democracy, Federalism, and Nationalism in Multinational States" in Ramón Máiz and William Safran, *Identity and Territorial Autonomy in Plural Societies*, London, Frank Cass, 2000; Requejo, Ferran, *Multinational federalism and Value Pluralism*, London, Routledge, 2005; Norman, Wayne, *Negotiating Nationalism*, Oxford, Oxford University Press, 2006; Gagnon, Alain-G., *Au-delà de la nation unificatrice: Plaidoyer pour le fédéralisme multinational*, Barcelona, Institut d'Estudis Autonòmics, 2007; Gagnon, Alain-G. and Raffaele Iacovino, *Federalism, Citizenship, and Quebec*, Toronto, University of Toronto Press, 2007; Beaud, Olivier, *Théorie de la Fédération*, Paris, Presses universitaires de France, 2007.

9 Norman, *op. cit.*, p. 80.

society, public opinion and the political culture are revealed. In addition, the principles of justice are applied to the basic structure and should not reflect specific characteristics of society or of concrete political systems. Only once we begin to lift the veil of ignorance and we see the general characteristics of our society (cultural pluralism, for example) can we design institutions which attend to these specific characteristics, with these institutions always following the patterns marked by the principles of justice that we have previously chosen in the original position, under the veil of institutional ignorance.

Among other things, this model implies that the parties in the original position accept *de facto*: (1) the foundational irrelevance of a multilevel distribution of political power in contrast to claims of sovereignty; and (2) the consideration of the borders of the state as natural, as given and existing in "perpetuity"[10]. The first assumption means that the plurality of political wills and constitutional and legislative spheres within a state of states constitutes a minor detail, irrelevant in any case for the theory of justice. The second implies that the really existing political community (nation-state) and with it the overlapping of political and cultural dimensions are considered prior to justice and equity, and the question of the homogeneity and unity of the *demos* (a question, i.e. who are the people of the state, which is in reality, from the point of view of logic, prior) is considered normatively resolved by factual history. The naturalist fallacy which the model incurs, deducing from the "is" (construction of a nation-state) a "should be" (the equation state = nation) thus incorporates, without any elaboration, a postulate which conceals from us *ab initio* the possibility of a normative foundation on the basis of unity and diversity.

It should be noted that these premises lead to a self-evident and undisputed corollary: the *unitary national state* is the model taken as the basis for the theory of justice. And this is true in a dual sense, first, as the theory considers – contradicting without any explanations the North American constitutional tradition – that the federal dimension of the republic, its character as a "compound republic", lacks foundational importance in regards to principles. And secondly, the overlapping of political and cultural borders is taken for granted in the theory – in this case following the constitutional-nationalist tradition of the US of "centralized federalism"[11] – and the interpretation of the *national state* in a monistic manner as *nation-state* is considered as self-evident. This position is, of course, common to all egalitarian liberalism[12].

---

10 Rawls, John, *Political Liberalism*, New York, Columbia University Press, 1993, p. 278.

11 Riker, William, *The Development of American Federalism*, Boston, Kluwer, 1987.

12 Dworkin, Ronald, *A Matter of Principle*, Cambridge, Harvard University Press, 1985.

The result is that the decisive dimension of the "compound republic" (Madison), of a state of states, of the articulation of self-government and shared government, the overcoming of the concept of sovereignty – as a means (1) to construct democracy in states of wide territorial dimensions, in addition to (2) providing innovative "republican remedies for republican diseases" – is elided in the foundations of a theory which aspires to provide the normative guidelines for a just political order. Based on the "veil of ignorance" *federalism* is irrelevant as the *federation* is considered to be an institutional peculiarity of second order, derived from specific historical circumstances, its theoretical nature discarded in a radical way by implicitly postulating that it should not enter into the principles of justice or the basic structure of society. Only once the principles of justice are established is it the moment to partially lift the veil of ignorance and begin to descend the ladder of abstraction to take into account the particularities of public culture and the economy of each society in designing institutions. For Rawls, only in the subsequent descent toward the level of constitutional and legislative law would the federal dimension perhaps appear as relevant[13].

However, to take state borders as given and to exclude the plurality of centres from which political will generates as an element of the basic structure, the theory of Rawls and, in general, egalitarian liberalism, adopt two extremely problematic hypotheses. These hypotheses are (1) in contrast to Madison, the hypothesis of sovereignty, the concept of the sovereign state endowed with a single (or ultimate or original) centre from which political power emanates; and (2) in contrast to Calhoun, (apart from other considerations) the hypothesis of the nation-state, the coincidence between cultural and political borders, the theoretical impossibility that the *demos* can consist in a plurality *of demoi*, and the existence of minority communities that can suffer the eventual oppression or exclusion under the state's protection of the majority community. A theory of justice which implicitly begins from these propositions is a seriously flawed theory on its own terms, as it assumes postulates in debt not *to principles of justice* that are object of an eventual overlapping consensus, but rather to a *particular idea of the good*; namely, the imposition by the state of a comprehensive doctrine (majority nationalism) regarding one of the most disputed problems among contemporary states and international society.

One would think that in the contemporary republican perspective we would find the normative-theoretical elaboration of federalism absent

---

13 King, Loren, "The federal structure of a Republic of Reasons", *Political Theory*, vol. 33, nº 5, 2005, pp. 629-653.

from liberalism[14]. But that is not at all the case. A good example of this is a work of reference in contemporary republican theory: *Republicanism* by Philip Pettit. In responding to the question, how can the state be organized so that state interference is not arbitrary, in other words, to address republican forms of constitutionalism and democracy, Pettit postulates three fundamental conditions. These are (1) the rule of law, (2) separation of powers, (3) that the law be relatively resistant to the will of the majority. However, only in regards to the second condition is "the decentralization of power that is achieved by having a federal system" admitted as one of the measures possible. He concludes with an empirical observation that leaves the federal dimension of republicanism without theoretical elaboration. "It is no accident that republicans have been traditionally in favour of federations"[15]. What is more, in addressing the deliberative dimension of republicanism, the absolute necessity that people "be able to coalesce around group identities that were previously suppressed"[16] is recognized, but this observation referring to individuals and groups is not complemented by a reinterpretation of what institutional framework is capable of reconciling unity and diversity and plurality with overlapping identities, which are principal elements of federalism. It is also striking, regarding the same issue, that Mauricio Viroli, for example, could write a book called *For Love of Country*, and despite its subject, "an essay on patriotism and nationalism", there is no mention of the federal republican tradition[17].

Nevertheless, the contribution of federalism to a theory of the *just society*[18] is of normative foundational importance that goes far beyond the mere adjectival and *ad hoc* concretion that is conceded in the last phases, that is, far from the "constitutional essentials" of the Rawls' model or its condition as one mere "measure" among many others that institutionalize the republic (Pettit). There are important reasons to assume that federalism should be inscribed into the very heart of the normative theory of democracy.

To begin with, we should remember the centrality of federalism in the republicanism of Kant. In effect, even though this is often neglected in

14 Maynor, John, *Republicanism in the modern world*, Cambridge, Polity, 2003; Laborde, Cécile and John Maynor, *Republicanism and Political Theory*, London, Blackwell, 2008.

15 Pettit, Philip, *Republicanism*, Barcelona, Paidós, p. 234.

16 *Ibid.*, p. 254.

17 Viroli, Maurizio, *For Love of Country*, Oxford, Oxford University Press, 1995.

18 LaSelva, Samuel, *Moral Foundations of Canadian Federalism. Paradoxes, Achievements, and Tragedies of Nationhood*, Montréal-Kingston, McGill-Queen's University Press, 1996; Gagnon, *Au-delà de la nation unificatrice : Plaidoyer pour le fédéralisme multinational*, *op. cit.*

many classic and modern interpretations[19], it is not only (1) the separation of legislative and executive powers as well as (2) the form of representative government that constitute the factors that are the core of Kantian republicanism. In the "second definitive article" of *Zum ewigen Frieden* (*For a Perpetual Peace*), written in 1795, he adds a third factor; namely: "The law of nations shall be *founded on* a federation of free states". In this way "a federation of nations (*Völkerbund*) which, however, should not be an worldwide, international state (*Völkerstaat*)" is postulated as an alternative scenario to war[20]. Certainly, in Kant we find an ambiguous use of the concept of federalism, sometimes as federation and other times as confederation, induced by his classic concept of sovereignty as absolute power (unlimited and indivisible). Yet, in his view, in contrast to Madison, only under sovereignty can the full condition of a state of law be reached and hence the ultimate aspiration of a *world republic*[21]. However, the ultimate objective of a *world republic* (*Weltrepublik*), of a state of nations (*Civitas Gentium*) is, first, too distant for a world of states that rejects *in hipótesis* what is just *in tesis*. The federation of states raises the normative horizon of the possible. "The practicability (objective reality) of this idea of federation (*Idee der Föderalität*), which should gradually spread to all states and thus lead to perpetual peace, can be proved"[22].

Secondly, and above all, the Kantian world republic is shaped as a federal republic. Thus, in the work, *Die Religión innerhalb der Grenzen der blossen Vernunft* of 1793, he postulates a "state of perpetual peace based on a league of peoples, a world republic (*auf einen Völkerbund als Weltrepublik gegründeten*)"[23]. This is, then, the so often neglected key. *Völkerbund als Weltrepublick* is, in other words, a world federal republic, *a Staatenverein Republik freir verbünder Völker* (a republic of free federated nations), not only as an alternative to the "monstrosity" (*Ungeheuer*) of a world monarchy, but also to a unitary world republic in debt to a single sovereignty. Thus, Kant's view was that, given the regulative nature of the idea of reason, a unitary world republic would

---

19 Vlachos, Georges, *Fédéralisme et raison d'État dans la pensée internationale de Fichte*, Paris, Pedone, 1948; Bobbio, Norberto, *Diritto e Stato nel pensiero di Emanuele Kant*, Torino, Giappichelli, 1969; Philonenko, Alexis, *Théorie et praxis dans la pensée morale et politique de Kant et Fichte en 1793*, Paris, Vrin, 1968.

20 Kant, Immanuel, *Zum ewigen Frieden Akademie Textausgabe*, vol. VIII, Berlin, De Gruyter, 1968 [1795], p. 354.

21 Pogge, Thomas, "Kant's Vision, Europe, and a Global Federation" in Luigi Caranti (ed.), *Kant's Perpetual Peace. New Interpretative Essays*, Rome, Luiss University Press, 2006, pp. 75-98.

22 Kant, *op. cit.*, p. 356.

23 Kant, Immanuel, *Die Religion innehalb der Grenzen der blossen Vernunft Akademie Textausgabe*, vol. VI, Berlin, De Gruyter, 1968 [1793], p. 34.

only ever constitute the horizon of an always unfinished trend, while he conceived of an international order for a new plural and cooperative world.

Third, the federal association (*föderative Vereinigung*) not only constitutes for Kant a superior alternative to that of a world government, the fusion of states under one power which will control all the others, but is also preferable from the point of view of the very diversity of humanity[24]. Nature, as he says in the first Supplement of *For a Perpetual Peace*, "wisely separates nations (*weislich die Völker trennt*)". "She employs two means to separate peoples and to prevent them from mixing: differences of language and of religion" (*der Verschiedenheit der Sprachen und der Religionen*)[25]. In short, what is a source of war and conflict, the plurality of states and nations, is also for the philosopher from Königsberg/Kaliningrad a source for the possibility of international accommodation and political cooperation. The departure from the state of war, conceived as a natural state of states and the emergence into a new cooperative, federal order, does not mean the construction of a new world sovereign. And in this way is indicated, in the very core of Kantian political philosophy, the incipient normative republican foundation of the pluralist federal synthesis of self-government plus shared government, and unity in diversity.

We see then, some of the basic components of the major normative contribution of federalism to republican democracy. First, federalism makes it possible to overcome the interpretation of the state based on the concept of *sovereignty*, this image that is so difficult to let go of, referring to the necessary existence of a single monopolizing centre of political power which governs the whole society. In contrast, federalism unequivocally points to a system of multilevel government, integrated by diverse spheres of decision-making and control. It posits the necessity to overcome the unilaterally vertical, hierarchical and pyramidal vision of the state[26], replacing it with a more *horizontal* version, with political power exercised and coordinated from diverse spheres.

Federation consists of a *state of states* based on an integrated, cohesive and supportive institutional design. In other words, strictly speaking the *federation is not a state*, but a new kind of polity. Federalism involves the substantive and guaranteed self-government of the federated

---

24 Marini, Giuliano, *La filosofia cosmopolitita di Kant*, Rome, Laterza, 2007.

25 Kant, *Die Religion innehalb der Grenzen der blossen Vernunft Akademie Textausgabe*, *op. cit.*, pp. 366-367.

26 Friedrich, Carl Joachim, *Trends of Federalism in Theory and Practice*, New York, Praeger, 1968; Elazar, *op. cit.*; Ostrom, Vincent, *American Federalism*, San Francisco, ICS Press, 1991.

units; but also requires, and to no small degree, co-government, shared government and the involvement and participation of the federated units in the general political will of the federation. But even more so, federalism links autonomy with solidarity and difference with cohesion in an indivisible manner. Said in another way, the two Rawlsian principles of justice, reformulated in a territorial key, become inseparable: the *liberty* of federated communities with inter-territorial *equality*. Thus, the loyalty to the federation and its correlate, respect for the self-government of the federated states, constitutes only one decisive dimension of the constitutional loyalty which is the cement of egalitarian liberalism, of a social and democratic state of law. Federalism could have as its emblem, with greater legitimacy than any other political system, the celebrated republican triad: liberty, equality and fraternity. In contrast, as the Spanish federalist Pi I Margall wrote many years ago, "a centralized republic is a monarchy in disguise with a Phrygian cap".

A federal state is, by definition, a *constitutional state without a sovereign*, considering that all its powers are distributed in different spheres, as well as being limited and subject to the constitution of the federation and the constitutions/statutes of its member states. And under the principle of *competence*, which substitutes for that of *hierarchy*, there is no place for any supposedly originating or unlimited power of the state or of the federated states. As Harold Laski recognized, from a liberal pluralist perspective, a federal system implies not only "the abandonment of the sovereign state", but that "because it abandons the principle of sovereignty, it abandons the principle of hierarchy also"[27].

Focus on the reach of all this. Federalism opposes itself to the theory of unitary popular sovereignty (*demos*) as constituting power and constitution in singular (Sieyès), with the theory of a pluralist popular sovereignty (*demoi*) as constituting power(s) and compound constitution(s) (Madison), or better still, a complex *Multilevel Constitution*, *Verfassungsverbund* (Pernice). Federalism, in short, unequivocally points to "*demoicracy*"[28], or more specifically, the presence of a *plural and shared constituting power* among various (co)constituting subjects: the people of the federation and the singular peoples of each community or federated state. The guarantee of a guardian of the constitution in service to its effective superiority, in other words, a constitutional court – to the effects that interest us here, constitutionally protected territorial autonomy – leads to, moreover, at

27 Laski, Harold, *A Grammar of Politics*, London, Allen & Unwin, 1925, p. 271.

28 Nicolaidis, Kalypso, "The Federal Vision Beyond the Federal State" in Kalypso Nicolaidis and Robert Howse (eds.), *The Federal Vision. Legitimacy and Levels of Governance in the United States and The European Union*, Oxford, Oxford University Press, 2001, pp. 439-482.

least two additional normative requirements. They are (1) on the one hand, the territorially sensitive integration of the constitutional court, and (2) the indeclinable participation of federated units in the reform of the federal constitution.

The federal state adds to the horizontal division of powers between the legislative, judicial and executive, an additional division, also horizontal of constituting and constituted powers, like a state of states[29]. The latter redounds in a democratizing complexity of self-governing scenarios, facilitating the articulation of differentiated preferences and a political richness which the existence of subsystems of parties reflecting those preferences entails. It even permits the manifestation of diverse intensities of preferences, based on the participation in different elections (general, regional or local). It facilitates, in short, the widest experimentation and, in the best republican tradition, it multiplies the accessibility to and the scenarios for political participation and encourages greater accountability in public policy and different institutional solutions to problems of equality and welfare.

But in addition, federalism, in debt to the idea of a pact between communities to carry out a common project, cannot be represented normatively as an institutionally crystallized structure[30]. Connected, as we have seen, by definition to the idea of limited power, to a constitution, but also to the idea of multilevel government and the pact, it is configured as an open *process* of interaction between institutional actors, which reaches successive states of equilibrium due to the forces generated by the experience of self-government and the challenges that changing internal and external contexts raise. What from the perspective of positive theory could be seen as indetermination, openness to successive renegotiations of the pact and incentives for eventual opportunistic behaviour on the part of the actors (who make the very rules of the game a matter of debate), is from a normative perspective a possibility to reach successive equilibriums in response to changing contexts and needs; which converts the federation in, to use the now classic terminology of Elazar, "a continuing seminar in governance"[31]. In addition, it situates a principal dimension for a normative theory of federalism in a republican key in the foreground, namely, the overcoming of the horizon of a mere aggregation of interests and attention on the political production of preferences through deliberation[32].

---

29 Bednar, Jenna, "Federalism: Unstable by Design", Paper proposed to the *American Political Science Association* meeting, Atlanta, 1999; Bednar, Jenna, *The Robust Federation: Principles of Design*, New York, Cambridge University Press, 2009.

30 Friedrich, *op. cit.*

31 Elazar, *op. cit.*, p. 85.

32 Máiz, Ramón,"Deliberación e inclusión en la democracia republicana", *Revista Española de Investigaciones Sociológicas*, vol. 113, nº 6, 2006, pp. 11-48.

However, a basic element in the renegotiation of equilibriums and the common commitment upon which federation is grounded is the *redistribution* of economic resources following universal criteria of solidarity between different communities, which also permits the development of self-government and cohesion. In the classic terms of Althussius: "the symbiotes pledge themselves each to the other, by explicit or tacit agreement, to mutual communication of whatever is useful and necessary for the harmonious exercise of social life"[33]. Thus, federalism, as mentioned earlier, as a state of states, contains a principal dimension of equality, of solidarity, an unwavering calling for equality between territories as the foundation for the justness of the collective project. Inter-territorial solidarity, financial self-sufficiency for the exercise of self-government, but also, and to no less extent, fiscal co-responsibility, all constitute basic pillars of its structure and institutional dynamics which possess a necessary cooperative dimension, although not exclusively (as federalism always contains a certain competitiveness between the different units to stimulate better service to the citizenry). In this way, federalism, and we must insist on this, integrates not only liberty in its dimension of collective self-government, but also social equality, cohesion and the strengthening of the welfare state. Do not all these arguments then, reinforcing the republican dimension of democracy, oblige us to revise the foundational, in short, normative exclusion of federalism from the basic principles of egalitarian liberal/republican theory of a just society?

But in addition, pluralist federalism permits us to overcome the seemingly so self-evident but unsustainable equation: *state = nation*, implicitly or explicitly assumed both in the postulate that each state must contain only one nation, as in the idea that each nation, by the very fact of being one, in inexorable logic, must possess its own independent state. Plurinational federalism permits the practice of not only non-violent accommodation, but also an accommodation which is mutually beneficial and culturally, economically and politically enriching for the various nations within the same state, reaching consensus on a common project for co-existence. Thus, non-monistic federalism allows for ("unity in diversity") the recognition of the profound moral significance that national identities have for individuals, which provide the cultural context through which politics is accessed[34], but does so without subscribing to the theses and the language of communitarianism and nationalism (the unilateral right of self-determination, secession, etc.), offering an alternative of

33 Altusio, Juan, *Política*, Madrid, CEPC, 1990 [1603], p. 15.

34 Kymlicka, Will, *Finding Our Way. Rethinking Ethnocultural Relations in Canada*, Toronto, Oxford University Press, 1998.

accommodation and co-existence through union ("self-government and shared government")[35].

Plurinational federalism becomes then a possible meeting place which, without aspiring to "resolve" or "finish with" nationalisms of the state or against the state, but contributing a differentiated solution of meaningful self-government and willingness to co-govern, can provide a sufficiently attractive sphere for negotiation and pacting with multiple winners. This is in contrast to other alternatives that are much more costly, conflictive and impoverishing (monistic federalism, confederation, secession), if not directly unviable in cultural, political, social and economic terms.

Thus, federalism democratically institutionalizes ideological, cultural and territorial pluralism, not only as an irremediable *fact*, but as an authentic political-constitutional value which, more than being preserved as a given, has to be constructed and shaped among all. Plurinational federalism does not reify identities, it does not institutionally bind them so that they become closed or exclusive, it does not isolate different communities, in short, *it is not multi-communitarianism*. Rather, it conceives identities, both as a whole and individually, as democratic processes of participation, internal diversity and deliberation, and reorients them so that they are, without eroding their differences, compatible and overlapping. Federalism involves an active recognition, but always from the perspective of an encounter, a negotiation and pact (*foedus*), of supportive co-involvement from positions of difference. As a result, federalism is completely distant from closed identities, forever crystallized in the past. Its normative core cannot be reduced to the passive recognition of the organic, cultural or historical basis of its constituent units. Rather, it is built around collective decisions and political compromise, democratically generated through pluralism, participation and deliberation. In view of everything mentioned there are no major theoretical reasons for the foundational exclusion of federal *autonomy* from a hypothetical discussion of the principles of justice in the original position; nor are there reasons to negate the contextual value, giving sense to democracy, of the different cultures for many citizens in plurinational federalism[36].

---

35 Máiz, "Democracy, Federalism, and Nationalism in Multinational States", *op. cit.*; Caminal, *op. cit.*; Requejo, *op. cit.*

36 Kymlicka, Will, "Territorial Boundaries: A Liberal Egalitarian Perspective" in David Miller and Solail Hashmi, *Boundaries and Justice*, Princeton, Princeton University Press, 2001; Gagnon, "The moral foundations of asymmetrical federalism: a normative exploration of the case of Quebec and Canada", *op. cit.*; Gagnon and Iacovino, *op. cit.*; Norman, *Negotiating Nationalism*, *op. cit.*; King, *op. cit.*

2. A Federal-Republican Concept of Nation

The fact that federalism consists in coordination which generates mutual benefits to its different parts – the federal state and federated states – and is not a contract based on the coercive authority of a sovereign power, leaves open, especially in the case of plurinational states, the question of the ties that should link the members of the federation. Federal coordination requires a difficult balance between self-government and shared government, between autonomy and a common project, and each of these dual aspects are equally unrenounceable.

This implies that we should carefully consider, from the perspective of the normative theory that concerns us here, the connections that ground the institutions. The key question is whether, discarding the centrality of *negative* incentives (the sanctioning power of an external sovereign power) as the foundation for the stability of the federation, *selective positive* incentives are enough, that is, the common interest that emerges from both the common benefit of the union, as well as the greater comparative cost of coordinating on another solution (secession, for example, or centralism). Or in other words, to formulate it in Rawlsian concepts: Is a mere *modus vivendi* sufficient as the basis for interfederal trust? The latter, following Rawls' criteria[37], would indicate that the parts of the federation possess established objectives and interests and the union rests exclusively on the fact that the foundational federal agreement represents a mere equilibrium. That is, the terms of the agreement for federation under the *modus vivendi* are formulated in such a way that their unilateral violation does not generate any benefits for any of the parts. However, the *modus vivendi* is based on a conception of zero-sum power, or what is the same; each one of the parts is always ready to pursue its preferences to the cost of others, and the stability of the system thus depends on contingent circumstances that maintain a fortuitous confluence of interest. This results in an endogenous instability. A state, for example, that has been the beneficiary for a period of time of federation, could become disloyal the moment in which it becomes a net contributor to the federation; or a state might oppose the consolidation of a "hyper solidarity" in favour of other communities that would negatively impact its own level of wealth, etc. In short, the ties that bind a federation as mere *modus vivendi*, the interests, the benefits or, possibly the loss of profits from the "exit" and "voice" options, do not resolve the problem of self-enforcing coordination and are prone to endemic instability. It seems necessary then, that *expressive* incentives somehow be added to the selective incentives, such as ties of a cultural or moral type, in other words, of an identitary nature. These will reinforce the federation as a plural and ethical community, endowed

---

37 Rawls, *op. cit.*, p. 245.

with certain empathy and even, in a wider sense, moral obligations which emanate from a commitment toward a future of shared co-existence.

However, does this lead us to a normative conception of federation from the opposite angle, that is, a *comprehensive* vision of federalism? Must citizens of the federation share the same idea of the *common good*, the same set of shared substantive values? Does federalism require a sort of communitarism as its foundation? Must we say that all federations must be grounded, in a monistic manner, on only one nation? The response to these questions has to be negative, as stability cannot be achieved at the price of the oppression that results from a communitarist or nationalist vision of the state, imposed from above on all the units of the federation, these possessing very different interests, desires and representations. And this is so for two reasons: (1) because federalism implies *autonomy*, in other words, the possibility of making political and differentiated decisions and not merely administrative or executive decisions. This means that different majorities in the states produce different preferences (and even intensity of preferences) and have their own political will not only in regards to public policies but also regarding the global vision of the state. In addition, there exist diverse manners to evaluate and understand the federation, a product of history, language, culture, social structure, identities, ideologies and interests. And (2), because above all, plurinational federalism implies a diversity of cultures, traditions, institutions, identities, etc. that are incompatible, by normative definition, with a comprehensive or monistic and ultimately nationalist vision of the state of the federation. Everything, therefore, points to the federation requiring ties that involve a common bond more tenuous than those of a comprehensive moral doctrine, but certainly more solid than a mere circumstantial interest, the relative mutual indifference of a *modus vivendi*.

Does the political philosophy of federation demand a normative horizon of *overlapping consensus* between the states?[38] Certainly, it cannot be denied that the Rawlsian model of liberal-egalitarian legitimacy is of interest here: political power exercised based on a constitution, which would be expected to be accepted by all citizens as free and equal (and autonomous), rational and reasonable individuals, based on principles and ideals acceptable to common human reason. And this affecting not only the constitutional essentials, but also the legislative issues that develop from it: a political conception of federal justice whose acceptance on the part of the citizenry and the states can reasonably be expected to serve as the basis for public reason.

[38] Norman, Wayne, "Les points faibles du modèle nationaliste libéral" in Guy Laforest *et al.* (eds.), *Libéralismes et Nationalismes*, Québec, Les Presses de l'Université Laval, 1995, pp. 81-93.

However, this leads us in an inexorable manner, from the perspective of normative theory, to postulating federalism as a political-moral conception that involves not only constitutional formulas, but also principles, values and political virtues (a federal culture), through which those principles are expressed and materialize in public life. This, in turn, obliges us, for the moment, to broaden Rawls' two restrictive principles of justice, *liberty* and *equality*, with the federal principle of *autonomy*, formulated from a federal perspective of fraternity. This latter principle being, in effect, closely tied to the first two, as the collective dimension of the very liberty of autonomous political wills and equality rooted in the solidarity and equity of federalism.

Of course, *overlapping consensus* contributes greater stability in contrast to a *modus vivendi*, dependent on favourable circumstances and the circumstantial correlation of forces which, in the case of change, can convert the very rules of the game into an object of political competition. It is also in contrast to the *comprehensive* vision that state nationalism would involve (but not "republican patriotism", as there is no civic nationalism that does not contain inevitable ethno-cultural components), which imposes a single, hegemonic vision of the community based on the culture, myths, narrative and interests of the majority community in the territorial sphere concerned. But the optic of *overlapping consensus* is, nonetheless, ultimately not sufficient grounds for a plurinational federalism, taking into account its excessively procedural and scarcely republican nature. Among other reasons this is because: (1) it greatly reduces the public agenda, the public uses of reason, apart from the identitarian, cultural and political demands of the citizenry; (2) it is formulated as an ideal reasoning process which imposes hyper-rational standards on the citizenry, ignoring the world of feeling which resides within language and the political value of the mythic-symbolic dimension; and (3) it is designed, as we have seen, taking the coincidence between political and cultural borders for granted, based on an uncritical acceptance of the nation-state.

In contrast, the configuration of national identity itself, its plural or singular character, its self-comprehension of us/them, the familiar/unfamiliar, its future as a space of assimilation or multiculturality, its relation with other eventual nations within the state, etc., are all issues that cannot be dealt with limited by the inheritance of tradition, resolved once and for all in a past perceived by successive generations as an essential, pristine and untouchable origin, not permitting any re-evaluation. In contrast, all of this must be the central object of open public discussion. Thus, *deliberation*[39] constitutes a principal dimension, not reducible to a

[39] Máiz, Ramón, "On Deliberation: Rethinking Democracy as Politics Itself" in Ernest Gellner (ed.), *Liberalism in Modern Times*, London, Central European University

mere overlapping consensus, in the democratic construction of nations, even more so plural and contested nations. *Nation as deliberation* means that the selection of myths and symbols which are never neutral, the historical narrative fraught with decisions regarding what is remembered and what is forgotten, the language differences protected by institutions and statutes regarding minority languages, the relationship with other nations and the state, the definition of the common future regarding economic and social aims and in relation to justice, these and other issues have to explicitly enter into the public sphere so they can be debated by majority and minority groups. The placement of deliberation in the very heart of the nation, far from meaning a transformation of a *philosophical* argument over autonomy and the cultural context of decision making into a *political* argument[40], *also* subjects the very cultural core of the nation to public debate, to criticism and to the exercise of autonomy and *judgment*. For this reason, the radical interpretations of the *modus vivendi* such as the comprehensive vision of communitarianism or the overlapping consensus of liberalism are insufficient. If it is about how to make it possible for the diversity of individuals and territorial communities of late-modern societies to coexist in common institutions which everyone accepts as legitimate[41], a normative theory of pluralist federalism of a clear republican spirit gains in importance in contrast to both state nationalisms and the "mosaic" of (multi)communitarianisms.

At the same time, something fundamental which escapes from the Rawlsian model of overlapping consensus as the normative horizon of federalism is the extent of the republican thesis (and if federalism loses its republican theoretical substance it becomes a caricature of itself) that the same thing happens to collective rights to self-government and cultural-territorial autonomy as to individual rights; namely, that the recipients of said rights can only acquire complete autonomy as a group to the extent that they understand themselves as authors of the decisions and institutions that regulate them. For this reason the political autonomy of nations as a collective right is closely linked to the construction of a public space which, through participation and deliberation, issues of interest, cultural and linguistic difference and the relevant criteria for recognition and self-government are elucidated. In other words, we must remind ourselves once again, that it is necessary to incorporate within the logic of self-government what Habermas referred to as an "internal conceptual

Press, 1996, pp. 145-173; Máiz, Ramón, "Nation and Deliberation" in Ramón Máiz and Ferran Requejo, *Democracy, Nationalism and Multiculturalism*, London, Routledge, 2005, pp. 58-79.

40 Benhabib, Seyla, *The Claims of Culture*, Princeton, Princeton University Press, 2002.

41 Gray, John, *Las dos caras del liberalismo*, Barcelona, Paidós, 2001, p. 141.

connection" (*begrifflich notwendingen Zusammenhang*) between rights and democracy[42]. This is because there is not, to the effects that interest us here, a plurinational pact of accommodation within a federation without a demanding democracy, which converts its beneficiaries into its authors, the protagonists of agreement through representation, pluralism, participation and deliberation. It is difficult to formulate the collective rights to self-government and cultural autonomy in a non-paternalistic manner if the very members of the nation do not previously articulate and ground their aspirations, objectives, demands and the scope of their own unavoidably plural national culture in public discussions exempt from coercion.

However, federalism formulated as a space *for* deliberation is not intended to overcome the conflict of multi-nationality through a yearning for a chimerical harmonious society or an earthly "communion of saints"; nor to eliminate from the political scene the comprehensive nationalist visions of the state or those against the state, their demands for self-determination and secession, nor deny their legitimacy as long as they comply with the normative requirements of pluralist democracy. Rather, its intent is the very opposite, to facilitate a normative focus which prescribes spheres for negotiation and deliberation, multilateral and bilateral spaces of convergence and divergence or conflict, in the interest of achieving a partial compromise and a common project for coexistence that can be revised based on the genesis of compatible and overlapping identities.

But the normative horizon of this *deliberative federal nation*, which aspires to construct a plural community, superimposed on internal communities, requires *internal* effects to construct its own logic. These are not only the abandonment of a state nationalism (national federalism) for being too all-embracing, but also the overcoming of a merely institutionalist and legalist reading of *federation* in an exclusively state key, for being excessively in debt to an insufficient and proceduralist *overlapping consensus*. It requires, in short, the reformulation of the very idea of the nation, the abandonment of organic nationalism, the liquidation of the idea – both impossible and unjustifiable – of a homogeneous and monocultural community, in favour of a theory of the nation as a *plural* political community, integrated by majorities and minorities which share, debate and renegotiate a common project at the same time as they construct it. In other words, it demands a *non-nationalist conception of the nation*, towards a concept which is, (1) *political* (not culturalist, although culture plays more than a minor role) and (2) *pluralist* (not monistic, both as a totality and within each of the communities). *A federalist concept of the nation*, or to be more precise, beyond the false dichotomy ethnic/civic

42 Habermas, Jürgen, *Faktizität und Geltung*, Frankfurt, Suhrkamp, 1996, p. 142.

nationalism, *a republican-federalist concept of the nation*, is one which reconciles unity and diversity in all of the federal and sub federal units, as a correlate to the synthesis of self-government and shared government, and illuminates overlapping identities. This is something unthinkable both for the principle of the nation-state, as for the principle of nationalities; and both from centralist Jacobin nationalism as well as from the national federalism of the "compound Republic" – an authentic people of peoples in their dimension as *nation of nations*.

Conclusion: Toward a Normative Theory of Federalism

The obvious shortcomings of liberal egalitarian and republican theory and its underlying (and poorly reasoned) normative dimension in many analyses of the positive/empirical theory of federalism demand the elaboration of a complementary substantive normative theory of federalism. A theory, in other words, which serves as a prescriptive guide in the orientation of political debate and which helps in the formulation of empirical questions, as well as providing a basis for the evaluation of really existing federations. A normative theory which, as a result of what has been discussed here, must address at minimum the following core arguments:

1. Federalism is not only an institutional model for the territorial organization of power – the federation – but also a *political theory of justice*, a normative political theory grounded in accommodation, trust and pact (*fides/foedus*) and based on the articulation of three basic principles: liberty, equality and *autonomy*.
2. Federalism is, above all, an alternative to the theory of sovereignty; being, in reality, a theory of a *constitutional state without a sovereign*, based upon all powers being distributed in different spheres and limited by the constitution. The basic federal mechanism is multilateral coordination between different political units through endogenous genesis and moral and political mechanisms of self-reinforcement (solidarity, recognition, loyalty).
3. In addition, federalism, in its pluralist formulation is a normative alternative to the national state and it basic equation (state = nation) as it is a *multinational federalism*, in other words, a pluralist and deliberative setting which aspires to accommodate various nations within the same polity. To this end it involves multilateral and bilateral spheres of negotiation and deliberation, a complex system of parties (parties at the state and non-state levels) and overlapping and compatible identities. But it must also reformulate a non-nationalist (plural and inclusive) concept of the nation (as *a pluralist nation of pluralist nations*).

4. The core of federalism is the integration and articulation of *self-government* and *shared government*, through the principle of competence against that of hierarchy. And its normative model is a horizontal matrix of the distribution and interaction of powers, a polycentric structure, networked not pyramidal, of political power.
5. Federalism is a *process*, more than a definitive and stitched together structure, of interaction among actors and institutions that reaches successive states of equilibrium. As such it has no closure, by definition being contestable and open to periodic renegotiations. Thus, federalism consists of a *federalization* with rhythms, requirements and experiences specific to each community, through interaction based on broad autonomy and joint involvement in the interest of a general political will.
6. Federalism points to a system of multilevel government based on the principles of subsidiarity and proportionality, with recognition and autonomy constitutionally guaranteed (through *complex constitutions*: a constitution of the federation and that of member states, which safeguard the different spaces of self-government). This multi-centric system opens upward toward complex units (for example, the European Union in a federalist interpretation) or downward toward more elemental units, reinforcing local democratic government (new municipalism).

The normative theory of federalism, in short, goes beyond the theoretical framework of egalitarian liberalism and requires the widening of the model of *republican democracy.* This contributes a fundamental vector of normative evaluation: a concept of strong citizenship, through the complex overlapping of the dimensions of liberty and equality, and articulating in an innovative manner, with the end of constructing both a state of states and a nation of nations, the classic principles of representation, deliberation and inclusion. But, all of this necessitates rethinking from a republican perspective, not only *the state* but also *the nation* itself beyond the false ethnic/civic dichotomy. In the same way that we cannot postulate republicanism as a total rupture, as a sort of world apart with respect to liberalism (or socialism); nor should we abandon the political uses of the nation to its communitarist and organic-nationalist variants.

CHAPTER 2

The Federal Ideal

Empirical and Normative Explorations

François ROCHER

Professor, School of Political Studies, University of Ottawa

The literature on Canadian federalism is characterized by two particular phenomena. First, Quebec Francophone scholars have, in large measure, attempted to illustrate that the spirit which marked the adoption of a federated state in Canada has been betrayed. Federal initiatives are invariably judged by these authors to be contrary to the initial division of powers. Conversely, scholars from English Canada have dealt with more pragmatic questions. Their approach to political institutions has been influenced by three dominant questions. On one hand, they have studied the links between federalism and democracy. On the second hand, they have explored the capacity of governments to develop public policies responsive to the needs of their citizens. Finally, they have focused on federalism as a way to manage Canada's diversity and reduce tensions by giving territorially concentrated minorities control of institutions which would allow them to protect and promote their distinctive features. In this presentation, I would like to argue that a third perspective has been absent from the reflections on federalism in Canada in the sense that the principles and normative dimensions of federalism are rarely discussed, at least compared to studies on federalism's political and institutional dimensions.

The modes of representation of federalism and its ideals have not solicited much attention. Without suggesting that the idea of federalism should determine its practice, it is important to recognize that representations are crucial bases for the evaluations that we make.

1. Federation, Federalism, Federal Society: From Organizational Principle to Normative Model

Federalism is foremost conceived of as a mode or principle of institutional organization. However, the concept of federalism also refers to the principle, the idea and the belief upon which the federal system is built.

The taking into account of the normative dimensions of federalism carries with it practical consequences that are important to mention before we start. The notion of federalism refers to both the collection of federal institutions and the collection of principles which must precede the putting into place of these institutions. In this regard, the analysis of federalism cannot only pay attention to the organization of power. Rather, it requires a detour for the exploration of ideas, representations, values and ideals. What philosopher Daniel Weinstock calls the normative justification of federalism consists of examining the desirability of the values that a federal system of government allows to be realized. This justification contrasts with another justification, which is purely instrumental, in which the choice of a federal system is only the fruit of a calculation of the advantages to be obtained and the relations of forces which are present. It is also a question of attitude.

The power of a central structure is not and should not be absolute. Rather, it must co-exist with the autonomy of federated entities. The recognition of autonomy must be substantial enough to permit groups participating in a federation to manage their own affairs with the means at their disposal. In summary, it is not the majority who governs the minorities, but the minorities who are self-governing. The federation organizes this heterogeneity and does not oblige the "minorities" to bow to demands defined by the general government. The sharing of powers guarantees the autonomy both of the federated entities and the general government. It presupposes that federated entities are exempt from all guardianship by and hierarchal links with the general government. The notion of non-subordination comes from this conception of a lack of guardianship and, thus, liberty within the areas where the federated government is presumed to be autonomous.

The autonomy and the multiplicity of powers within the federated governments and the general state should be balanced by the necessity to establish reciprocal contacts. The federation organizes this solidarity through common institutions. The imperative of autonomy is tied to the requirement of cooperation and participation.

Further, federated communities should be conscious of the fact that the decisions that they make, even within their own sphere of autonomy, could affect the other communities constitutive of the federal space. This interdependence obliges the putting in place of mechanisms to ensure dialogue and cooperation among the federated communities (horizontality) and between the federated communities and the general government (verticality).

Federalism calls for a collective transformation of societal consciousness. For Elazar, "the first step is a shift of minds of men from thinking statist to thinking federal. Once begun, the possibility for combining various arrangements of different degrees of scope and intensity has wide limits". Thus, for the federal experiment to function well, it is required that the different federal components (states, groups, collectivities) abandon the idea that a concentration of power constitutes the best way to govern. In other words, a federal culture has to be valorized, promoted and respected. Federalism, like all other forms of government, constitutes a response to the values present in societies characterized by diversity and pluralism. While federalism cannot be reduced to bargaining, its study should include that of the negotiation process. Societies claiming to be federal can call upon a diversity of political arrangements but these must reflect the diversity out of which the society is constituted. Therefore, while the political act which directs a society towards the federal style of organization could be guided by economic or military considerations, or is the result of a "reasonable marriage" to use Maurice Lamontagne's expression, the ultimate success of federalism depends on the correlation which exists between governmental structures and social consensus. Thus, the management of territorially defined social cleavages – whether of an ethnic, cultural, linguistic or religious nature – becomes a major preoccupation.

* *
*

These general institutional and normative considerations allow us to put into focus four aspects that will illuminate our path to understanding the evolution of the federal idea in Canada. First, in a federal state, structures and attitudes are closely connected. There must be a level of congruence between the mode of organization and societal values.

Second, the presence of several orders of autonomous governments, and more generally a federal culture, implies both a double loyalty and a shared identity. Loyalty expressed towards the general state, which coordinates solidarity, is as important as the reinforcement of the autonomy of the constitutive groups of a federation.

Third, the federal order, which encompasses a multiplicity of powers which are both autonomous and interdependent, cannot be definitive. It is important to mention that the federation evolves not only because it is exposed to internal conflicts, but because it permits the expression and affirmation of such internal conflicts.

Fourth, the significance accorded to normative principles in relation to institutional arrangements underlines the importance of the function of legitimacy. Federal legitimacy is, in large measure, dependent upon the capacity to reflect normative principles. Moreover, federal legitimacy is reinforced by the necessary linkage between the presence of a federal culture and the institutions which nourish it. The absence of either a federal culture or the institutions to sustain that culture could only plunge the federal political regime into a profound crisis. This crisis would not take the form of disagreements over certain choices but the fundamental questioning of the conditions which allow the continuance of the federal political community.

2. The Evolution of the Canadian Political System or the Negation of the Federal Ideal

It is my argument that the contemporary representations of federalism have been consistently articulated for several decades. In Quebec, the dominant understanding of federalism and federal institutions has its origins in the Tremblay Report, named for the president of the Quebec provincial government's Royal Commission on Constitutional Problems, published in 1956. Since then, while evidently being adapted for particular political conjunctures, the Quebec-Canada debate has taken place almost exclusively within the argumentative framework set out in the report. Similarly, English Canadian literature on federalism, as well as the practice of federalism by the general government, follows the argumentation advanced by the Rowell-Sirois Commission, named for co-presidents of the Report of the *Royal Commission on Dominion-Provincial Relations*, which published its report in 1940.

These two documents have shaped the manner in which intergovernmental relations and citizen-state relations are understood in Canada. The reasoning that we find in these reports has nurtured the way in which political actors and intellectuals have understood the evolution of the Canadian federal system and have interpreted the key events, such as the putting into place of the Canadian welfare state; the constitutional debate which culminated in the repatriation of the Constitution of Canada, which included a Charter of Rights and Freedoms and an amending formula; the saga of the Meech and Charlottetown Accords; the creation of NAFTA (inspired by the recommendations of the Macdonald Commission); and more generally, the diminishing role of the general government which paralleled the increasing power of the provinces. The representations of federalism contained in the Rowell-Sirois and Tremblay reports, as well as the understanding that flows from these reports, do not respect the ideal and normative federal project articulated within the above triptychs that have as their central element the twin notions of autonomy and interdependence. The dominant understanding of the English Canadian literature on federalism pays no heed to the notion of autonomy in favor of the notion of efficiency, while Quebec Francophone scholars and the practices of the Quebec provincial government have not adequately taken into account the notion of interdependence. If the institutional problems concerning the functioning of the federal system which are raised in the literature are often pertinent, the understanding of such problems is embedded in a mode of thought which leaves little place for a federal conception of the nature of relations that should characterize a federation.

2.1 A Double Obsession: Pact and Autonomy

The work on the evolution of federalism emanating from Francophone Quebec emphasizes the Canadian federal regime's invariably centralizing character and desires the rehabilitation of the original federative idea. This interpretation must recognize the fact that the political regime put in place in 1867 was not completely federal and, in fact, subordinated the provinces to the general government. The political regime of 1867 did not respect the principle of autonomy of the provinces nor did it permit the provinces to participate in the decisions taken by the general government. Essentially, the above interpretation follows the principal arguments of the Tremblay Commission and adapts them to contemporary realities.

The definition of federalism for the authors of the Tremblay Report was explicitly inspired by the classic works of Albert Dicey, Kenneth C. Wheare and Georges Burdeau. The emphasis is placed on both the balancing of unity and pluralism, and the presence of two orders of equal and co-coordinated governments. The regional governments have the mission to protect the particular interests of their political communities. The Tremblay Commission insisted that the actions of each order of government should be limited to its proper sphere of jurisdiction, within which it has independence *vis-à-vis* the other order of government. The principle of non-subordination thus occupied a place of privilege within the structure of federal institutions. Non-subordination was even presented as the "first and general idea of the regime, which applies to all authentically federal states".

The question of the origins of the political system is central because it determines the way in which the federation is evaluated and its evolution judged. The reading of the *BNA Act* of 1867 by the Tremblay Commission illustrates the clash of two tendencies: the unitary spirit embodied by

John A. Macdonald and the federal spirit articulated by those who wanted provinces to have real autonomy and sovereignty.

The spirit of the federation rests on the implicit recognition of the equal treatment of two national peoples as associates and partners, each possessing rights regarding and ensuring the survival of their group within the Canadian union.

While the Tremblay Commission's report is almost entirely devoted to the philosophical, historical, judicial and institutional justification of the principle of provincial autonomy (and therefore the principles of heterogeneity and non-subordination), it devotes only six pages to the matter of how the principle of interdependence should be materialized. The issue of the coordination of policies, which is nonetheless essential to respecting federal principles, merits only superficial consideration in the Commission's report.

This imbalance constitutes no less than the distortion of the federal ideal, a distortion which subsequently had a profound influence on the way political discourse was articulated around the question of the Quebec-Canada dynamic.

For Quebec governments, the Quebec-Canada dynamic is illustrated through several concepts: attachment to the principle of autonomy, respect for and the expansion of provincial jurisdiction, achieving a distinct status, and asymmetrical federalism. The position of Quebec governments (and the majority of intellectuals) is not one of holding back Quebec. Rather, the position of Quebec governments aims at the construction and legitimatization of a "national" political space which corresponds to the proclaimed and proven particularities by which Quebec defines itself as a "complete society". It is remarkable to note that this construction has taken place, both at the discursive level and concerning Quebec-Canada state relations, on the basis of the non-participation of Quebec in the building of the Canadian political community. In other words, Quebec's relationship with the rest of Canada is primarily utilitarian (Premier Robert Bourassa spoke of a "profitable federalism").

2.2 A Double Preoccupation: Performance and Legitimacy

The interpretation of the federal regime within English Canadian literature emphasizes the transition from a highly centralized system, in which the general government could intervene in provincial jurisdiction using declaratory powers of reservation and disallowance, to one of the most decentralized federations in the world. The narrative is generally that the recourse to unitary mechanisms has diminished over time to the point where the power of disallowance has not been exercised since

1943. Responding to the demands of the provinces, including Ontario, the JCPC in London rendered several decisions which contributed to the "federalization" of the Canadian political regime through the forcing of the general government to respect the original division of powers. Therefore, the authority of the provinces was confirmed and their subordination to the general government was reduced.

Ultimately, the growth of the Canadian state made the compartmentalized model of federalism obsolete. The increase in the size of the Canadian state was accompanied by an interpretation of the federal regime which aimed less at accommodating its constitutive communities and more at a "pragmatic" approach to the sharing of jurisdictions. Postwar federalism was characterized by a dense overlapping of jurisdictions, an interdependence of policies and a greater level of intergovernmental competition. Thus, several mechanisms of "intergovernmental collaboration" were put into place though the increased practice of executive federalism.

In summary, federalism within English Canadian literature is presented first, foremost and above all as a *formula* or an *arrangement* relative to the exercise of power. Viewed through the lens of functionality, the overall evaluation of the Canadian political regime is generally positive despite the inevitable tensions it creates.

On the whole, the criteria used to evaluate the evolution of the Canadian political regime make little reference to the dimensions pertaining to the normative federal project. Richard Simeon remarked that recent studies have mostly emphasized the analysis of the efficiency of public policies. The value judgments contained in these studies are not concerned with notions of autonomy or interdependence but with the themes of democracy and access to the exercise of power, social justice, equality and, only secondarily, with the accommodation of the constitutive communities (Quebec and First Nations).

This mode of understanding Canadian federalism with its insistence on efficiency, transparency, legitimacy and, more specifically, the capacity to deepen democracy is not new. Already in 1940, the Rowell-Sirois Report displayed a political discourse in which the concepts of efficiency, rationalization, (fiscal) equity between the two "orders" of government, constitutional flexibility and national unity occupied a central place. Indeed, the quest for efficiency and the rebalancing of federal-provincial relations was at the heart of the mandate of the Rowell-Sirois Commission. However, since the publication of the report, observers have noted the absence of deep reflection on the underlying principles of the Canadian federal regime. Nonetheless, similar to the Tremblay Commission, the Rowell-Sirois Commission played a determining role in the understanding of federalism throughout Canada.

The general philosophy of the Commission attempts to legitimize a more functional approach to the federal regime. Thus, the principle of provincial autonomy was never directly questioned in areas of health, social assistance and education. In the same vein, the centralization of powers was never favoured in order to respect regional particularities.

The novelty of the approach put forth by the Rowell-Sirois Report was not in its search for a new division of powers which would favour the general government, but its argument for the decompartmentalization of federalism. In this respect, the notion of interdependence is well represented in the Report.

This change in perspective permitted the Canadian federation to gradually transform itself without having to make numerous formal modifications to the Constitution. Inter-governmentalism, presented as the vector of flexibility[1], became the principal preoccupation of elites and political analysts in Canada.

Further, the judgments and opinions of the Supreme of Court of Canada have also shifted towards emphasizing functionality over principles.

It is clear that the return of the compact or *covenant* thesis becomes increasingly less likely as the Canadian political community consolidates itself. According to the new principles which have accompanied the re-founding of Canada, such as the primacy of individual rights as guaranteed by the Charter and the formal equality of the provinces entrenched by the amending formula of the Constitution, the demands formulated by the "federalist" political elites in Quebec are incompatible with the modern representation of the pan-Canadian civic republican nation. For Cairns, only this new type of Canadian nationalism could correspond to the new constitutional foundations of the Canadian federation.

What remains of the normative federal political project as defined by the literature? Honestly, very little. The principles of autonomy, non-subordination and heterogeneity are contradictory to the managerial approach that has gradually taken over since the work of the Rowell-Sirois Commission emphasized notions of efficiency, performance and formal equality in 1940. Even the normative principle of interdependence, which arises from the multiple mechanisms of federal-provincial collaboration, only seeks participation as part of the quest for efficiency.

Conclusion

This analysis invites us to re-visit the terms on which the debates and analyses of Canadian federalism rest. The interpretative frameworks have

[1] Wheare, Kenneth C., *Federal Government* (4th ed.), London, Oxford University Press, 1963, p. 227.

evolved very little over time. In the case of Quebec, the dominant way of understanding the Quebec-Canada dynamic is based upon the work of the Tremblay Commission which took place over a half a century ago. Similarly, the preoccupations which animate English Canadian literature on federalism have their roots in the work of the Rowell-Sirois Commission whose mandate was defined in 1937. Perhaps, it is time suggest a small paradigmatic revolution.

Part II

Recognition and Empowerment

CHAPTER 3

Empowerment through Different Means

Nationalism and Federalism in the Canadian Context

Alain-G. GAGNON

Canada Research Chair in Quebec and Canadian Studies, Department of Political Science, UQAM

In a world that is said to be post-nationalist and post-sovereign, why do nations said to be without states get so much attention? The golden age of nation-states is said by several authors to be over, but this is far from meaning that nations and national identities have lost their relevance and power to mobilize. To the contrary, far from having lost their appeal and importance, national communities remain key actors in current-day politics. In this chapter, I will be focusing on two main dimensions. First, I will be discussing why nations are still relevant actors in the struggle against unfair practices in a world led by neo-liberal practices and second, I will be advancing the argument that multinational federalism could provide major instruments to institutionalize a fairer representation of political claims in complex political settings. The argument that will be developed here is that the optimal way to bring communities together and to develop trust in such settings is through a policy of empowerment of communities rather than through the imposition of a strategy that would consist in constraining minority nations in their desire to assert themselves.

Pierre Elliott Trudeau has been both a strong advocate of federalism and Canadian nationalism and has expressed during his life-time a firm opposition to separatism. Here is a revealing quote from Trudeau that gets to the heart of his political thought and constituted the cornerstone of his approach to politics:

> One way of offsetting the appeal of separatism is by investing tremendous amounts of time, energy, and money in nationalism, *at the federal level*. A national image must be created that will have such an appeal as to make any image of a separatist group unattractive. Resources must be diverted into

> such things as national flags, anthems, education, arts councils, broadcasting corporations, film boards; the territory must be bound together by a network of railways, highways, airlines. [...] the whole citizenry must be made to feel that it is only within the framework of the federal state that their language, culture, institutions, sacred traditions, and standards of living can be protected from external attack and internal strife[1].

Trudeau's argument was that, especially in cases of pluriethnic and multinational states, a pan-nationalism would be the best option to advance in order to avoid what he portrayed as a slippery slope toward secession. In this chapter, I will proceed in three steps with a view to exploring the concept of empowerment and conciliation under the ambit of two distinct domains: nationalism and federalism. First, let's turn our attention toward the idea that nationalism could offer a fertile ground to advance fairer public policies in a multinational liberal context. Quebec-Canada dynamics will be at the very heart of this essay and will constitute a central building block for a series of reflections on the management of deep diversity in multinational federations.

1. Empowerment through Nationalist Mobilization

Sociologist Marc Renaud wrote a useful summary of the social and economic conditions prevailing in the 1960s in Quebec. At the time, francophone Quebeckers represented 80% of the population of the province and owned 50% of the enterprises, but controlled barely 15% of the value added in the industrial sector[2]. In short, francophones controlled the least profitable sectors of the economy, those sectors being, first and foremost, agriculture, and to a much lesser degree, retail trade, services, and construction. Let me quote an excerpt from Renaud's account:

> [...] quite a few French Canadians had the formal training enabling them to fulfill top managerial, professional, and technical jobs in the economy and, after the educational reforms of the mid-1960s, their number considerably increased. In effect a new middle class was born [...]. This new middle class is, in essence, different from Quebec's old middle class and traditional elites whose power and status derived above all from their position vis-à-vis the religious order.
>
> In the early 1960s, this new middle class was confronted with a private economy quite incapable of generating new job outlets and quite inhospitable to certified French-Canadian skills. The expansion of the state in this context came as a miracle. It provided job outlets to university – and technically

1 Trudeau, Pierre Elliott, *Trudeau and the French Canadians*, Toronto, Macmillan, 1968, p. 193.

2 Renaud, Marc, "Quebec New Middle Class in Search of Social Hegemony" in Alain-G. Gagnon (ed.), *Quebec: State and Society*, Scarborough, Methuen, 1984, p. 160.

trained French Canadians, thus securing the survival of that class within Quebec[3].

The implementation of such overwhelming changes helped to give Quebec's state actors legitimacy as they were viewed as being responsible for the upward mobility of francophone Quebeckers. In turn, state nationalism was advanced as the main mechanism for transforming economic and political conditions, and for providing francophone Quebeckers with equal job opportunities. The task was gargantuan considering that, in 1959, fewer than fifty specialists in the human and social sciences (including economists, urban planners and social workers) were employed by the Quebec government, and that almost a third of all public sector employees had less than five years of formal education. At the same time, more than half of the public sector employees worked in the administration of justice, highways, Hydro-Québec, or the Liquor Commission[4]. It is in this context that the Parent commission in the area of education was set up to bring about a major reform.

The 1961 commission was set up to bring the key field of education under state control. Its report, tabled in 1966, found that the state

> must see to social and economic progress, provide for the general welfare, protect the community, correct injustice, help the weak. In view of this, it may be said that the modern state can no longer leave a part of its people in ignorance without jeopardizing the progress and peace of society and without complicity in inequities which it has a mission to redress. Thus it is obligated to provide, directly or indirectly, for the education of all, and this is one of its essential functions, of which it will never again be able to divest itself[5].

The work of the Parent commission corresponds to a period in Quebec politics when state nationalism was also on the ascent in public consciousness. For many Francophone Quebeckers the only way for them to reverse the power structure was to call upon the state to tame forces of private capital.

Most francophone Quebecers also saw state nationalism as a potent instrument for advancing democratic practices, for developing solidarity and social cohesion, for attenuating discrimination, for increasing social inclusion, for stimulating public investment, for advancing privatization or for undermining liberal economic practices. Within this context, I would

3 *Ibid.*, p. 169.

4 Brooks, Stephen and Alain-G. Gagnon, *Social Scientists and Politics in Canada: Between Clerisy and Vanguard*, Montreal and Kingston, McGill-Queen's University Press, 1988.

5 *Report of the Royal Commission of Inquiry on Education in the Province of Quebec*, Quebec City, Department of Education, Pierre de Marois Printer, 1966, pp. 13-14.

submit that all political parties within the Quebec National Assembly have defended, from the 1960s onwards, some form of state nationalism.

Francophone Quebecers have been spared from the dark side of nationalism; instead they have focused on its potential for a transformative and emancipative politics. I remember very well the unfettered excitement of Québécois youth when René Lévesque was first elected Premier on 15 November 1976. There was a feeling in the air that things had begun to change for the better. A sense of confidence had been imprinted in the public consciousness.

Let's clarify the Québécois enthusiasm for state nationalism. To be clear, nationalism is a polysemic concept. For some, nationalism is a reactionary movement that seeks to advance an ethnic project based on primordial ties and opposition to liberal values. For others, nationalism is the expression of a social movement that seeks to transform power relations and redress past injustices. Still, for others, it is a quest for identity in a world that is caught between forces of integration and disintegration[6]. So, both Canadian majority nationalism and Quebec minority nationalism have at times adopted different postures with respect to culture, economy, and identity politics. That being said, my general understanding of these two forms of nationalisms in Canada is that, over the last thirty years, they have overwhelmingly tended to push for liberal values in their respective nationalist projects.

So nationalism is not always an ugly thing. American political scientist Craig Calhoun invites us to avoid discussing nationalism simply

> through instances of passionate excess or successful manipulation by demagogues. For nationalism is equally a discursive formation that facilitates mutual recognition among polities that mediate different histories, institutional arrangements, material conditions, cultures, and political projects in the context of intensifying globalisation. Nationalism offers both a mode of access to global affairs and a mode of resistance to aspects of globalization. To wish it away is more likely to invite the dominance of neoliberal capitalism than to usher in an era of world citizenship[7].

The main point then is simply to underline that we should not jump too quickly to conclusions when we are addressing nationalism as a socio-political project. The requirement of national solidarity has been particularly well illustrated by pacifists such as Mohandas Gandhi (1869-1948) in the case of India, Martin Buber (1878-1948) in the case

---

6 Laforest, Guy and Douglas Brown (eds.), *Integration and Fragmentation. The Paradox of the Late Twentieth Century*, Kingston, Institute of Intergovernmental Relations, 1994.

7 Calhoun, Craig, *Nations Matter: Culture, History, and the Cosmopolitan Dream*, London and New York, Routledge, 2007, p. 166.

of Israel, as well as by protestant theologian Paul Tillich in Europe and catholic theologian Jacques Grand'Maison in Quebec[8]. In other words, nationalism can help to empower communities that have been ignored, neglected or taken for granted. This brings us to our discussion of federalism as a potent tool for recognition and the empowerment of communities and societal cultures in a pluralist context.

2. Empowerment through Multinational Federalist Mobilisation

In addition to nationalism, federalism can be understood as an instrument for empowering communities. Federalism facilitates inter-state relations, intra-state linkages and inter-community relations. Elsewhere I have identified five main uses of federalism in divided political settings[9]. These were federalism as a conflict management mechanism, as a shield for minorities and territorial interests, as a device to search for an equilibrium between forces of unity and forces of diversity, as a system of representation in dual if not multiple expressions of democratic practices, and as a social laboratory propitious for developing innovative socio-political programmes. What has been lacking in most accounts of federalism is an understanding that it can also serve as a mechanism for empowering minority cultures and nations in complex political settings. I have tried to address this oversight in some recent writings among which are included *Multinational Democracies, The Case for Multinational Federalism: Beyond the All-Encompassing State* and, recently, *L'Âge des incertitudes: essais sur le fédéralisme et la diversité nationale.*

In *Multinational Democracies*, my colleague James Tully introduces this new distinctive type of political association in the following manner:

> First and foremost, multinational democracies, in contrast to single-nation democracies (which are often presumed to be the norm), are constitutional associations that contain two or more nations or peoples. [...] Since the nations of a multinational democracy are nations, their members aspire to recognition not only in the larger multinational association of which they are a unit, but also to some degree in international law and other, supranational legal regimes (as for example, the four nations of the United Kingdom). Accordingly, multinational democracies are not traditional, single-nation democracies with internal, sub-national minorities, seeking group rights

8 For a detailed account of these personalities and their position with respect to nationalism, refer to Baum, Gregory, *Nationalism, Religion and Ethics*, Montreal and Kingston, McGill-Queen's University Press. 2001.

9 Gagnon, Alain-G., "The Political Uses of Federalism" in Michael Burgess and Alain-G. Gagnon (eds.), *Comparative Federalism and Federation: Competing Traditions and Future Directions*, Toronto, University of Toronto Press, 1993, pp. 15-44.

> within, but societies of two or more, often overlapping nations that are more or less equal in status.
>
> Second, multinational democracies are not confederations of independent nation-states, plural societies of separate peoples or multinational empires. […] The jurisdictions, modes of participation and representation, and the national and multinational identities of citizens overlap and are subject to negotiation. […]
>
> Third, the nations and the composite multination are constitutional democracies. That is, the legitimacy of both the nations and the multinational associations rests on their adherence to the legal and political values, principles and rights of constitutional democracy and international law. […]
>
> Fourth, multinational democracies are also multicultural. Both the nations and the multinational association as a whole are composed of individuals and cultural, linguistic, religious and ethnic minorities who struggle for and against distinctive forms of representation and accommodation of their cultural diversity. In response, the nations and the multinational association develop procedures and institutions for the democratic discussion and reconciliation of these forms of diversity […][10].

Tully has done a superb job in depicting and seeing the potential of this distinctive type of political association for the advancement of justice and political stability in advanced democracies.

Pierre Trudeau's writings, prior to his entry into federal politics in 1965, have much in common with Tully's perceptive account of multinational democracies. Trudeau, in fact, once argued in favour of a political project known as the *multinational option* in which federalism and democracy could be advanced simultaneously. In these writings, Trudeau argued that the classic Westphalian model of the state could not provide a satisfying response to minority claims or contribute to the advancement of plural communities. Tully has recently revisited some of Trudeau's earlier writings on multinational federalism and found it deserving of high praise as it is based on "grass-roots democratization, local and regional experiments in socialism, and a plurality of national, ethnic, democratic, regional and economic associations" and in which "English-Canadian and French-Canadian nationalisms would co-exist within the federation and be civic and plural rather than ethnically homogeneous"[11].

However, following his entry into federal politics, Pierre Trudeau chose not to pursue his own conceptualization of the "multinational option".

10 Tully, James, "Introduction" in Alain-G. Gagnon and James Tully (eds.), *Multinational Democracies*, Cambridge, Cambridge University Press, 2001, pp. 3-4.

11 Tully, James, "Federations, Communities and their Transformations" in André Lecours and Geneviève Nootens (eds.), *Dominant Nationalism, Dominant Ethnicity*, Brussels, PIE Peter Lang, 2009, p. 196.

He showed also a clear discomfort with the idea that Canada could be imagined as a "community of communities"[12]. Rather he defended the idea that all *Canadians* should fall under the scope of undifferentiated recognition and that individual rights should prevail over all other forms of political recognition. In other words, institutions, culture, identity, belonging, history, gender and indigeneity should not interfere with concrete political life.

2.1 The Time of Uncertainties[13]

It is crucial to connect with Trudeau's earlier writings as we now find ourselves in an age of great uncertainty. This age is defined by the creation of a global market and economic standardization, by a rising tidal wave of cultural Americanization, by the decline of political literacy and civic engagement, by a growing uniformity between formerly distinct societies and cultures, and by the continuing atomization of the individual. Taken together, these phenomena constitute an unprecedented threat to the survival of minority cultures, identities, and nations. Thus there is a pressing need for minority groups to reassert themselves and to resist the homogenizing imperatives of the *age of uncertainty*.

Within this context, one can identify how multinational polities can most effectively attend to the recognition of diversity and respond to the claims of minority nations. Since its inception, Canada has had to address these issues and, as such, the Canadian case provides an informative account of the manner in which minority and majority nations have been engaged in an evolving institutional and ideational dialogue. In turn, we will attempt to elicit, from this particular context, broader lessons that may be applied both to other federal polities and states undergoing the process of federalization. We will also link the Canadian case with the Spanish case. An examination of these two polities provides a new launching point from which one can advance a model for the continuing survival and advancement of minority nations. In doing so, let's sketch the principles that are vital to ensure that national minorities and national majorities coexist under the auspices of just and equitable intercommunal relations and through which minority nations can fulfill their legitimate and democratic aspirations.

---

[12] See, Bickerton, James, Stephen Brooks and Alain-G. Gagnon, *Freedom, Equality, Community: The Political Philosophy of Six Influential Canadians*, Montreal and Kingston, McGill-Queen's University Press, 2006.

[13] This section borrows in part from my most recent book *L'Âge des incertitudes: essais sur le fédéralisme et la diversité nationale*, Québec, Les Presses de l'Université Laval, 2011.

The relationship between international organizations and national minorities underwent a significant transformation between 1995 and 2005. Instead of promoting the rights of national minorities, as they once did, international organizations now tend to focus on protecting the rights of individuals *within* minority nations. To be clear, the plight of the national minorities of Kosovo and East Timor have been brought to public attention via the intermediary of international organizations. However, these cases represent exceptions to the developing trend that has taken hold in the supranational sphere and that has meant a tradeoff between the recognition of national minorities for the promulgation of a global society constituted of culturally diverse groups. This development is perhaps best captured in a 2004 United Nations Development Programme Report on Human Development bearing the title: *Cultural Liberty in Today's Diverse World.*

In order to ensure their long-term survival, national minorities must overcome a major hurdle. National majorities have historically downplayed or ignored national minority claims-making under the pretext that, if this were to be done, it would threaten the state's position in international organizations and/or in international economic competition. Confronted with threats emanating from minority groups, representatives of the encompassing state have demanded the unquestioned loyalty of national minorities. However, within the context of unfettered cultural and economic globalization, the dual threat of cultural erosion and declining international relevance is potentially far more devastating for minority nations.

These nations must not only counteract the homogenizing forces of globalization, they must also resist the pressure of cultural uniformity generated from within their own state. In Canada, Aboriginal peoples are the ones that are arguably most affected by these global phenomena.

The loyalty and unity that national majorities demand of national minorities cannot be accepted unless they are also reflected by the adoption of commensurate measures meant to ensure the protection of liberty, freedom and democracy within the multinational polity. It is an issue of conditional trust[14].

Here the words of Lord Acton resonate across time. Lord Acton argued that modern multinational federalism entailed finding a balance between unity and liberty; avoiding the reconciliation of these two ideas would have damaging consequences on any state. On the one hand, despotism

14 For a thorough discussion of conditional trust argument, see the work produced by the Research Group on Plurinational Societies (GRSP) and most recently Dimitrios Karmis and François Rocher (eds.), *La dynamique confiance/méfiance dans les démocraties multinationales*, Québec, Les Presses de l'Université Laval, 2012.

would prove to be the logical outcome if the goals of unity were served at the expense of liberty. On the other hand, the entrenchment of liberty without attention to unity would lead inevitably to anarchy. For Lord Acton, the institutionalization of multinational federalism presented a means to avoid both of these paths. Lord Acton made clear that

> The presence of different nations under the same sovereignty [...] provides against the servility which flourishes under the shadow of a single authority, by balancing interests, multiplying associations, and giving to the subject the restraint and support of a combined opinion. [...] Liberty provokes diversity, and diversity preserves liberty by supplying the means of organisation. [...] The coexistence of several nations under the same State is a test, as well as the best security of its freedom[15].

In the last segment of this chapter, I will offer my own take on how liberty, diversity and unity can be reconciled in this age of uncertainty. In turn, I hope to outline the contours of a new political project for multinational states that is rooted in the ideals of *liberty*, *recognition* and *empowerment*. I contend that a political project based on these ideals will open new vistas for minority and majority nations to engage in frank and honest dialogue and will allow for the mutual and compatible coexistence of difference, trust, and liberal communitarianism within the context of modern democracy. However, the adoption of this new political project is not a given. It will require that minority nations follow the path laid before them by indigenous movements and, in turn, resist with determination those that seek to maintain or promote the status quo.

3. Towards a New Politics in Multinational Polities: Moderation, Dignity and Hospitality

The enshrinement of a new political project in favour of multinational polities requires cultivating three principles: the principle of moderation, the principle of dignity and the principle of hospitality. These three principles are the fibers that, when sown together, create the canvas of a politics based on liberty, recognition and empowerment.

3.1 The Principle of Moderation

Montesquieu's excursus on creating "balance" in political societies provides the theoretical basis for the first principle. In the nineteenth century, Montesquieu argued both for the separation of legislative, executive and judicial powers and for the unrelenting pursuit of diversity. The principle of balance, which underlies both of these objectives, is

15 Acton, John Emerich, "Nationality" in Gertrude Himmelfar (ed.), *Essays on Freedom and Power*, Glencoe, The Free Press, 1949, p. 185.

vital for the enshrinement of a new politics within the context of the age of uncertainty. Balance, according to Montesquieu, is a necessary buttress against the development of autocratic, totalitarian and tyrannical systems of government. As such, the entrenchment of balance and "good government" via separation of powers and the pursuit of diversity requires that political ambitions and intentions be tempered or "moderated".

History is, however, rife with countless instances where political actors have defied the principle of moderation and, instead, have attempted to impose their will on constituents and political subjects. The First Nations of the New World have paid the price for the unfettered ambition of colonial powers. So too have minority nations been subject to the creation of structures of domination. This is most readily brought to light, within the Canadian context, by the landmark works of Eugénie Brouillet, John Conway, Michel Seymour and James Tully which document the process of cultural, religious and linguistic homogenization that the Quebec and Acadian nations have had to resist since the foundation of the Canadian state.

3.2 The Principle of Dignity

Other great thinkers have focused on human nature and the conditions for the creation of a just society. David Hume (1748) and John Rawls (1971), in particular, have addressed the need to design rules that lead to and sustain justice. In turn, Alain Renault has attempted to apply these precepts to the contemporary context. In doing so, Renault has translated Hume's "condition of justice" as the "condition of diversity". To cite Renault: "I define the 'condition of diversity' as the totality of factors that have led contemporary societies to question the nature of the rules that they themselves must adopt in order to recognize that human nature is intrinsically differentiated and that it is only by acknowledging this fact that it can be treated with dignity[16]". This acknowledgement constitutes the basis for the second principle that must undergird relations among nations in modern democratic societies.

While the rhetoric of dignity is no longer a core component of majority-minority interaction in Canada, it is central to the persistent inter-national conflict in another multinational polity. In recent years, Spain has seen a growing conflict between state nationalist forces and sub-state national movements in the Basque country, Catalonia and Galicia. The nature of this conflict is effectively captured in a comprehensive editorial (signed by twelve Catalan newspapers) published on the 26th of November 2009. The editorial strikes at the heart of the conflict between Bourbon-style

16 Renault, Alain, *Un humanisme de la diversité. Essai sur la décolonisation des identités*, Paris, Flammarion, 2009, p. 73.

nationalists and advocates of multinational federalism. To quote the editorial:

> The foundational pact that has allowed Spain to prosper over the last thirty years is now being questioned. At this time it is best remember one of the founding and indispensable principles, drawn from Ancient Rome, that underlies our legal system: *Pacta sunt servanda*. Agreements must be kept.
>
> Catalonia is in the grips of real fear and it is necessary for all of Spain to recognize this… Catalans fear, above all, a loss of dignity[17].

These quotes reveal that majority-minority relations could very well be at a turning point. Whether it is in Catalonia, Scotland, or in contexts where national minorities have engaged in similar political projects, the idea of dignity has become the rallying cry for the re-entrenchment of democracy.

In Spain, demands for the enshrinement of dignity have not fallen on deaf ears. Although it is unclear what the future holds for the Catalan people, we have nonetheless witnessed a return to national mobilization that rivals the power and numbers of those movements that emerged in the waning years of the Soviet empire. Within this more recent context, dignity is inextricably linked to the recognition of national diversity.

3.3 The Principle of Hospitality

The two first principles require that national majorities embrace moderation and respect national dignity. The third principle – and the most important of the three principles – that underlies the creation of a new political relationship between national groups requires that national minorities adopt an ethic of hospitality. The principle of hospitality is meant to enlarge contexts of choice and acts as a means to counteract the atomizing effects of procedural liberalism.

Philosopher Daniel Innerarity has recently devoted an entire book to the idea of an ethic of hospitality. According to Innerarity, adopting hospitality as a prime imperative permits one "to appropriate an interpretive approach for understanding the rich strangeness of life, the ways of others, and the often opaque and hostile cultural context that we find ourselves immersed in and that, nonetheless, drives us to seek out what is new, to enter into contact with what is different and to seek out harmony in the disparity that constitutes our existence[18]". This way

---

17 "La Dignitat de Catalunya", *Avui*, 26 November 2009, editorial published simultaneously by 12 newspapers with headquarters in Catalonia.

18 Innerarity, Daniel, *Éthique de l'hospitalité*, Québec, Les Presses de l'Université Laval, 2009, p. 4. Author's translation.

of understanding reality casts new light on the political world and gives primacy to a good life rooted in society and inter-communal relations.

The principle of hospitality will undoubtedly lead to deliberation and to periods of uncertainty. However, all mature democratic societies must embrace a certain degree of uncertainty and, accordingly, must be open to the possibility of change. It is only through inter-communal interaction (or creative tensions to use Trudeau's terminology) that a modern society can implement a political project that listens to all voices and that encourages political participation within and across communities. Minority nations, even more so than majority nations, must embrace the ethic of hospitality. They must address a series of challenges entailing, inter alia, the accommodation and integration of migrant populations, maintaining the predominance of majority languages, addressing the disappearance of a sense of community, counteracting citizen disengagement, and moderating the cultural and economic impact of globalization. When confronted with these phenomena, minority nations are at risk. As such, they must find new ways of sustaining mobilization and activism both in the intra and inter national arenas.

The principle of hospitality requires the adoption of a genuine politics of interculturalism. The intercultural model allows for healthy dialogue between the constituent members of a diverse society and, in turn, for the articulation of an authentic pact between groups. This model also allows, on the one hand, for the continued cultural and ideational diversification of the national minority and, on the other hand, it provides an opportunity for the national minority to exist and thrive over time. While intercommunal dialogue may lead to the voicing of profound ideological disagreements, interculturalism is a necessary mechanism for ensuring the survival and democratic evolution of minority nations. As Daniel Innerarity states: "Democratic renewal will not be instigated by the drive for consensus but rather under the auspices of reasonable disagreement. Although democracy is impossible without a certain degree of consensus, it must nonetheless be open to the expression of diversity and to the articulation of collective identities rooted in different traditions[19]".

By Way of Conclusion

Throughout this paper, I have presented the politics of recognition and the politics of empowerment as necessary for the deepening of democracy. Through the evocation of the notions of regionalism, nationalism and federalism, I have sought to question policies that led

19 Innerarity, Daniel, *La démocratie contre l'État: essai sur le gouvernement des sociétés complexes*, Paris, Flammarion, 2006, p. 129. Author's translation.

to uneven development and regional disparities; to challenge policies insensitive to national minorities; and to suggest how we might advance political autonomy in line with a principle of the non-subordination of power in federal regimes.

My argument was developed over a series of four reflections. The first reflection explored regional mobilisation as a means to empower citizens inhabiting remote areas that are affected by uneven development. The second reflection had to do with nationalist mobilization in a politico-economic context influenced by forces of globalisation, forces that can undermine the life of national communities within the world order. The third reflection dealt with models for the management of linguistic and national diversity, focusing equally on models rooted in communal rights and models rooted in individual rights. In that third reflection, I was keen to examine multinational states as new institutional forms of constitutional association. I contended that political autonomy ought to be seen as a form of voluntary and consensual enfranchisement and not as a means to exclude the "Other". The fourth reflection evaluated different conceptualizations of "community", "autonomy", and "empowerment" in nationally diverse states. Multinational federalism was presented as the most promising framework for the management of diversity within these states. In that reflection, I reassessed paths towards community reconciliation by reifying and deepening three federal instruments drawn from the past: the need to find a proper balance between forces in tension; the urgency to advance a politic of dignity that builds on a continually renewed trust; and the need to nourish a politics of hospitality so that no one feels excluded from the policy process and the path to democratic renewal.

In closing, and to reach beyond the points I have addressed in this lecture, if there is one message I have sought to communicate it is that as individuals we have a key role to play in advancing principles of fairness and justice. Empathy is an essential feature to be emulated at all levels. It could be at the level of municipal politics, at the provincial level, or with Quebec's national affirmation and at the multinational level as I have been advocating for some time now. Seeking to advance those causes can only bring dignity to people and make the "Other" know of the importance of acting in good faith, otherwise trust will weaken and unravel.

CHAPTER 4

The *Canadian School of Diversity's* New Influences on the Theory of Collective Rights in Spain

A Critical Review of Seymour's Contribution

José María SAUCA

Professor of Philosophy of Law, Carlos III University of Madrid

1. The Debate about Collective Rights in Spain

The recognition of collective rights has been one of the most heavily debated questions in Spanish political and legal philosophy in the last decade. The prominence of this topic is not unique to the Peninsula; there has been a good deal of international debate on the same question. One can, however, note local characteristics, singling out the authors who have led these debates. In this vein, I believe it is only fair to recognize the pioneering role of López Calera's monograph on this subject, while also recognizing that texts by Requejo[1], De Lucas[2], and Cruz Parcero[3] may have provided some preliminary context. The text by López Calera[4]

1 See Requejo, Ferrán, "Cultural Pluralism, Nationalism and Federalism: A Revision of Democratic Citizenship in Plurinational States", *European Journal of Political Research*, vol. 35, nº 2, 1999, pp. 255-286.

2 De Lucas, Javier (ed.), *Derechos de las minorías en una sociedad multicultural, Madrid*, Consejo General del Poder Judicial, 1999, especially pp. 251-312.

3 Parcero, Juan Antonio Cruz, "Sobre el concepto de derechos colectivos", *Revista Internacional de Filosofía Política*, nº 12, 1998, pp. 95-115. Also see his *El lenguaje de los derechos. Ensayo para una teoría estructural de los derechos*, Madrid, Trotta, 2007, pp. 101-126.

4 Calera, Nicolás López, *¿Hay derechos colectivos? Individualidad y socialidad en la teoría de los derechos*, Barcelona, Ariel, 2000. The proposals in this text were also addressed in a previous book entitled *Yo, el Estado. Bases para una teoría sustancializadora (no sustancialista) del Estado*, Madrid, Trotta, 1992, and, as I see it, reflect some of his older works, especially *Hegel y los derechos humanos*, Granada, Universidad de Granada, 1971.

disseminated the argumentative strategies of Kymlicka, Raz, and Hartney in Spain and supported an eminently juridical thesis that linked the justification of collective rights to the confirmation of their effective juridical recognition. I believe that the anthology published by the *Bartolomé de las Casas* Human Rights Institute in Madrid[5] transformed the question into the object of a wide-ranging disciplinary debate. In general terms, the debate reproduced the majority view that rejected collective rights. That rejection was only tempered by the inclusion of moderate *philosophical culturalist* theses and positive juridical perspectives, both at the national and the international level. From that point on, a series of monographs have been produced that represent the distinct lines of international thought on the question. I believe the work of García Inda[6] – which also incorporates other critics' ideas, most notably Souza Santo's – presents a thesis that is openly in favor of recognizing collective rights. Cruz Parcero, in the aforementioned work, follows a strategy of dismantling or, at least, relativizing criticisms directed at the category. Albert Calsamiglia[7], in the more specific area of cultural collective rights, opts for a justifying approach that is more political than juridical. Neus Torbisco[8] offers a complete reconstruction of collective rights as group rights, clearly following Kymlicka. Rodríguez Abascal[9] presents a systematic critique of the category of collective rights. Much of the most forceful doctrine of Spanish human rights (Garzón Valdés, Laporta, Peces Barba, Pérez Luño, Eusebio Fernández, Ruiz Miguel, Savater, etc.) is behind this thesis.

To my way of understanding, the specificities of the debate have revolved around two ideas. On the one hand, its political distinctiveness responds to the multinational character of the Kingdom of Spain. Regional multilingualism and the centrifugal tendencies of the people from some of the historical autonomous communities set the stage for the defense or criticism of collective linguistic rights and the eventual right to self-determination on the part of those peoples. On the other hand, one of

5 Roig, Francisco Javier Ansuátegui (ed.), *Una discusión sobre derechos colectivos*, Madrid, Instituto de Derechos Humanos Bartolomé de las Casas, Dykinson, 2001.

6 Inda, Andrés García, *Materiales para una reflexión sobre los derechos humanos colectivos*, Madrid, Instituto de Derechos Humanos Bartolomé de las Casas, Dykinson, 2001.

7 Calsamiglia, Albert, *Cuestiones de lealtad. Límites del liberalismo: corrupción, nacionalismo y multiculturalismo*, Barcelona, Paidós, 2000.

8 Casals, Neus Torbisco, *Group Rights as Human Rights. A Liberal Approach to Multiculturalism*, Dordrechts, Springer, 2006.

9 Abascal, Luis Rodríguez, *Las fronteras del nacionalismo*, Madrid, Centro de Estudios Políticos y Constitucionales, 2000, and also "El debate sobre los derechos de grupo" in Elías Díaz and José Luis Colomer (eds.), *Estado, justicia, derechos*, Madrid, Alianza, pp. 409-434.

the effects of Spain's constitutional debate at the end of the 1970s and the subsequent establishment of democratic institutions has been Spain's very close connection to the doctrine of fundamental rights. From the academic point of view, the extensive production of material generated during those years is striking. Thus, the starting point for the debates that have arisen from the theoretical point of view, both by those who defend their conceptualization as moral rights and those who sustain a historical-positivist thesis[10], has been a common proscription of collective rights. González Amuchastegui's work[11] may be considered the best expression of this general convergence.

In this brief reconstruction of the evolution of the theoretical treatment of collective rights in the Spanish academy, we can clearly see the influence of Canadian theoretical writings. The majority view that is critical of collective rights has discovered one of the most solid arguments on which to base their criticism in Hartney's conceptual treatment. On the other hand, minority thinkers who favor acceptance have focused on the proposals of important Canadian authors. In addition to the significant influence of Kymlicka, contributions by Carignan[12], Sumner[13], McDonald[14], Réaume[15], Cardinal[16], and Karmis[17] are worth noting, as well as the work included in the highly influential monographic number

---

10 See Toubes, Joaquín Rodríguez, *La razón de los derechos. Perspectivas actuales sobre la fundamentación de los derechos humanos*, Madrid, Tecnos, 1995.

11 Amuchastegui, Jesús González, *Autonomía, dignidad y ciudadanía. Una teoría de los derechos humanos*, Valencia, Tirant lo Blanch, 2004.

12 Caringan, Linda, "De la notion de droit collectif et de son application en matière scolaire au Québec", *Revue juridique Thémis*, vol. 18, 1984, pp. 1-103.

13 Sumner, Wayne L., *The Moral Foundation of Rights*, Oxford, Oxford University Press, 1987.

14 McDonald, Michael, "Collective Rights and Tyranny", *Revue de l'Université d'Ottawa*, vol. 56, n° 2, 1986, pp. 115-139; "Indian Status: Colonialism or Sexism", *Canadian Community Law Journal*, vol. 9, 1987, pp. 23-48; "The Personless Paradigm", *University of Toronto Law Journal*, vol. 37, n° 1, 1987, pp. 212-226; "The Forest in the Trees. Collective Rights as Basic Rights" in Guy Lafrance (ed.), *Éthique et droits fondamentaux/Ethic and Basic Rights*, Ottawa, Les Presses de l'Université d'Ottawa, 1989, pp. 230-241; "Liberalism, Community and Culture", *University of Toronto Law Journal*, vol. 42, n° 2, 1992, pp. 113-131.

15 Réaume, Denise, "Individuals, Groups and Rights to Public Goods", *University of Toronto Law Journal*, vol. 38, n° 1, 1988, pp. 1-27; "Groups Rights and Participatory Goods" in Guy Lafrance (ed.), *Éthique et droits fondamentaux/Ethic and Basic Rights*, Ottawa, Les Presses de l'Université d'Ottawa, 1989, pp. 242-249.

16 Cardinal, Linda, *Une Langue qui pense: la recherche en milieu minoritaire francophone au Canada*, Ottawa, Les Presses de l'Université d'Ottawa, 1993.

17 Karmis, Dimitrios, "Cultures autochtones et libéralisme au Canada. Les vertus médiatrices du communautarisme libéral de Charles Taylor", *Canadian Journal of Political Science*, vol. 26, n° 1, 1993, pp. 69-96.

of the *Canadian Journal of Law and Jurisprudence* in the summer of 1991[18].

In the context of the *Canadian School of Diversity*'s influence[19], I believe the book by Quebec author Michel Seymour entitled *De la tolérance à la reconnaissance* [*From Tolerance to Recognition*][20] may again become a relevant work for this material. I will spend the rest of this study considering that text.

2. *De la tolérance à la reconnaissance* as a General Theory of Collective Rights

Seymour's book is a generous monograph that exceeds seven hundred pages. Its structure consists of three formally differentiated sections that are organized hierarchically in such a way that the first two present the basic research designed to justify the theses sustained in the third. The first section of the book, entitled *Legacy of a Concept*, addresses a genealogy of the concept of *recognition* starting with Hegel's *phenomenology of spirit*. The Hegelian readings of Kojève, Habermas, Honneth, and Taylor, alongside a multiplicity of complementary works, configure the basic conceptual frame of reference. Its reception outside of the Hegelian tradition of critical thinking is approached through the analysis of works from the liberal tradition (Appiah, Barry, Johnson, Kukathas, and Waldron), the democratic liberal tradition (Benhabib, Gutmann, and Nussbaum), and particularly, from within the Canadian academy (Taylor, always omnipresent, Tully, Kymlicka, Carens, Margaret Moore, Melissa Williams, Eisenberg, Blattgerg, Maclure, Nadeau, and Nootens, among others). From the last group, Seymour dedicates, in the fifth and last chapter of this section of the book, a meticulous study of Will Kymlicka's contributions, viewing them as the most elaborate effort made by a liberal theoretician to justify group rights. His central thesis emphasizes that, to the extent that Kymlicka maintains his connection to liberalism with an individualistic stamp, he is incapable of laying the foundation for collective rights, presenting a sugar-coated version of rights through the formula of the rights of differentiated groups.

---

18 I am referring to works by Peter Benson, Leslie Green, Jan Narveson, Nathan Brett, Joseph Pestieau, Lesley A. Jacobs, Moshe Berent, and Don Lenihan published in the *Canadian Journal of Law and Jurisprudence*, vol. 4 nº 2, 1991, pp. 217-422.

19 See Gagnon, Alain-G., "Reconciling Autonomy, Community and Empowerment. The Difficult Birth of a Diversity School in the Western World" in Alain-G. Gagnon and Michael Keating (eds.), *Political Autonomy and Divided Societies*, Basingstoke, Palgrave Macmillan, 2012, pp. 49-59.

20 Seymour, Michel., *De la tolérance à la reconnaissance. Une théorie libérale des droits collectifs*, Québec, Boréal, 2008.

The second section, entitled *Political Liberalism*, is central to his argumentative strategy and is characterized by the attempt to shift the liberal approach's center of gravity from the concept of individual autonomy to the concept of tolerance. This movement is substantiated through two impulses that unfold in opposite directions. On the one hand is a constructive strategy based on laying the foundations for the moral relevance of a type of collective subject whose configuration maintains continuity with the justification of what is called the Principle of the Value of Cultural Diversity (PVCD). On the other hand is a critical strategy that consists of confronting this thesis with the standard liberal thinking that is, in different ways, receptive to the acceptance of claims of cultural diversity, centering on Appiah, Buchanan, Kukathas, Johnson, and Kymlicka.

The third section deals, in the strict sense, with the exposition of the *theory of collective rights*. The challenges of this objective refer, first, to the evaluation of the ethical-normative conditions that allow a group to be included within the category of rights bearer. In the second place, it refers to spelling out the conditions required for the stakeholder to be the genuine object of collective rights. In the third place, it refers to the determination of subjects obligated by collective rights and, finally, to the specification of a typology to describe plausible collective rights. Beyond that, the exposition is once again developed in a continuous dialogue with the critics or with the theses exposed by eventual critics among whom, in addition to those already mentioned, Narverson, Tamir, and particularly Hartney stand out.

To conclude this overview of Seymour's text, I will point out three characteristics that I believe summarize the central traits of its nature. In the first place, the book is a *revolutionary* text. This is obvious from its style, the persuasive prose, the construction of the argument, and finally, the effort to concretize theoretical reflections with specific examples of societies, countries, or simply specific political problems. If Margalit's distinction between "e.g. [exemplum gratia] philosophers and i.e. [idest] philosophers" is meaningful[21], Seymour would, without a doubt, fall within the first category.

Nevertheless, the most meaningful revolution is found deep down. "The theme of this text [says Seymour] is the multinational State as a model of political organization. It deals, equally, with national minorities at the heart of the nation state as well as the people as a whole incorporated into supranational organizations"[22]. The connection with the theme of

21 Margalit, Avishai, *The Ethics of Memory*, Cambridge, Harvard University Press, 2002, p. IX.

22 Seymour, *op. cit.*, p. 11.

collective rights is found in an implicit nexus between the two questions; I am referring to the concept of nationhood. It is the theme of nationalism that is profiled as the fundamental substratum of this theory of collective rights and infused with the central pulse of its development. "This text [he concludes], while based on theoretical questions, participates in the political conflict by taking a position that seeks to find a balance between minority and majority nations"[23].

In the second place, it is a task that could be called *interstitial* within the liberal tradition. Its construction is buttressed by reconstructions and the support of collateral elements and, on some occasions, by generally accepted arguments in the tradition from which we attempt to garner the greatest utility for the defended argument. We can see this interstitial character most clearly in the detailed reading that follows Rawls in *Political Liberalism* and very particularly in *The Law of Peoples*. In the latter, the Harvard professor maintained that this vision "conceives of liberal democratic peoples (and decent peoples) as the actors in the Society of Peoples, just as citizens are the actors in domestic society"[24]. He also equates them to individual agents in the method established in *A Theory of Justice*[25]. On the basis of this recognition of the quality of the subject in the area of a normative theory regarding what constitutes a well-organized international society, Seymour articulates an argument that crosses the domestic and international spheres. He promotes, on the one hand, the competence of individuals, as individual right bearers, to act in the international arena and, on the other hand, the competence of the people as a whole, as collective rights bearers, to act in the domestic realm. His thesis is explicitly presented as a coherent, and to a certain extent, natural development of the Rawlsian thesis. Rawls simplified that thesis for methodological reasons, reducing the framework of the well-organized society to a homogeneous nation state within a single timeframe because of the change to identifying cultural components that migratory processes generate. A similar strategy is also employed in relation to Kymlicka. While the references to discrepancies are frequent, one of Kymlicka's concepts reveals substantial Seymourian influence and specifically recognizes him. I am referring to the idea of societal culture as a conceptual framework for the definition of the idea of a people[26]. According to Seymour, the whole construction of the reflection of the idea

23 *Ibid.*, p. 668.

24 Rawls, John, *The Law of Peoples with "The Idea of Public Opinion Revisited"*, Cambridge, Harvard University Press, 2001, p. 23.

25 *Ibid.*, p. 55.

26 Kymlicka, Will, *Liberalism, Community, and Culture*, Oxford, Clarendon Press, 1989, pp. 166-168 and also *Politics in the Vernacular. Nationalism, Multiculturalism and Democracy*, New York, Oxford University Press, 2001, pp. 50-66.

of a people or a nation – whenever the two terms are used interchangeably – refers to their determination as a culture that is not substantial, narrative, or relative to values, but is an institutional construction of culture. In this way, all culture "is a structure of culture, in other words, a language, institutions, and a common public history inscribed in a crossroads of influences, and it affords a context of choice"[27]. Incidentally, this interstitial note also operates as a description of the *liberalizing* lectures that Seymour develops on other occasions. This approach affords a special place for addressing Taylor. We can see it in the following example:

> It is true [recognizes Seymour] that referring to Taylor in the framework of my argument was perhaps not very fortunate [...] but if the communitarian biases that are at the center of Taylor's thesis are eliminated, liberalism 2 can be reformulated without a communitarian perspective. Liberalism 2 will appear, however, as an anti-individualist and anti-collectivist version of liberalism [and] will recognize the primacy and inalienable character of the individual rights of individual persons and the collective rights of the people without creating a hierarchy out of the two types of rights[28].

Finally, as emphasized in this quote, the third characteristic that stands out in Seymour's work is what could be called *explorations of the limits of liberalism*. Concretely, it assumes the need to configure a profile of liberalism close to the idea of tolerance rather than focusing on the thesis of autonomy. This last liberalism, which he calls *individualistic liberalism*, is characterized by three central theses from which others can be inferred. The first thesis is that "the person is an individual regardless of any finality, any value or any project". This carries four consequences. First, the person can be subject to certain socioeconomic determinations but can renounce, at the identifying level, any ideological determination that refers to beliefs, purposes, values, and projects. Second, the person is in a position to be able to distinguish personal identity from any specific moral identity. Third, the rational autonomy of the person consists of his or her ability to revise individual conceptions of the good and continue being the same person. Fourth, the people would be a voluntary grouping of individuals.

The second thesis of individualist liberalism is that "the individual is the ultimate source of legitimate moral vindication", which leads to two corollaries. On the one hand, any justification of policies applied to a group should, ultimately, serve the interests of the individuals, and its principal justification should be those individual interests. On the other hand, fundamental individual rights have absolute priority over the rights of the group.

---

27 Seymour, *op. cit.*, p. 270.

28 *Ibid.*, pp. 535-536.

The third thesis consists of affirming that the individual should have primacy over the group, which means that autonomy is the liberal value par excellence. The final conclusion to these three theses, to say it in Dworkin's words, means affirming that no restriction, limitation, or obligation imposed on fundamental rights is acceptable unless it is because of another fundamental right[29].

The alternative proposal that is called, following Rawls, *political liberalism* is distinguished from the previous one by the three alternative theses it offers. Political liberalism's first thesis is to maintain a political conception of the person based on his or her institutional identity. In that way, the political person is the citizen at the heart of a society, which in Seymour's terms, is at the heart of an institutionally organized people. In this way, the institutional identity of the person corresponds with a diversity of metaphysical conceptions of personal identity and, specifically, corresponds to a communal conception as much as to an individualist conception. To that extent, it aspires to a degree of neutrality in relation to the debates between those who think their identity depends on beliefs, purposes, values, and projects and those who are defined as indifferent to any belief, purpose, value, or project. This institutional person has two moral faculties: the sense of justice and the rational ability to act according to his or her purpose. For that reason, the person is presented as an equal citizen who has a certain degree of rational autonomy, but who does not necessarily have significant autonomy.

For their part, the people as a whole, understood in the political liberalism sense, can be defined as a *society* in the sense that Rawls develops in his book entitled *Political Liberalism* or as *societal culture* in Kymlicka's sense. Rawls's conception of a society would be "a system of social cooperation for mutual benefit", or a "social union of social unions", or a "base structure" that includes the union of economic, social (e.g., education, health), legal, and political institutions. It is sometimes understood as an "independent political community" and, on exceptional occasions, as the people organized into sovereign states. With all this, it is in his *The Law of Peoples* where he turns to a definition of the people beginning with their institutional identity, eliminating all reference to comprehensive theories about their identity as a free association of individuals, organic community, collective body, or macro-subject where individuals share the same beliefs, values, and purposes.

---

29 *Ibid.*, pp. 265-267. The authors who Seymour has in mind when he reconstructs this general framework include Anthony Appiah, Brian Barry, Charles Beitz, Allen Buchanan, Simon Caney, David Held, Stanley Hoffman, Andrew Kuper, Will Kymlicka, Martha Nussbaum, Thomas Pogge, Amartya Sen, Yael Tamir, Kok-Chor Tan, and Jeremy Waldron.

The second thesis of political liberalism maintains that both the person and the people as a whole are autonomous sources of valid moral vindications. They would be joined by legal entities, NGOs, labor unions, companies, and supranational organizations.

The third thesis of political liberalism maintains that rather than autonomy, tolerance – understood in its political sense as *toleration* and not as an attitude, *tolerance* – is the liberal value par excellence.

The equivalent corollary to Dworkin's aforementioned thesis is that reasonable restrictions on individual rights and liberties can be justified[30].

In conclusion, Seymour defends his theory as a genuinely liberal theory connected to the tradition of the more mature Rawls and places his trust in the greater potential it affords to manage the challenges of recognition as a central question of a theory of justice. Let me conclude with his own words: "Fortunately, recent unexpected changes at the core of liberal thought allow us to glimpse a broader opening in the implacable, plural diversity of national cultures, the rights of the people, the rights of minorities, immigration, and indigenous peoples. For liberalism to grant a true place for collective claims, it is necessary to free oneself from moral individualism without, however, endorsing communitarianism"[31].

3. The Characterization of Collective Rights According to Seymour's Thesis

The starting point of Seymour's theory on collective rights is found, as has already been stated, in the consideration of the moral agent from a political perspective. In this way, he sketches some of the limits of the problem that leave outside of the field of study all the ontological aspects of the category of collective beings and the diverse conditions of their existence. Similarly, in a moral sense, it leaves outside of the analysis the substantive aspects related to ideas of goodness or the good life, any element related to the narrativities that constitute group identity, as well as any consideration related to the necessary connection between morality and individuality, understood as a metaphysical thesis that exceeds the arena of public space.

Building on the foundations of the moral agency of this political perspective, he articulates twelve conditions that should be satisfied to sustain the plausibility of the justification of collective rights. I believe this dodecagon can be condensed into four central aspects. In the first place, there is the determination of the subject of collective rights. Second, there is the delimitation of the content or object of collective rights. Third

30 *Ibid.*, pp. 265-267.

31 *Ibid.*, p. 271.

is the articulation between subject and object of collective rights. Fourth is the exposition of the justifying principle of collective rights. Let us take a look at each of these issues.

3.1 The Subject of Collective Rights

Subjects who bear collective rights regarding a particular interest should be minimally institutionalized groups of individuals who view themselves as members of a single group. The links that constitute this connection are a language (or languages), an institutional framework, and a common public history. Seymour understands that the only collectives that meet these requirements are the people or subsets of the people (see Pogge[32] or Buchanan[33] for an opposing view). In this way, groups that do not meet these requirements such as religious associations, labor unions, corporations, NGOs, and companies can be subject to rights but not to collective rights as such. Similarly, women, gay men and lesbians, and racial groups can be subject to rights, but they are nothing more than groups of individual interests. In order to be accepted as a subject of collective rights, a group must guarantee the configuration of a context of choice for its members. The only group capable of doing so is a people, or a fragment of the same, understood in the previously mentioned institutional sense[34].

In addition to the conceptual delimitation of those who bear collective rights and on the basis of the collective interest that we will discuss below, the particular group must be large enough to represent a sufficiently elevated number of individuals. It does not need to specify a methodology to estimate the number of individuals necessary to make a group large enough to merit the holding of rights, but it appeals to approximate strategies of delimitation in which the central references are what unite enough individuals to nurture the institutional framework of its own collective as well as safeguarding, *rebus sic stantibus*, the reasonable durability of the group. This calculation of a minimum personnel basis for the configuration of the group for these purposes does not correspond, however, to the introduction of cost/benefit analysis[35]. Once the minimum requirements regarding permanence and the dynamics of the group are

---

32 Pogge, Thomas, "Group Rights and Ethnicity" in Ian Shapiro and Will Kymlicka, *Ethnicity and Group Rights*, New York, New York University Press, 1997, pp. 187-190.

33 Buchanan, Allen, "What's So Special about Nations?", *Canadian Journal of Philosophy*, vol. 22, 1998, pp. 283-309.

34 Within this category, he notes seven types of peoples or nations on the basis of the criteria regarding the type of connections they share, but they are nothing but manifestations of a uniform category (he talks about ethnic, cultural, civic, diasporic, sociopolitical, multisocietal, and multiterritorial nations). Seymour, *op. cit.* p. 35.

35 *Ibid.*, p. 483.

satisfied, the center of gravity for the recognition of collective rights is found in the will of the people to satisfy the desire of living together. I do not think it is excessive to believe that Seymour is of a mind here to respond affirmatively to the small indigenous communities that are attempting, in spite of their demographic limitations, to preserve their traditional way of life.

Finally, regarding the question of the subjectivity of collective rights, he addresses the determination of the obliged subject by understanding that one of the necessary conditions for the existence of the right is the reciprocity of being able to identify a subject while being delimited by the obligation to satisfy the collective interest that constitutes its objects. The subject is, initially, the State in which the group in question is located. However, this assertion of obligation operates through citizen rearrangement. The individuals in the group, as well as other individuals who are members of other State groups, should also be prepared to assume certain obligations stemming from the affirmation of collective rights of the peoples in question. The strategy of determining the obliged subject is once again based on giving examples:

> The civic nation has obligations regarding contiguous diasporas and the minorities that come from immigration. The multisocial or multinational nation also has obligations regarding these same minorities as well as the minority or majority nations at the heart of the State. Supranational organizations have obligations regarding the aforementioned groups and also regarding multiterritorial nations and the nations that constitute States, whether they are civic or multisocietal[36].

3.2 The Content of Collective Rights

Seymour remains ambivalent about the content or object of collective rights, connecting them, on the one hand, to the idea of interest and, on the other, to the idea of will. Following the long tradition of Bentham and Ihering, the content of collective rights is an interest, and the object of that interest should be an institutional, collective, and identifying good. Institutional goods are participatory goods that have a constitutive character for the group and from which no one can be excluded[37]. Typical examples include language, collective memory, etc. They are characterized because some element of one's own good is the act of participating in the process of its production and/or enjoyment. Collective goods are defined in contrast to individualizable goods. Thus, it implies the belief that the adjective *collective* signifies that those goods are not limited to a mere aggregation of satisfied individual interests.

36 *Ibid.*, pp. 483-484.

37 Réaume, "Groups Rights and Participatory Goods", *op. cit.*

> Collective objects [states the author] cannot be reclaimed, possessed, produced, and consumed except by a collectivity. Of course, the collectivity cannot enjoy these rights unless the members themselves can enjoy them. It is absurd to imagine that the interest of the group can be satisfied without the members of the group satisfying some of its interests. [...] But this need not make us conclude that group interest is nothing more than the interest of the members[38].

Finally, identifying goods are those that are focused on preserving the identity of the group understood as an institutional identity. Among all the stakeholders in a national group, only a subset can access the status of the object of collective rights: this includes groups that attempt to retain their ability to create, maintain, develop, or control their own institutions.

Seymour does not resort to an abstract display of categories in the development of his argument, but to a strategy of direct definition. In this way, collective goods are seen as: the protection of the hunting and fishing rights of native peoples as ancestral inhabitants of certain territories, thus justifying the individual rights of indigenous peoples to hunt or fish in certain reserves; the rights of the Francophone community in Canada, which justifies the individual right of Francophone children to be taught in their own language if the number of affected people is sufficient; the community's right to provide itself with institutions and with representatives of those institutions, which thus presumes the individual right to vote; and the right of the people as a whole to promote and preserve the institutions that favor economic, cultural, social, and political development, that is, the right to self-determination[39]. A paradigmatic example of an institutional, collective, and identifying good is language. It is institutional because the language is presented in the public space as a practice controlled by constitutive rules. These rules are characterized by the fact that they are shared by a collectivity, which implies its collective side. It is identifying to the extent that it cannot be reduced to its usefulness or instrumental function.

Regarding will, Seymour's second consideration, he maintains that the mere existence of interest is not definitive and should be complemented with the existence of a collective volition as a safeguard of that interest. Thus he notes that "not all peoples should have political institutions, but they have the right to them if the people decide to reclaim them"[40]. Thus, it is necessary for people who reclaim the collective interest, object of the collective right, to want to live together and want the protection of their people. Without this claim on the part of the people, it does not do any

---

38 Seymour, *op. cit.*, p. 478.

39 *Ibid.*, pp. 479-480.

40 *Ibid.*, p. 481.

good to promote the protection of group identity. Collective rights are only predictable in favor of those peoples who endorse their own recognition. We cannot allow any paternalism on this question. Democratic will is not sufficient reason for the affirmation of collective rights, but it is a necessary condition for recognition. The context for this component of will is the possibility of sustaining the existence of a moral right to self-determination that is projected in the aspiration for constitutionalization as an element of stability in multinational states, given that the recognition of stateless nations is a condition *sine qua non* of this stability.

Now that we have examined Seymour's general argument on the content of collective rights, I think it would be useful to consider a specific problem that I believe is central to the question: the character, aggregative or not, of collective interest that shapes collective rights. The strategy that the author develops in his discussion continues in a debate that focuses on critiques of Michael Hartney[41], who has probably presented the most complete account of the conception of collective interests as individualizable interests[42]. Hartney's discussion is presented as the standard of the thesis of moral individualism (he uses the term *value-individualism*, following Raz and Sumner's lead)[43]. This individualism does not imply an ontological thesis because he accepts the existence of groups that are ontologically irreducible. In the same way, he recognizes that the existence of the group and its development can, in a certain sense, be considered a good for the group and that they do not clearly afford benefits for individuals considered separately. But these theses do not affect the moral question, and those goods are not morally pertinent since the existence and development of the group are, in his opinion, non-moral goods. Group goods can have moral and conditional relevance, but not intrinsic relevance. Goods only become morally pertinent if they are placed in relationship with intrinsic goods and the only intrinsic goods are individual (moral individualism). The dilemma is inescapable. Either there is an instrumental justification for collective goods and a liberal thesis is maintained; or there is a justification of collective goods as intrinsic goods, in other words, as goods not derived from the value that is given them by individuals, and a

41 Hartney, Michael, "Some Confusions Concerning Collective Rights", *Canadian Journal of Law and Jurisprudence*, vol. 4, nº 2, 1991, pp. 293-314. Also in Kymlicka, Will (ed.), *The Rights of Minority Cultures*, Oxford, Oxford University Press, 1995, pp. 202-227. Also see Seymour, Michel, "Le concept juridique de droit collectif" in Guy Lafrance (ed.), *Ethic and Basic Rights*, Ottawa, Les Presses de l'Université d'Ottawa, 1989, pp. 264-273.

42 See Abascal, *op. cit.*, p. 414; Parcero, *op. cit.* p. 110.

43 Raz, Joseph, *Morality of Freedom*, Oxford, Oxford University Press, 1986, pp. 208-209.

non-liberal thesis is maintained. *Tertium non datur*[44]. Thus all collective interests are explicable as an aggregate of interests[45] and when it is said (e.g., by authors such as Réaume[46], Waldron[47], or Green[48]) that collective interests are not reducible to a group of individual interests, it can mean one of these two things: either that it is an interest shared by members of a group in such a way that the interest is non-individualizable or that it is an interest of a group above and beyond the interests of its members. The thesis is that neither of these possibilities is morally plausible[49]. Seymour believes Hartney's thesis here is founded on an error. On the one hand, the understanding that goods are enjoyed individually does not explain why members of the group have this good and those who do not belong to the group do not. He believes that the reason these individuals have the individual right is because they belong to a group that presupposes the existence of a right for that group. The typical example is of immigrants who do not have an individual right to receive an education in their language while the members of an indigenous people do have that individual right. This asymmetry is justified not, as Kymlicka[50] says, because immigrants have implicitly renounced their language, but because immigrants do not possess collective rights of a cultural nature from which to derive their individual right to an education in their own language[51]. The justification of this differentiated treatment is not strictly individual, but collective. Furthermore, the eventual intercultural linguistic and pedagogical policies would not constitute an obligation of the host society but, instead, advocacy measures adopted in order to facilitate non-traumatic integration. In short, "if the individual has the right to protect his cultural belonging […] it is because he belongs to a national community present in the land that can reclaim institutional goods of this type. Individual cultural rights are an individual benefit that derives from the satisfaction of collective rights that the community bears to provide itself with cultural institutions"[52].

---

44 Hartney, "Groups Rights and Participatory Goods", *op. cit.*, p. 207.

45 *Ibid.*, pp. 207-208.

46 Réaume, "Individuals, Groups and Rights to Public Goods", *op. cit.*, pp. 10-13; "Groups Rights and Participatory Goods", *op. cit.*, pp. 243-244.

47 Waldron, Jeremy, *Liberal Right. Collected Papers 1981-1991*, Cambridge, Cambridge University Press, 1993, p. 346.

48 Green, Leslie, "Two Views of Collective Rights", *Canadian Journal of Law and Jurisprudence*, vol. 4, nº 2, 1991, pp. 315-327.

49 Hartney, *op. cit.*, pp. 208-210.

50 Kymlicka Will, *Multicultural Citizenship: A Liberal Theory of Minority Rights*, Oxford, Oxford University Press, 1996, pp. 76-106.

51 Seymour, *op. cit.*, p. 596.

52 *Ibid.*, p. 598.

On the other hand, and in line with the example proposed in its day by Dworkin and taken up again by Réaume regarding the interest the members of an orchestra would have in maintaining and promoting their own group, Seymour critiques Hartney who does not grasp the difference that exists between the formation of a collective will out of the aggregate of individual wills and the formation of a collective will by individual wills to the extent that individual wills are formulated as part of a collective will. In his own words:

> the confusion resides in the fact that the collective will is in a certain sense individualizable. The people's will is in a way dependent on the interpretations that individuals make of this collective will. But equally, if individuals contribute to the formation of collective will, the opinion regarding the formation of collective will, in other words, the opinion regarding collective interest is not an aggregate of opinions that rests on individual interests. It is, at the most, an aggregate of opinions interpreting collective will. For all these reasons, collective interest cannot be reducible to a sum of individual interests[53].

3.3 Subject-Object Articulation

The group that is presented as the subject of collective rights should report a decisively relevant structural qualification. The interest whose satisfaction justifies the existence of the collective right should be included on the track record of the identifying connections of all agents even though it need not constitute a primary social good according to all of them. For that reason, only national social cultures are in any position to satisfy this requirement: "Nations have the particularity of being the *only entities* that appear on the track record of connections of all the citizens of the world"[54]. The approach is, therefore, clearly objective because, correctly or not, it affirms the empirical confirmation that the only collective reality that is found in all contemporary individuals – including a negative reaction by those who are stateless – is the connection with one's own people. This objective fact is, incidentally, resistant to the fact that there are individuals who manifest obvious disinterest for this type of identifying connection. What ends up being

> without a doubt necessary [maintains Seymour] is that the group in question truly plays an important role in maintaining the representation that people make of their own person, but it is not necessary for individuals to themselves grant the group the statute of principal social good. What is important is, however, that the concerned group be present in the self-representation that

53 *Ibid.*, p. 601.

54 *Ibid.*, p. 485. Italics are mine.

> the agents make of themselves without being concerned about its place on the track record of connections[55].

This approach ends up considerably reducing the class of groups admissible as collective rights bearers. Those who reclaim diverse individual interests and express different ideas of the good life or the common good (associations, communal groups, corporations, non-governmental organizations, etc.) do not "play a role in the imaginary of all citizens, no matter the importance that is granted to these groups"[56]. This objectivism lays the foundation for the lack of importance that the characteristics of the nation can have for *each* individual's self-understanding. Their justification is found in that this context of national choice drives the self-representation of the institutional identity of the individual. Regardless their degree of closeness to substantive connections, their configuration as citizen is established through that group.

> The groups [concludes his argument] that are subject to collective rights do not have to be conceived as sources of an involuntary belonging from which they [individuals] cannot remove themselves. However, they are not simple associations to which we link ourselves by simple acts of will [...]. They have the characteristic of inviting all members into identifying representation[57].

The shadow of anti-individualist arguments by Putnam, Burge, Pettit, or Taylor is explicit. This membership is no more than the thought experiences that allow us to structure the representation that we make of ourselves.

This qualification of the collective-rights bearing group regarding the type of interest it protects will be specified by the application of three criteria that are implicitly understood in the requirements of its nature as a societal culture. In the first place, groups that hold collective rights should fulfill the requirements of political qualification. The institutions of the interested group should favor or make possible individual freedom and equality. This possibility of individual freedom and equality can only be realized by the group that affords the individual a context of choice within a national societal culture. That is the only thing that can offer the range of moral, cultural, and political options that are the condition of freedom and equality. There are two types of groups that can give the individual this opportunity. In the first place are fully democratic societal cultures, understood as liberal societies. In the second place are democratic communal societies. This type of society would be based on some substantive ideal related to ideas of goodness but, even if they had

55 *Ibid.*

56 *Ibid.*

57 *Ibid.*, p. 487.

no universalist projection, they would maintain a democratic structure to allow for the possibility of transformation. This intense normative component in democratic demand attempts, as I understand it, to respond to the application of the traditional liberalist criticism of communitarianism that stresses its defects when it comes to accepting the moral dissent of the individual. However, Seymour estimates that, for pragmatic reasons that are not specifically laid out, the recognition of the collective rights of decent hierarchical societies can be accepted[58].

In the second place, he maintains that the structure of collective-rights bearing groups must be cultural and not religious. The interested group must be characterized by the structure and not the character of their culture. This excludes religious communities that are defined by a conception of the good life or the common good. They have *character* but not *structure*. The differentiation attempts to construct a concept of acceptable collective rights in a liberal society.

> It presumes a distinction between the public and private identity of the group, between the structure of the culture and the character of the culture, between language conceived as a system of conventions and language conceived as a vector of a certain conception of the world, between the group inscribed in a context of choice and the group conceived as a community of destiny inscribed in a certain teleological objective or in a certain narrativity[59].

The exclusion of communitarian perspectives as a consequence of this differentiation has, however, one exception: certain cultures that make use of ideas about the good life as a basis for adopting democratic structures and interiorizing the possibility of change within the community itself. Finally, it confronts difficult cases such as the question of orthodox Jewish communities that are stably housed within broader societies or the conditions under which communities created by immigration can reproduce their social culture of origin within their host country. To the extent to which they guarantee stability and permanence, they would be eligible for official approval as a diaspora and, therefore, eligible to bear collective rights.

Finally, collective-rights bearing groups should satisfy a condition of permanence. As was mentioned above when discussing the quantitative aspect of the subject, it is necessary for groups to have a presumably permanent existence that is designated as reinforced stability. Groups that have an ephemeral existence without the intervention of an intermediary cannot be collective rights holders. This would exclude, for example, groups of immigrants until they reproduce their sociocultural conditions

58 *Ibid.*, p. 474.

59 *Ibid.*, p. 488.

in a stable manner, probably in an intergenerational fashion. Having permanence as a condition of temporality is limited to the demand for a likely reproduction of the group in question, barring an action meant to dissolve it (even if by the group itself).

3.4 Justifying Principle of Collective Rights

The final or independent justificatory principle that Seymour promotes as a justifier of collective rights is what is called the Principle of the Value of Cultural Diversity (PVCD). The concrete application of this principle is central to the construction of Seymour's theory of collective rights since it, while promoting their recognition, restricts these rights only to the people. The starting point, which would be typically liberal, consists of clearly affirming that the people are understood as social cultures and that their value is not intrinsic, but merely instrumental. In other words, they are valuable to the extent that they favor making a system of rights and freedoms available. This argumentation would lead to constructing a justifying strategy of the recognition of some moral value in *one* societal culture but not *my* societal culture. In this way, the attempt to justify the moral value of the plurality of societal cultures requires supplementary support: the PVCD.

I will explain this argument more fully. Seymour begins with the idea that the political conception of the people presumes a national self-representation at the core of a critical mass of citizens over a given territory and a collection of common institutions that cement relationships between those citizens[60]. This political conception of the people does not presume either moral individualism or collectivism but, in the opinion of the author, it makes it possible to have collective claims in the public sphere. The basis of the argument is his repeated reading of liberalism:

> Political liberalism does not consider people as primitive and undeniable entities that should be conceived as ends in themselves. Instead, they are entities that have the institutional personality of a citizen. Therefore, nothing prevents introducing nations conceived as entities that have an institutional identity alongside the people understood in the same fashion[61].

However, until this point, this conception does not justify why we should promote a double regime of rights, one for people and another for the people as a whole. To answer that, Seymour articulates three focal points. The first understands that the people, in their role as participants in the public sphere, are worthy of respect. The second shows that political

60 *Ibid.*, p. 343.

61 *Ibid.*, p. 403.

liberalism establishes the PVCD. The third affirms that the people today continue to be important sources of cultural diversity[62].

The first argumentative focal point begins with generally accepting that collective entities, even though their undeniable nature in relation to individuals is recognized, are only important because they are essential for individual wellbeing[63]. Therefore, why should the people be important? From a sociological and psychological point of view, it is because as societal cultures (in other words, institutional wholes such as a political, economic, educational system and other cultural institutions), they make it possible to have a context of choice and a system of rights and freedoms that, in turn, condition the possibility of creating other groupings. It would be a Rawlsian conception of the nation as a "social union of social unions".

However, this argument does not justify the granting of rights to all the peoples in particular[64]. The construction of the people operates by recurring to the idea of tolerance understood as a mere *modus vivendi* generator of stability. Thus, overcoming eventual violent conflicts between peoples on the international level leads to reaffirming the necessity for a *modus vivendi* that serves progressively to generate stability in relationships and, in the long run, to transform a mere *modus vivendi* into tolerance understood in the sense of respect. This is the point at which it can be affirmed that the dignity of every people is justified.

As a second argumentative focal point, this dignity does not imply admitting that the people as a whole are moral agents[65] or justifying their importance through the considerations that refer to the individual. Instead, they are justified because they can have a strictly political, and not a metaphysical characterization, with a basis in their institutional identity. When we talk about the people here, it signifies a strictly institutional entity, not a group of people assembled around a collection of beliefs, values, purposes, and projects. Some of their beliefs, values, purposes, and projects are eventually flat out rejectable, and this is not the way for the people to reclaim respect. Political liberalism establishes tolerance-respect with regard to all the peoples as institutional political agents.

The third focal point emphasizes transforming respect into active policies. Respect is not by itself sufficient to justify policies of difference, policies of cultural pluralism, or policies of affirmative action. Respecting is not valuing, and we need to attribute value to the existence of the

62 *Ibid.*, p. 345.

63 Kukathas, Chandran, "Are There Any Cultural Rights?", *Political Theory*, nº 20, 1992, p. 112. Also in Kymlicka, Will (ed.), *The Rights of Minority Cultures*, Oxford, Oxford University Press, 1995, pp. 228-256.

64 Seymour, *op. cit.*, p. 347.

65 *Ibid.*, p. 350.

institutional framework to justify these actions. For that, we need to establish a connection between the people and cultural diversity: the idea is that the people are important sources of cultural diversity. Seymour offers two reasons that support a favorable answer. On the one hand, the people are a source of external diversity to the extent that they are different from other peoples. On the other hand, they are the source of internal diversity to the extent that they offer their members a context of choice. Thus, a nationalism that restricts diversity, whether external or internal, will be, to that same extent, morally unacceptable.

This argumentative strategy challenges the use of arguments that have a compressed nature, such as saying that the PVCD creates benefits for the individual or that it is intrinsically valuable. This strategy makes it clear that political liberalism requires arguments that are not compressed but are based exclusively on public reason. The people are, as has been said, sources of valid moral claims and important sources of internal and external diversity but the justification of this approach requires argumentation based on the exercise of public reason. In this sense, there are five justifying arguments[66] that can be summarized regarding the increase of true international consensus in favor of the use of diversity; some historical evolution in the same sense; the distinction between the political notion of *toleration* rather than the psychological notion of *tolerance*[67]; and toleration among different collective moral identities and among the institutional identities of the people. In conclusion, his thesis is that if cultural diversity is a value that must be defended and promoted, and people serve the cause of that diversity, it is then necessary to defend and promote the worth of the people. The basic reason underlying the PVCD is that it is a demand derived from the equality of all people's worth. It presumes the transition from respect to valuing[68].

Finally, because of these connections between subject, content, and justifying principle, Seymour concludes that there are four large categories of groups capable of bearing collective rights: majority nations, minority nations, contiguous diasporas, and the groups resulting from immigration. All of them presume populations enjoying varying amounts of institutional goods, that is to say, they are more or less complete societal cultures. Each type of group corresponds to different kinds of rights. In other words, he

66 *Ibid.*, pp. 357-360.

67 *Ibid.*, p. 443.

68 *Ibid.*, p. 356. We must also point out that Seymour establishes an analogical argument between the principles of cultural diversity and what is called the Principle of the Value of the Diversity of the Natural Resources of the people (PVDNR) and the Principle of the Value of the Diversity of Individual Talents (PVDT). This last is developed in the Rawlsian manner of *justice as equity* and sustains that "sharing talents is a common good for the entire society." See Seymour, *ibid.*, pp. 364-365 and p. 493.

distinguishes three different types of collective rights: a) Poly-ethnic rights or a politics of cultural pluralism for non-contiguous diasporas (including immigrants who have consolidated as a group), b) Institutional rights for contiguous diasporas, and c) Rights to self-determination and self-government for the people[69].

In conclusion, for Seymour collective rights are "rights that the people possess that affect participative goods, produced and consumed in groups. They reference the maintenance, development, or creation of institutions that allow us to guarantee the integrity of the people as a people"[70]. In order to justify these rights, we need not subscribe to any moral assumptions about social ontology or adopt any comprehensive theory or fall victim to essentialism, communitarianism, collectivism, or authoritarianism. The alternative is to invent a non-individualist version of liberalism capable of gathering the collective entities sympathetically and constituting them into moral agents once they are considered in their institutional identity[71].

4. Critical Evaluation of the Characterization of Collective Rights According to Seymour's Thesis

In this last section, I would like to present some thoughts about the dissonances that I find in Seymour's work. First of all, I must recognize the originality of his thesis and the courage needed to seriously and systematically confront the important risks that accompany any intellectual question that attempts to open new paths that go beyond the commonplaces that enjoy – with or without basis – consensuses that are stable or becoming consolidated.

I will focus on two questions to organize this discussion: Seymour's proposal for political liberalism and the connection between collective rights and nationhood.

On the first question, the construction of political liberalism on the basis of the critique of individualist liberalism presupposes a strong theoretical commitment whose consequences are far reaching. I will not try to evaluate what the prevalence of tolerance can afford in multiple cases as its most inclusive nature, the reality of the division and limitation of political and social power, or the defense of pluralism, but I believe it is a stretch to attempt to build theories in order to unambiguously justify the category of collective rights. In short, an eventual consequence of this reformulation of the liberal paradigm can be made concrete in the

---

69 *Ibid.*, pp. 474-475.

70 *Ibid.*, p. 631.

71 *Ibid.*, p. 636.

affirmation of collective rights, but I do not believe that the attempt to justify them operates as a driving force behind change.

Similarly, I believe that at least four comments are relevant to the most singular attempt to anchor the justification of collective rights in the contributions of late Rawls. In the first place, it seems plausible to sustain a *methodological* interpretation of Rawls in the sense of understanding that the justifying model of his theory of justice is a simplified model that presupposes cultural homogeneity of the group and its invariability over time. However, increasing the complexity of Rawls's approach by introducing these cultural variables means a variation on liberalism whose continuity is not guaranteed. The fundamental reason it is also feasible rests on a Rawlsian interpretation such that *all* cultural aspects belong to the private field and are, therefore, beyond the public exercise of reason. I consider this last interpretation less suitable, but it is clearly feasible and is even the most widely accepted interpretation, so the necessary continuity between the ideas put forth by Seymour and Rawls is not guaranteed.

In the second place, I believe Seymour's reading of *The Law of Peoples* is strained. The recognition of the people's moral agency on the international plane operates as an alternative to the classic formula that attributes subjectivity to the states, and it would be truly difficult to justify which of the two rights is best suited to acquiring moral agency to the detriment of the people when it comes to configuring the conditions of a well-ordered international society. In a similar fashion, we could claim that the people deserve the presumption of equal respect, like individuals and unlike the states, which do not necessarily receive that respect. However, Rawls's thesis does not suggest that the domestic space for the exercise of public reason be reformulated to incorporate new agents who are not individuals, much less in order to recognize their rights on an equal footing. I do not find it foolish to propose an expansion of the interests that were considered in the original position in order to incorporate questions related to cultural and ethnic rights or the rights of group representation. These are aspects that should be kept in mind when configuring a well-organized domestic society, especially in the case of future generations, but I do not believe they lead to an affirmation of new instances of moral agency from the Rawlsian point of view.

In third place, and in the opposite vein, it is complicated to accept Seymour's criticisms of the abandonment of Rawls's universalist ideal in the international field without appealing, in turn, to the adoption of criteria of moral individualism, the criticism of which is the basis of Seymour's theoretical construction. The proposed argument supporting the idea of a globally based structure[72] as a third alternative would correspond, in any

[72] *Ibid.*, p. 318.

case, more to the exposure of hypothetical alternative empirical processes than to maintaining a novel moral principle.

Finally, it is difficult to justify collective rights in the domestic realm as derived from the principle of difference as a second principle of justice. The problem is double. On the one hand, Rawlsian logic would allow analogical justification of the adoption of policies of recognition – including those related to the defense of the Principle of the Value of Cultural Diversity (PVCD) – in the same way it justifies the logic of policies of wealth redistribution, but it does not follow that it establishes the justification of rights. On the other hand, and more importantly, eventual collective rights would be lexicographically subordinated to the rights of the first principle of justice, which would make it difficult to maintain the axiological parity between individual and collective rights that Seymour defends as one of his theory's central tenets.

On the second question, which is related to the connection between collective rights and nation, I find that there are certain discrepancies that merit a more detailed analysis. His central thesis maintains that only the people can bear collective rights because only they can be configured as societal cultures, that is, as cultural structures that imply a crossroads of influences and a context of choice. In this way, all the substantive realities, ideals of the good, conceptions of the good life, narrativities in the identifying configuration of the group, etc., are removed from the idea of the people, and the strategy of a strictly institutional characterization of the nation is employed. This demand for a reduction in cultural density is justified by two things. On the one hand, there is the liberal demand to maintain neutrality in the public space that should not be considered constricted by the attribution of moral agency to the people. In this way, the recognition of these moral agents in the public sphere leads to taking only some of the items that define the people or nation into consideration: the ones that are relevant as a context of choice. On the other, the support for political liberalism – unavoidable when attributing collective moral agency – also implies a reduction of the cultural components of the nation in a much more intense way than required by the thesis of individualist liberalism since, in the case of individualist liberalism, the justification of group rights can be broader because the rights continue to be held by an individual and are justified to the extent that they guarantee that individuals maintain this collection of cultural elements that afford them useful parameters for the determination of their own life plans[73]. The result of this process of the loss of the nation's cultural density to justify

[73] Kymlicka, *Multicultural Citizenship: A Liberal Theory of Minority Rights*, *op. cit.*, p. 107.

its moral agency is the cost of leaving behind what was the first principle of the argument, specifically, the defense of cultural diversity.

This problem gravely affects the three basic realities that constitute this light version of the concept of the nation as bearer of collective rights: common public language, institutional structure, and common public history (in some cases, the list is expanded to include up to eight characteristics: "Explicit or implicit constitution, language, institutions, history, national consciousness, desire for life in common, network of influences, and context of choice"[74]). Regarding language, the process is clear. To the extent that it is unburdened of elements related to conceptions of the world and is restructured around participatory social good, the instrumental side of language continues to be emphasized and its cultural components are diluted. To the extent to which the assessment of language is confined to the arena of public life, that is, to the exercise of public reason, its substantive meaning remains unread. To the extent to which it allows the convergence of more than one language as an identifying element and that it even affirms that the loss and substitution of one language by another dominant language is not decisive for the disappearance of the nation, it seems clear that its identity does not come from cultural realities. In addition, Seymour's references to language as a manifestation of external plurality do not clarify whether it is a contextual defense (for example, the survival of the use of French in North America) or whether it operates in absolute terms (for example, the disappearance of Cree languages among Aboriginal peoples in Quebec). In relation to institutional structure, there are also problems around the possibility that a people have suffered an expropriation of their institutional framework and that the individuals who constitute the people as a whole conserve a certain representation of themselves as members of those peoples. In this sense, it seems that Seymour[75] continues to recognize something in them regarding the holding of rights. Finally, regarding common public history, it seems to imply the suppression of the constitutive narrativities of the people, as well as the configuration of one's own historical memory. Therefore, if the idea of the people that is needed to sustain the theory of collective rights requires a negating of the elements that define it, the question we need to ask ourselves becomes obvious: What role does the recognition of a collective right play for a collective that does not need its signs of identity?

On the other hand, it is useful to note that there are difficulties regarding this centrality of the concept of nation when it comes to collective rights. Among them, we could emphasize the fact that it artificially rejects the

---

74 Seymour, *op. cit.*, p. 589.

75 *Ibid.*, p. 520.

possibility that other institutions can assume the functions of context of choice that are exclusively attributed to the nation. This fragmentation can operate in groups smaller that the people as a whole as well as on a larger scale. Smaller groups could include religious organizations and communities and alternative forms of socialization. Larger groups could include broader contexts of choice such as supranational orders, imperial territories, or simply, civilizations. In both groups, it is not difficult to imagine situations in which these contexts of choice are prioritized over the context of nations.

In short, it is not excessive to believe that Seymour's construction of the category of collective rights takes as a central objective the moral subjectivization of an institutional framework as a resource, mechanism, or technique through which that institutional framework can make the decision to establish itself as a new frame of reference of individual rights. In this way, collective rights would come together as a right of internal cohesion and an affirmation of subjectivity. In the end, the closing clause of the universe of collective rights would lead back to the right to self-determination understood as the jurisdiction of a constitutive collective action of new spaces for the exercise of individual rights. This path does not resolve the question of whether that collective action is exercised by a confluence of individual rights or by a collective agency constituted by individuals as well as public agents.

In conclusion, Seymour's proposal presumes an articulated and complex exercise in rereading the foundations of liberalism to recognize the collective rights of nations, or fragments of them, that come together under the authority of constituting them as legitimate subjects of the decisions regarding their own institutionalization, both within international and state structures, while understanding the relativity of multinational states. The most relevant question that would remain on the table is whether this complex collective moral agency is necessary for that objective or if the traditional option of the exercise of individual rights complemented by differentiated group rights leads to a more acceptable solution.

Chapter 5

After the Bouchard-Taylor Commission

Religious Accommodation and Human Rights in Quebec[1]

Jocelyn Maclure

Professor, Department of Philosophy, Laval University, Quebec City

Introduction

The issues surrounding secularism and the management of religious diversity in contemporary societies gain from being approached from a contextual and comparative perspective. Liberal democracies come to these thorny issues from very different historical pathways, but they all have to grapple with the challenges raised by moral and religious diversity. My own contribution to this comparative research agenda is to talk about the Quebec experience with a particular emphasis on Quebec's *Consultation Commission on Accommodation Practices Related to Cultural Differences* (CCAPRCD), and its aftermath.

Quebec and Canada are highly stimulating contexts for those who study questions related to identity and diversity. The issues that were mainly debated until perhaps 2006 were nationalism and the right to self-determination, federalism, and immigration and integration models such as multiculturalism and interculturalism. Since 2006, these issues were overshadowed by the debates around secularism and the management of religious diversity, including the issue of religious accommodations.

In 2007, a high-profile public commission – the CCAPRCD[2] – was put together by the Government of Quebec. The Commission was co-chaired

1 I wish to thank the workshop participants for their very helpful questions and comments, as well as Dominic Cliche for his first rate editorial work.

2 Bouchard, Gérard and Charles Taylor, *Building the Future: A Time for Reconciliation: Report*, Consultation Commission on Accommodation Practices Related to Cultural Differences, Les Publications du Québec, 2008.

by the philosopher Charles Taylor and the historian Gérard Bouchard. Its mandate was fourfold: first, to take stock of accommodation practices in Quebec; second, to analyze the attendant issues, bearing in mind the experience of other societies; third, to conduct an extensive public consultation on this topic; and fourth, to formulate recommendations to the government to ensure that accommodation practices conform to the values of Quebec society as a pluralistic, democratic, and egalitarian society.

The co-chairmen quickly decided to opt for a wide interpretation of their mandate. Rather than focusing strictly on the legal obligation to accommodate as it was defined in the jurisprudence, they chose to tackle the related but larger issues raised by citizens, such as the meaning of secularism, the place of religion in the public sphere, immigration and integration, and the fate of Quebec identity. Addressing all these issues in a comprehensive fashion was of course not possible, but it is doubtful, however, that the Quebec public would have been satisfied with a narrow and legalistic interpretation of the mandate.

In this paper, I will first zero in on the debate over "reasonable accommodation". I will try to define the legal obligation to accommodate and specify what are its limits. I will then try to pinpoint the meaning of secularism and defend what I will call a liberal and pluralist conception of secularism. Finally, I will discuss the main piece of legislation that was passed in the aftermath of the Bouchard-Taylor Commission, viz. Bill 94.

1. Reasonable Accommodation

1.1 The Definition of a Reasonable Accommodation

The legal norm of "reasonable accommodation" was at the heart of the debate in Quebec, as an important number of citizens felt that the accommodation of religious diversity was going too far and that it was threatening basic public values. The concept of a "reasonable accommodation", though, was not very well understood. One of the positive contributions of the CCAPRCD was that the media and members of the public came to a better understanding of the legal duty to accommodate.

In the Canadian jurisprudence, reasonable accommodation is a rather well defined and circumscribed legal norm that stipulates that there is a duty on the part of an employer or an institution to offer accommodation measures to someone who is adversely affected by a rule or a policy that seems *prima facie* neutral, but that indirectly discriminates against the members of a group. The discriminated individual can be a part of a religious group, but it can just as well consist of, for instance, people living with disabilities or pregnant women. The notion of reasonable accommodation was thus conceived as a way to correct indirect and involuntary discrimination, i.e. cases when a norm of general application can be shown to be discriminatory against members of a group on the basis of some their attributes, such as their physical condition, gender, age, ethnicity, language, or religion. For example, there is no explicit discrimination in a rule prohibiting headgear at a school, for it does not target any particular group. In its application, however, the rule constrains those whose faith requires wearing headgear, while those whose conscientious convictions do not include the wearing of headgear can more easily harmonize their freedom of religion and their right to a public education. This does not mean that the rule itself cannot be legitimate. Maybe it would not be a good idea, generally speaking, to allow high school students to wear headgear in class. But a religious obligation (or any other deeply-held, meaning-giving belief) is not the same thing a personal preference[3], and this is why accommodation measures are sometimes necessary. Similarly, it is easy to understand why prisons or hospitals have rules that prevent patients or detainees from choosing their meals – this would be too costly and impractical. However, few people believe that vegetarians (either for religious or secular reasons) should not benefit from an exception[4]. This is why fairness sometimes requires a differential treatment even if the rule does not explicitly discriminate against anyone[5].

The duty to accommodate is thus a jurisprudential creation. It originates from the interpretive work of the courts rather than from an explicit legislative act. it is not explicitly stated in the *Canadian Charter of Rights and Freedoms*[6]. But the courts established that the norm of

---

3 For a defense of that argument, see the second part of Maclure, Jocelyn and Charles Taylor, *Secularism and Freedom of Conscience*, Cambridge, Harvard University Press, 2011.

4 See, for instance, the decision by the Federal Court of Canada in the case *Maurice v. Canada (Attorney General)*, 2002 FCT 69, [2002] 2 F.C. D-47, 186.

5 The Supreme Court of Canada explicitly formulated the legal obligation of reasonable accommodation for the first time in 1985 in the *Simpson-Sears* ruling. As a member of the Seventh-Day Adventist Church, the plaintiff had to keep Sabbath, which for this Church extends from sundown Friday to sundown Saturday. This entailed that she could not work on Friday evenings as well as on Saturdays. Arguing that her religious obligation was incompatible with the employment policy of the company for full-time sales clerks, *Simpson-Sears* discharged the plaintiff on the basis of her refusal to work on Saturday. The Supreme Court claimed that the refusal on the part of Simpson-Sears to take "reasonable steps to accommodate the complainant" constituted a form of indirect discrimination. See *Ontario Human Rights Commission (O'Malley) v. Simpson-Sears* [1985] 2 S.C.R. 536.

6 Canadian constitutional culture, I think, partly vindicates Ronald Dworkin's interpretive theory of constitutional adjudication. When it is confronted with hard cases, such as claims for accommodations, end of life issues or the right of a province to secede, it readily invokes implicit principles of political morality.

reasonable accommodation is a logical corollary of the equality rights and freedom of religion that are enshrined in the *Charter*[7]. It stems from a material, rather than a purely formal, conception of equality; its purpose is generally to enable a member of a minority or a vulnerable individual to take advantage of an opportunity or of a public good[8]. For example, accommodation measures can remove the obligation to choose between two basic human rights, such as having an equal right to apply for a position and practicing one's religion, or having access to a public good (such as education, health care, or all kinds of permits) and respecting the prescriptions of one's faith.

One misunderstanding that the CCAPRCD Report helped correct was that the duty to offer reasonable accommodation measures was thought by many to apply in all possible cases of accommodation claims. What needed to be reminded is that there has to be discrimination for the duty to accommodate to apply. As the Report suggested, "reasonable accommodation" ought be distinguished from "concerted adjustment". The former is derived from more general human rights, whereas the latter is the result of voluntary negotiations between consenting parties who wish to cooperate, to live together peacefully as neighbors or to establish a business relationship.

In order to illustrate this distinction, consider one of the cases that was at the origin of the reasonable accommodation controversy: the so-called "YMCA case". The YMCA is a sport center located in a neighborhood of Montreal where an important Hassidic Jewish community lives. The YMCA is right next to a Hassidic primary school. The pupils, when they were playing in the school's yard, could see inside the gym where people, including women, worked out. The school board asked the YMCA whether they would mind frosting the windows so that the young children would not see inside, and offered to pay for the new windows. The board of the YMCA agreed. But when some clients of the YMCA heard about the deal, they expressed their discontent and reported it to the media. The YMCA's decision was widely criticized. Many citizens thought that this was a clear demonstration that the accommodation of religious diversity was going too far and the norm of reasonable accommodation was in fact unreasonable.

This case, however, had nothing to do with the legal obligation to offer accommodation measures. There was no indirect discrimination involved

7 Woehrling, José, "L'obligation d'accommodement raisonnable et l'adaptation de la société à la diversité religieuse", *McGill Law Journal*, vol. 43, nº 2, 1998, pp. 325-401.

8 Bosset, Pierre, "Les fondements juridiques et l'évolution de l'obligation d'accommodement raisonnable" in Myriam Jézéquiel (ed.), *Les accommodements raisonnables: quoi, comment, jusqu'où? Des outils pour tous*, Cowansville, Éditions Yvon Blais, pp. 3-28.

and the YMCA was consequently under no obligation to frost its windows. This was a case of "concerted adjustment". The media were unfortunately not quick enough to correct the misperception. Combined with other cases, this fueled the public outcry with regard to the accommodation of religious diversity.

1.2 The Limits to the Duty to Accommodate

That being said, one of the main concerns expressed by citizens with regard to the legal duty to accommodate concerned the limits of such an obligation. Many feared that freedom of religion, as interpreted by the Court, would end up trumping other fundamental values such as gender equality, or the religious neutrality of the State, or fairness among co-workers. That fear was compounded by the "personal and subjective" conception of freedom of religion found in the jurisprudence. Before I get back to the question of the limits of the obligation to accommodate, I shall say a few words on the subjective conception of freedom of religion and, more generally, on how rulings of the Canadian Supreme Court are often perceived in Quebec.

In Canada, as well as in the U.S., the claimant requesting an adjustment or an exemption is not expected to demonstrate the objectivity of his or her belief. In the Canadian Supreme Court 2004 *Amselem* decision, the majority established that the claimants "need not show some sort of objective religious obligation, requirement or precept to invoke freedom of religion"[9]. For the Court, the crucial point is that the belief held by the claimants has "a nexus with religion", and that the petitioner sincerely believes that his or her faith prescribes a given practice or act. No authorized religious representatives or experts need to confirm the existence of the precept invoked for a request for an accommodation to be taken under advisement. The criterion used by the Supreme Court is thus that of the *sincerity* of belief: the petitioner must demonstrate that he or she truly believes he or she is obligated to conform to the religious precept in question.

The chief advantage of a personal and subjective conception of freedom of religion is that it spares the courts from having to act as interpreters of religious dogma and as arbiters of the inevitable theological disagreements that divide all religious communities. In relying on personal belief, they avoid having to choose between the contradictory interpretations of religious doctrines. They also circumvent the danger of falling back on the majority opinion within the religious community and thereby contributing to the marginalization of minority voices.

---

9 *Syndicat Northcrest v. Amselem*, 2004 SCC 47, [2004] 2 S.C.R. 55 at 4, 37.

The downside, however, is that this very broad conception can end up opening the door, first, to an excessive number of accommodations – this is the problem of proliferation – and, second, to the strategic or manipulative invocation of freedom of conscience and religion and of the legal obligation to accommodate – this is the problem of instrumentalization.

At this juncture, and this is probably something relevant in other multinational political associations such as Spain, the debate about the status of Quebec within the Canadian federation interfered with the debate about religious accommodations. Even if the support for the separation of Quebec is not particularly strong nowadays, there is a strong subset of the Quebec population which believes that some basic federal institutions and policies suffer from a legitimacy deficit. This mainly goes back to the events of 1981-82 when the new *Constitution Act* was passed without the consent of Quebec, when the *Canadian Charter of Rights and Freedoms* was designed and constitutionalized, and judicial review imported to Canada. Many believe, rightly or wrongly, that the Canadian Supreme Court cannot or will not properly recognize Quebec's rights and interests, and that many of its rulings prove it[10].

For instance, most observers agree that it was the Supreme Court's decision in the Multani case in March 2006 that kick-started the reasonable accommodation debate in Quebec. In that case, the Court allowed the young Multani, a Sikh schoolboy who wanted to bear a kirpan – the Sikh ceremonial dagger – at school, to do so under strict conditions. Up to this day, even though the Supreme Court said that the kirpan had to be worn under the shirt, placed in a case and wrapped and sewn in a cloth envelope that itself needed to be sewn to the shirt, more than 90% of the Quebec population believes that the Supreme Court was wrong. The decision was widely interpreted as another symptom of the Supreme Court's propensity to overrule legitimate laws passed by the Quebec legislative assembly (judicial activism), and of the imposition of Canadian-style multiculturalism in Quebec, a policy which is seen as encouraging ghettoization and fragmentation, and as conflicting with Quebec's own integration policy, that is, "interculturalism"[11].

This perception that the Canadian *Charter* and the Supreme Court, as well as the multiculturalism policy, go against the grain of Quebec's interest heightened the crisis. It did not create the crisis, but it amplified it. As I

[10] See Tully, James, "Introduction" in James Tully and Alain-G. Gagnon (eds.), *Multinational Democracies*, Cambridge, Cambridge University Press, 2001 pp. 1-34.

[11] For a critical discussion of the alleged difference between multiculturalism and interculturalism, see Maclure, Jocelyn, "Multiculturalism and Political Morality" in Duncan Ivison (ed.), *The Research Companion to Multiculturalism*, Ashgate Publishing Limited, Farnham, 2010, pp. 39-56.

pointed out, many feared that religious accommodations were threatening fundamental rights or public values. As a consequence of that fear, the idea of institutionalizing a formal hierarchy within fundamental rights gained some traction; many thought that gender equality, for instance, needed to trump freedom of religion in cases of collision between the two rights. But the answer to this fear, as it should become clear, lies not in the philosophically and morally unsustainable proposal to hierarchize basic human rights but in the notion that the accommodation claims ought to be "reasonable".

Courts have indeed specified that accommodation claims ought to be "reasonable". Courts can assess not only the sincerity of the claimant but also the effects of the desired accommodation measure on the rights of others and on the capacity of the institution to function efficiently and achieve its goals. We are moving here into the terrain of the "undue hardship" or, better still, "excessive constraint" (*contrainte excessive*) set of criteria that can be reconstructed from case law. The content of the excessive constraint set of criteria is not fixed and immutable, for it must always be specified with reference to the facts of the matter. But looking at a wide range of cases involving both public and private organizations reveals some general and transversal criteria. An accommodation claim cannot (1) create excessive functional constraints (in terms of cost and functioning), (2) compromise the ends of the institutions (making profits, educating, or providing health care or social services), or (3) infringe upon the rights and freedoms of coworkers or fellow citizens[12]. As is well known, individual rights were never seen as absolute by liberal philosophers from Locke to Kymlicka and through Mill and Dworkin; basic human rights can legitimately be restricted in the name of the rights of others or of compelling public interests[13]. Accommodation claims must be reasonable because exemptions, compensations, or adaptation measures modify, to varying degrees, the prevailing terms of social cooperation. The obligation to accommodate is meant to redress an injustice by correcting indirect discrimination; logically, it should not do so by creating new situations of unfairness. Yet, for an accommodation claim to be turned down, it must be shown that its deleterious effects are real and significant. Dissociating itself from its US counterpart, the Canadian Supreme Court points out in

12 Bosset, Pierre, "Limites de l'accommodement: Le droit a-t-il tout dit?", *Éthique Publique*, vol. 9, nº 1, 2007, pp. 165-168.

13 The "excessive constraint" set of criteria is thus consistent with s. 1 of the 1982 Constitution and with the Oakes Test, which is applied by Canadian courts to assess when a law can legitimately restrict individual rights. See *R. v. Oakes*, [1986] 1 R.C.S. 103. Since the limits to the duty to accommodate include not only deontological reasons (the rights of others must be respected), but also functional considerations, "excessive constraints" is more appropriate than the narrower "undue hardship."

Central Okanagan School District N° 23 v. Renaud that a minimalist and insufficiently demanding notion of excessive constraint would amount to a removal altogether of the legal duty to accommodate[14]. The burden of proof, in the Canadian jurisprudence, is placed upon the party who claims that a norm is reasonable *even* if it restricts the religious freedom of another party.

Accommodation claims can thus in some cases be legitimately turned down. For instance, a Canadian provincial Court of Appeal recently denied the right to civil marriage commissioners to decline to solemnize same-sex marriages even if doing so would be contrary to their religious beliefs[15]. The majority's *ratio* was that, although the freedom of conscience of the marriage commissioners was genuinely infringed by the obligation to solemnize same-sex marriages, the stakes of allowing them to opt out were too high. This would amount, according to the Court, to "perpetuate a brand of discrimination which our national community has only recently begun to successfully overcome"; this would have "genuinely harmful impacts", the refusal on the part of commissioners being perceived by gays and lesbian, as well as by other citizens, as an act as offensive as any racist or sexist one; and it would "undercut the basic principle that governmental services must be provided on an impartial and non-discriminatory basis"[16]. Consequently, the deleterious effects of the accommodation have been judged, in that case, to overweight the positive ones.

As the Canadian jurisprudence testifies, the notion of "reasonableness" that delineates the obligation of the accommodation measures is flexible enough to adapt to a wide variety of empirical situations but yet sufficiently well defined and robust to safeguard basic rights and common public values[17].

2. Secularism

The management of religious diversity also raises the question of the appropriate place of religion in the public sphere and of the relationship between public institutions and religious practice. All democracies, notwithstanding the fact that they are officially secular such as France

---

14 *Central Okanagan School District N° 23 v. Renaud*, [1992] 2 R.C.S. 970.

15 The Court of Appeal for Saskatchewan, [2011] SKCA 3.

16 *Ibid.*, at 17-18 and 40-42.

17 For other cases where accommodation claims were turned down by Canadian courts, see Maclure, Jocelyn, "Reasonable Accommodation and the Subjective Conception of Freedom of Conscience and Religion" in Avigail Eisenberg and Kymlicka, Will (ed.), *Identity Politics in the Public Realm*, Vancouver, University of British Columbia Press, 2011, pp. 260-280.

or Turkey or that they have a "separation" clause enshrined in their constitution, such as the U.S., or that some form of official recognition is granted to one or more religions, such as Denmark or the U.K., have to deal with religion and cope with the challenges raised by religious diversity.

France, for instance, is often thought to be the most secular society, but we know that 85 percent of the funding for private religious schools comes from the state (as opposed to 60% in Quebec); that the French state maintains and preserves Catholic and Protestant churches and Jewish synagogues built before the 1905 Law on the Separation of the Churches and State; that six Catholic holidays (Easter, Ascension, Pentecost, Assumption, All Saints' Day, and Christmas) are legal holidays; and that a concordat granting privileges to the Catholic, Protestant, and Jewish religions is maintained in Alsace-Moselle. Separation and neutrality, as the example of France attests, are never fully realized in practice.

Fully excluding religion from the public space is not, even in the most secular regimes, a real option. On the one hand, freedom of religion includes the freedom to act on the basis of one's beliefs, within reasonable limits. This is what the Americans call the "free-exercise of religion", which cannot be strictly confined to the private sphere. On the other hand, we cannot extract a society from its cultural and historical context. We will not require that churches stop ringing their bells; that all the villages or streets that borrow their names from saints be renamed; or that the cross that stands on top of the Mount-Royal in Montreal be taken down. No one seriously asks that we eliminate all the statutory Holidays that come from Christianity and design a deculturalized calendar like the French revolutionaries tried to do. Very few would suggest that spaces such as hospitals, prisons and armies stop offering religious or spiritual counseling.

A theory and practice of secularism that allow us to arbitrate the dilemma related to the presence of religion in the public sphere are thus needed. Elements for such a model were gathered in the CCAPRCD Report[18], and Charles Taylor and I further developed it in *Secularism and Freedom of Conscience*[19]. The Commission recommended that the government drafts and submits to the Quebec legislative assembly a "white paper" or a Policy statement on secularism. This formal recommendation was alas disregarded.

---

18 See Bouchard and Taylor, *op. cit.*, chapter 5.

19 Maclure, Jocelyn and Charles Taylor, *Secularism and Freedom of Conscience*, Cambridge, Harvard University Press, 2011. Originally published in French in 2010 under the title *Laïcité et liberté de conscience*, Boréal/La Découverte, Montréal/Paris. See also the spanish translation *Laicidad y libertad de conciencia*, Madrid, Alianza Editorial, 2011.

The CCAPRCD Report defended what Taylor and I called a liberal and pluralist conception of *laïcité*. It is liberal because it is a human rights-based conception. It primarily seeks to protect the equality and freedom of conscience of all. It is pluralist because it does not believe that a "difference-blind" conception of liberalism is appropriate under conditions of deep moral and religious diversity.

This model is called in the Quebec political culture "*laïcité ouverte*" (or open secularism). It is a model of *laïcité* that recognizes that strictly confining religion to the private sphere is a not real option and that is thus "open" to some forms of reasonable presence of religion within the public sphere. I now want to go over a few general guidelines that were sketched out regarding the place of religion in the public space and in public institutions.

2.1 Distinction between Institutions and Individuals

Broadly speaking, secularism requires that there is no organic connection between the state and religion. The secular state must take its orders from the people through their elected representatives and not from religion. But the state's religious neutrality demands that *public institutions* favor no religion, not that the *individuals* who find themselves in these institutions privatize their religious affiliation. What I mean is that there is an important difference between, on the one hand, allowing citizens, for instance, to display religious symbols in public institutions and, on the other hand, favoring a particular religion through public interventions.

For example, we must contrast the act, by a student, of wearing a religious symbol in class to parochial teaching or to the recitation of a prayer before the beginning of classes in public schools. The essential point, if we wish to grant students equal respect and protect their freedom of conscience, is not to remove religion in all its manifestations from school but rather to ensure that the school does not espouse or favor any religion. The same distinction applies to other public institutions such as municipalities or courts.

2.2 Should Public Officials Be Allowed to Wear Visible Religious Signs?

At this point, one obvious question that this theory raises is about the implications of the state's religious neutrality for state officials, that is, for those who represent it and allow it to perform its functions. In some countries, such as France and Turkey, civil servants cannot display religious symbols when they are on duty. The reason most often mentioned for prohibiting state officials from wearing religious symbols is that they represent the state and must consequently embody the values it promotes. Since the state is in theory neutral toward citizens' various religious affiliations, its representatives must exemplify that neutrality.

At first sight, that position seems reasonable and legitimate. As individuals, citizens are free to display their religious affiliations both in the private sphere and in the public sphere, understood in the broad sense. But as state officials, they must agree to embody or personify the state's neutrality toward religions. A state employee wearing a visible religious symbol might give the impression that he is serving his church before serving the state, or that there is an organic link between the state and his religious community, whereas a uniform rule prohibiting the wearing of such religious symbols avoids the appearance of a conflict of interest.

That being said, it is important to be aware that prohibiting public officials from wearing religious symbols bears a cost, namely, either the restriction of the freedom of religion or of the equal access to positions in the public administration. No right is absolute, but a liberal democracy must always have strong reasons for restricting fundamental rights and socio-economic opportunities. So the question is: Does the appearance of neutrality, which is the objective of the rule prohibiting the wearing of visible religious symbols by public officials, constitute a strong reason?

Although the appearance of neutrality is important, the Commissioners Gérard Bouchard and Charles Taylor did not believe that it justifies a general rule prohibiting public officials from wearing conspicuous religious symbols. What matters above all, according to them, is that such officials demonstrate impartiality in the *exercise* of their duties. State employees must seek to perform the mission attributed by lawmakers to the institution they serve; their acts must be dictated neither by their faith nor by their philosophical beliefs but rather by the will to accomplish the tasks associated with the position they hold.

But why think that the person who wears a visible religious symbol is less liable to demonstrate impartiality, professionalism, and loyalty to the institution than the person who wears none? Why, in that case, stop at external manifestations of faith? Logically, should not state employees be required to renounce all convictions of conscience, thus instituting a modern version of the Ironclad Test Oath that Catholics needed to take in order to have a public office after England took New France in 1760?[20] That would obviously be absurd. It is unclear why we should think *a priori* that those who display their religious affiliation are less capable of being professional and loyal to their employer than those whose convictions of conscience are not externalized or are so in a less conspicuous manner

[20] Milot, Micheline, *La laïcité*, Ottawa, Novalis, 2008, p. 99.

(the wearing of a cross, for example). Why deny the presumption of impartiality to one and grant it to the other?

Public officials must be evaluated in light of their actions. Do they display impartiality in the exercise of their duties? Do their religious beliefs interfere with the exercise of their professional judgment? It is possible to evaluate the neutrality of the actions performed by state officials without systematically restricting their freedom of conscience and religion. For example, when an employee wears a visible religious symbol and proselytizes at work, what would need to be proscribed is the proselytism and not the wearing of the religious symbol, which is not in itself an act of proselytism.

The position just outlined does not mean, however, that the wearing of all religious symbols by all public officials must be accepted. Rather, it implies that wearing a religious symbol ought not to be prohibited simply because it is religious. Other reasons may justify the prohibition, however. Here, we go back to the reasonable limits on freedom of religion that I sketched out in section 1.2. The wearing of a religious symbol must not interfere with the performance of one's duties. A teacher or a nurse, for example, could not wear a burqa or niqab at work and still adequately discharge her duties since the full veil hinders communication and raises security issues.

2.3 Heritage vs. Establishment

Another source of discontent about measures of accommodation for religious minorities has to do with the perceived asymmetry between what is required of members of the majority and what is required of members of minority groups. Some have trouble understanding why accommodations must be granted to individuals belonging to minority religious groups so that they can practice their religion in the public space, whereas the majority must accept, in the name of secularism, the privatization of some of their religious symbols and rituals.

Does secularism indeed require the sacrifice of a society's religious heritage? In particular, must public institutions and public places be purged of any trace of religion, and especially, that of the majority? Would that not amount to obliterating the past, severing ties between the past and the present?

An adequate conception of secularism must seek to distinguish what constitutes a form of establishment of religion from what belongs to a society's religious heritage. In Canada, the old Lord's Day Act, the privileges granted not long ago to Catholics and Protestants in the teaching of religion in public schools, the recitation of a prayer before the beginning of sessions of municipal councils, and the obligatory use of the Bible to swear an oath in court constituted forms of establishment of the majority religion. In all these cases, practicing Christians were favored and non-Christians compelled to respect a law or a norm that was at odds with their conscience. To put it differently, Christian beliefs were directly turned into positive law. But some practices or symbols that may have originated in the religion of the majority do not truly constrain the conscience of those who are not part of that majority. Such is the case for practices and symbols that have a heritage value rather than a regulatory function. The cross on Mount-Royal in Montreal, for example, does not signify that the City of Montreal identifies itself as Catholic, and it does not compel non-Catholics to act against their conscience. It is simply a symbol that attests to an episode in Quebec's history.

A religious symbol is thus compatible with secularism when it is a reminder of the past rather than a sign of religious identification on the part of a public institution. As the Quebec Human Rights Commission points out, a symbol or ritual stemming from the religion of the majority "does not infringe on fundamental liberties if it is not accompanied by any constraint on individuals' behavior"[21].

As always, there will be limit cases. Religious symbols in public institutions, like crosses in public schools, do not constrain individual behavior, but they do entail that there is a special link between the school and the religion of the majority; it creates a form of symbolic inequality, and for that reason I think they should be removed. It is necessary to keep practices that do constitute a form of identification on the state's part with a religion – usually that of the majority – from being preserved on the pretext that they now have only a heritage value[22].

3. The Aftermath of the Bouchard-Taylor Commission: Quebec's Bill 94

The post Bouchard-Taylor Commission debate was predominantly focused on religious signs in the public sphere. Some wished that the Quebec legislative assembly would follow Belgium and France and ban the burqa and niqab in the public space. This was not really taken up by legislators of the different parties. The more heated debate had to do with religious signs in the public administration. A majority among the public

21 Bosset, Pierre, *Les symboles et rituels religieux dans les institutions publiques* [Cat. 2.120-4.6], Commission des droits de la personne et de la jeunesse du Québec, Quebec, 1999, p. 10. My translation.

22 The European Court of Human Rights succumbed, I think, to this fallacy in *Lautsi and Others v. Italy*, Application no. 30814/06, 18 March 2011, Strasbourg, [Online]: http://cmiskp.echr.coe.int/tkp197/view.asp?item=1&portal=hbkm&action=html&highlight=30814/06&sessionid=71434273&skin=hudoc-en.

thinks that public officials should not be allowed to wear visible religious signs, an opinion voiced in parliament by the official opposition.

However, the government decided otherwise. In March 2010, it introduced "Bill n°94: An Act to establish guidelines governing accommodation requests within the Administration and certain institutions"[23], that it saw as its main legislative response to the CCAPRCD Report and to the ongoing debate on secularism and reasonable accommodations. Despite the political rhetoric of the government, the scope of the bill is fairly limited. For the main part, the bill gives an explicit legislative status to already existing positive legal norms. Articles 1, 4 and 5, for instance, simply reaffirm the duty to accommodate within reasonable limits as it was already defined in the jurisprudence. In addition, article 4 enunciates the principle of the "religious neutrality" of the State, which was until then indirectly inferred from the rights and freedoms granted to all citizens. The element of novelty in the bill is contained in article 6:

> 6. The practice whereby a personnel member of the Administration or an institution and a person to whom services are being provided by the Administration or the institution show their face during the delivery of services is a general practice.
>
> If an accommodation involves an adaptation of that practice and reasons of security, communication or identification warrant it, the accommodation must be denied.

The main target of this norm is to ban the wearing of the burqa and the niqab by public officials and to require women who wear such kinds of veils to remove them while they are transacting with a civil servant. The second paragraph of the article is a restatement that there are reasonable limits to freedom of religion, i.e., that motives related to security, communication and identification can justify turning down accommodation requests. Finally, article 7 stipulates that "the highest administrative authority of a department, body or institution is responsible for ensuring compliance with this Act", under the final authority of the Minister of Justice.

One of the positive effects of this bill is that all departments and bodies now have a legal duty to adopt guidelines related to the management of religious diversity and to monitor the practices of accommodation and non accommodation that are taking place on the ground. However, many, including the official opposition, think this bill does not go far enough.

---

23 National Assembly of Quebec, 2010, Bill n° 94, *An Act to establish guidelines governing accommodation requests within the Administration and certain institutions*, [Online]: http://www.assnat.qc.ca/en/travaux-parlementaires/projets-loi/projet-loi-94-39-1.html.

Conclusion

The debate in Quebec between the competing models of secularism is not settled yet. The Parti Québécois, the sovereignist party which currently is the official opposition in the parliament, is now preparing legislation on *laïcité* – that will perhaps take the form of a charter (*charte de la laïcité*) inspired by the *Charter of the French Language*[24]. The current liberal government maintains that Bill 94 testifies to their endorsement of *laïcité ouverte*. This where we are now in Quebec.

One of the pending issues in the current context is that more coercive rules regulating religious practice could easily be challenged before the courts and ultimately struck down by the Supreme Court of Canada. Going back to the intersection between the debate over the status of Quebec within the Canadian federation and the debate within Quebec on religious diversity, such an outcome could in turn fuel the resentment against Canadian federalism and the Supreme Court of Canada in particular. This is very speculative but, if the PQ defeats the currently very unpopular Liberal Party in the next provincial election, the internal debate over secularism and religious accommodation could lead to another round of constitutional debate over the future of Canadian federalism.

24 R.S.Q., chapter C-11, April 2011 [2010]. The Parti Québécois formed a minority government in September 2012 and embarked on such a project.

Part III

Human Rights, Political Rights and Institutional Pluralism

CHAPTER 6

Federalism and the Protection of Rights and Freedoms

Affinities and Antagonism[1]

José WOEHRLING

Associate Professor, Faculty of Law, University of Montreal

Introduction

What are the interrelations between federalism and the protection of human rights? Such a question arises not only in federations in the strict sense, but in all "compound" states that consist of two levels of government, each having substantial powers and enjoying true autonomy in relation to the other (as for example in "regionalized" countries like Spain or Italy). Given such a situation, each level of government can take positive as well as negative measures in respect to human rights: negative, in exercising its powers in ways that restrict the benefit of rights; positive, in so far as each level of government is able to adopt constitutional and legislative instruments aimed at protecting the enjoyment of rights. Thus, we shall examine in turn: (1) The effects that federalism has on the protection of rights and freedoms, where we shall see that the division of powers that characterizes federalism has mostly, albeit not only, beneficial consequences for the protection of the rights of individuals and minorities; and (2) The effects of protecting rights and freedoms through a national Bill of Rights and judicial review for the balance of powers in a federation. As we shall see, judicial review by federal courts under a national constitutional instrument can lead to more centralization of powers as well as to more legal standardization, both impinging on the values of federalism.

---

1 Reprinted, with revisions, from Requejo Ferran and Miquel Caminal (eds.), *Political Liberalism and Plurinational Democracies*, London, Routledge, 2011, pp. 139-156.

1. The Impact of Federalism on the Protection of Rights

Federalism, and more generally the compound nature of governmental power, furthers the protection of rights and freedoms in two different ways. First, from an institutional and political point of view, federalism divides and diffuses – and consequently limits – power, at the same time as it allows people to participate more actively in political affairs within smaller political units. In federations with national, ethnic or linguistic minorities, those groups large enough to form the majority of the population in one or several federated units will be able to attain a position of political majority. Secondly, from a legal point of view, by superposing two legal systems, federalism also allows for the existence of two layers of constitutional or quasi-constitutional instruments for the protection of human rights that will complement each other and together provide more comprehensive protections. However, in certain aspects the functioning of a federal system can also hamper the protection of rights and freedoms, especially in creating difficulties for the ratification and implementation of international human rights conventions.

A. Institutional and Political Benefits of Federalism for the Protection of Rights

1. The Rights of People in General

In a broad way, the benefits of federalism for the protection of rights and freedoms of people in general can be epitomized by two simple ideas. First, by dividing power, federalism limits and diminishes power and thus helps to prevent its abuse. From this point of view, federalism functions like a second form of separation of powers that complements the separation between the legislative, executive and judicial branches. This concept, which hardly needs further elaboration, has received a classical exposition in a famous text by James Madison, in the *Federalist Papers*:

> In the compound republic of America, the power surrendered by the people is first divided between two distinct governments, and then the portion allotted to each subdivided among distinct and separate departments. Hence a double security arises to the rights of the people. The different governments will control each other, at the same time that each will be controlled by itself[2].

Secondly, by decentralizing power, federalism enhances political and democratic rights inasmuch as citizens can participate more effectively in political life within smaller political units where the *locus* of power is situated nearer to them. Federalism confers more influence to smaller

2 Hamilton, Alexander, James Madison and John Jay, *The Federalist Papers*, New York, New American Library, 1961, p. 323.

groups by localizing a greater part of political authority at their level. It gives individuals the possibility to exercise more influence and control at the regional or local level than they can conceivably exercise at the national level. As well, by giving people the opportunity to participate in political affairs at more numerous levels of government, federalism helps to educate them in the practice of citizenship. Finally, in a federation, citizens have access to more than one source of governmental services and benefits; if one administration fails to provide a certain benefit, they can turn to another level of government. Thus, federalism forestalls a situation of monopolistic exercise of state power and, instead, creates a competition between different governments to the benefit of the electorate[3].

However, the localization of a substantial amount of political power at a level that is closer to the local population can also bring negative consequences for the protection of rights and freedoms, by increasing the likelihood of tyranny by sectoral interests. A political majority is easier to gain and to conserve at a local rather than at the national level, thus there are more risks that it is appropriated by a particular faction. Conversely, the localization of political power at the national level is considered to avert the tyranny of local majorities. In a larger context, the influence of the many pressure groups will be better counterbalanced. The national government usually can keep more distance in relation to local quarrels; it is often in a better situation to protect regional or local minorities. At the same time, the centralization of power can also bring a concentration of power that heightens the risks of abuse. A more distant government will also be less responsive to the needs and wishes of citizens. In consequence, both centralization and decentralization of political power can result in negative as well as positive outcomes for the protection of rights and freedoms. Federalism allows for a combination of centralization and decentralization in proportions that vary with each particular situation.

Finally, in so far as the different governments in a federation act as a check upon one another, there will result a supplementary limitation of political power to the benefit of the citizens. As Alexander Hamilton wrote:

> Power being almost always the rival of power, the general government will at all times stand ready to check the usurpations of the state governments, and these will have the same disposition toward the general government.

---

3 Conversely in so far as federalism divides powers between two levels of government, its functioning demands a high degree of coordination between the federation and the constituent units. Coordination mechanisms are generally dominated by the executive branch and inadequately controlled by elected assemblies and, thus, subject to a certain democratic deficit. Furthermore, the complexity of intergovernmental coordination mechanisms creates a lack of transparency for citizens, who no longer know which level of government is responsible for certain decisions.

> The people by throwing themselves into either scale, will infallibly make it preponderate. If their rights are invaded by either, they can make use of the other as means of redress[4].

Nonetheless, in a well-balanced federation each government must enjoy a sufficient autonomy in relation to the other in the use of its constitutional powers.

2. *The Rights of Minorities*

In a federal state, it is possible to adjust the political divisions of the territory in order to create one or more constituent units in which a group that is a minority nationally will form the majority regionally, and thus be in position to control the political institutions and power at the regional level. Several federal countries, like Canada, Switzerland, Belgium or India, have precisely chosen to become federations because it was considered a solution to the problems arising from the existence of ethnic, religious or linguistic minorities[5]. Of course, this kind of arrangement is only available to national minorities, as distinguished from immigrant groups (which in any case do not claim such territorial autonomy), and is only possible if the national minority is large enough and concentrated on a given territory. Furthermore, when internal federal borders are drawn in order to allow a national minority to become a majority in one or more constituent states, this will often create new minorities within the regional majority[6].

Another difficulty in using federalism in order to solve problems associated with minorities stems from the fact that the federal principle, as it is normally understood, does not easily admit asymmetric arrangements. In most multinational federations, only some constituent states, sometimes only one, are controlled by a national minority and thus insist on more local autonomy. The other constituent states, which are inhabited by the national majority, will more easily accept the trend toward a greater centralization of power at the level of the federation. A way of accommodating these different positions could be to accept more asymmetry in the powers allocated to the constituent states inhabited by a national minority, on the one hand, and to the states that serve as territorial subdivisions of the

---

4 *Ibid.*, paper n° 28.

5 However, in other federations like the United States, there has been a conscious effort to avert the possibility of federalism being used in order to allow national minorities to form the majority in one or several constituent units.

6 The political division of the State territory in order to create subdivisions in which a national minority forms the majority of the local population is also possible in "regional" States like Spain or Italy and even in unitary States, where certain regions can be given a special status, like Corsica in France or the Aaland Islands in Finland.

national majority, on the other. However, such an asymmetry is difficult to reconcile with the principle of equality between the constituent states as well as with equality between all citizens of the federation (as long, at least, as equality of treatment is understood as identical treatment rather than different treatment according to different situations).

The reluctance to grant territorial autonomy to national minorities is often explained by the fear of the national majority that it will nourish rather than assuage separatist claims or tendencies. Another concern is that an ethnic or religious minority exercising a measure of territorial autonomy may adopt policies or rules toward its own members, or members of the national majority inhabiting the minority territory, that are incompatible with human rights like sexual equality, freedom of religion or freedom of opinion, to the extent that such policies might be considered necessary to uphold traditional institutions and ways of life. Finally, dividing the territory along ethnic lines produces more homogenous majorities and, as James Madison argued, the more homogenous a majority, the greater the risks that it may become tyrannical toward minorities:

> The smaller the society, the fewer probably will be the distinct parties and interests composing it; the fewer the distinct parties and interests, the more frequently will a majority be found of the same party; and the smaller the number of individuals composing a majority, and the smaller the compass within which they are placed, the more easily will they concert and execute their plans of oppression. Extend the sphere, and you take in a greater variety of parties and interests; you make it less probable that a majority of the whole will have a common motive to invade the rights of other citizens; or if such a common motive exists, it will be more difficult for all who feel it to discover their own strength, and to act in unison with each other. Besides other impediments, it may be remarked that, where there is a consciousness of unjust or dishonorable purposes, communication is always checked by distrust in proportion to the number whose concurrence is necessary[7].

To protect minorities that cannot benefit from a system of territorial autonomy (or "minorities within the minority" that have appeared as a result of such arrangements), other methods are required. Minorities can be given a guaranteed representation within political bodies like legislatures or executives; veto rights and increased or double majority rules can provide minorities with a protection against injurious majority decisions. Note, however, that such designs are not particular to federal systems. It is also possible to design a system of "personal federalism"

---

7 *Ibid.*, paper n° 10, pp. 68-69.

(or "personal autonomy") in which a minority group will be given the power to adopt rules whose applicability is determined by membership in the group based on a personal characteristic like religion or language, rather than on residence on a particular territory[8]. Again, such an arrangement is not limited to federal systems (even though it can be considered inspired by the federal principle) and one of its most interesting contemporary implementations is to be found in Lebanon, which is not a federation. The 18 religious communities existing in Lebanon adopt the rules applying to their members in matters of marriage, divorce, adoption and other questions of personal and familial status. However, implementation of the personal autonomy principle has been quite limited in so far as modern democratic systems function under principles of political representation and criteria for the application of legal rules that are mainly based on considerations of territory.

One way of protecting minorities living within the constituent states of a federation is to give federal authorities the power to prevent, stop or redress the wrongs inflicted on them by the regional government. However, such mechanisms are difficult to reconcile with the autonomy that should be guaranteed in a true federation to each level of government in relation to the other.

Finally, the mobility and establishment rights guaranteed in the federal constitution constitute a last resort protection for minorities against their regional government. Members of a minority that are not satisfied with their position in their state of residence can move to another constituent state where the group they belong to forms the majority or, at least, where they can expect to be treated in a better way. It must be noted that in the United States this "right of exit", which allows a change of legal status through a change of jurisdiction, is often considered to be one of the advantages of federalism for the protection of the rights of people in general, not only of the rights of minorities. Such a view has been put forward by, amongst others, Robert Bork:

> If another state allows the liberty you value, you can move there, and the choice of what freedom you value is yours alone, not dependent on those who made the Constitution. In this sense, federalism is the constitutional guarantee most protective of the individual's freedom to make his own choices[9].

However, the most effective means for the protection of minorities that cannot benefit from territorial autonomy is the use of a constitutional

---

8 Kymlicka, Will, "Two Models of Pluralism and Tolerance" in David Heyd (ed.), *Toleration: An Elusive Virtue*, Princeton, Princeton University Press, 1996, p. 81.

9 Bork, Robert, *The Tempting of America. The Political Seduction of the Law*, New York, Simon & Schuster, 1990, p. 53. On this aspect, see also Stewart, Richard B., "Federalism and Rights", *Georgia Law Review*, 1985, vol. 19, nº 4, pp. 923-927.

instrument, applied by the courts, in order to place limits on majority rule. In a federation, this protection of rights and freedoms through judicial review can be enhanced by superposing two levels of constitutional instruments for the protection of rights, be it the rights of people in general or the rights of minorities.

At the same time, there exists a certain tension between the protection of minorities by systems of territorial autonomy, on the one hand, and judicial review on the other. In so far as judicial review based on rights and freedoms limits majority rule, it will of course limit the powers, and hence the autonomy, of national minorities that form the majority in a constituent state of a federation. Such a "minority-majority" will see its self-rule limited in favor of its own minorities. The most difficult situation appears when the minority living in a unit controlled by a national minority belongs to the national majority (for example, Anglophones in Quebec, Castillanophones in Catalonia or German-speaking Swiss in the French-speaking cantons). Groups that are a majority in a constituent state but a minority nationally will often feel culturally threatened and thus have a tendency to use their majority position to the fullest, in order, for example, to protect their language. Conversely, the majority at the national level, whose members are in the minority in a member state, can use its power position to force on the regional government very stringent obligations toward its minority, which that government will regard as unduly restricting its autonomy.

In sum, national minorities forming the majority on a part of the federal territory will be served best by a system of territorial autonomy that allows them to become a political majority and exercise a partial self-rule. Minorities too small or too scattered over the territory to be able to benefit from such an arrangement must be protected against majority rule by a constitutional instrument combined with judicial review.

B. Legal Benefits of Federalism for the Protection of Rights: the Two Layers of Constitutional Instruments and Judicial Review

In most federations, there are two layers of constitutional or legislative instruments for the protection of rights and freedoms, one at the national level, the other at the level of the constituent states. To illustrate this situation, we shall use the examples of Canada and the United States. In Canada, all provincial legislatures and the federal Parliament have adopted, in their respective fields of jurisdiction, human rights statutes that are not entrenched through a special amendment procedure, but possess nonetheless a "quasi constitutional" character giving them a limited kind of primacy over ordinary corresponding provincial or federal legislation. In addition, the Canadian Constitution contains, since

1982, a fully entrenched *Canadian Charter of Rights and Freedoms*[10]. In the United States, the situation is similar; along with the Bill of Rights entrenched in the American Constitution, one finds a State Bill of Rights in each of the State constitutions[11].

In these two federations, the state or provincial constitutional or "quasi constitutional" instruments often guarantee rights and freedoms that are not guaranteed, or not as effectively, by national instruments[12]. For example, the *Canadian Charter of Rights and Freedoms*, forming part of the Canadian federal Constitution, does not guarantee property rights or, more generally, social, economic and cultural rights, that are contained in some of the provincial Charters or Bills of Rights, most notably the Quebec *Charter of Human Rights and Freedoms*. In the United States, rights like the right to education are absent from the federal Constitution, but can be found in many of the State Constitutions.

Many other aspects of the complementarity between the Federal Constitution and the State constitutions in their role of protecting rights and freedoms have been documented in the United States[13]. In Canada, while the Canadian Charter only applies to public authorities (vertical effect), many of the provincial instruments apply as well to private relations (horizontal

---

10 Woehrling, José, "L'actualité constitutionnelle au Canada: la superposition et la complémentarité des instruments constitutionnels et "quasi-constitutionnels" de protection des droits et libertés", *Revue française de droit constitutionnel*, nº 53, 2003, pp. 187-203; Woehrling, José, "Superposición y complementariedad de los instrumentos nacionales y provinciales de protección de los derechos del hombre en Canadá" in Miguel A. Aparicio (ed.), *Derechos y libertades en los Estados compuestos*, Barcelona, Atelier Libros juridicos, 2005, pp. 65-100.

11 Collins, Ronald K. L., "Bills and Declarations of Rights Digest" in *The American Bench* (3rd ed.), Sacramento, Reginald Bishop Forster and Associates, 1985, pp. 2483-2523.

12 In Canada, the federal Supreme Court is the final interpreter of the federal Constitution as well as of provincial human rights quasi-constitutional instruments and the Court shows a tendency to interpret both sets of instruments in a similar way, even in cases where there exist significant differences in their respective wording. Such an attitude has both advantages and disadvantages. The main advantage is that it simplifies the legal situation. The disadvantage is that such an attitude tends in some situations to diminish the complementarity of the two sets of instruments. In the United States, the distinctive character of the State constitutions is more accented, to the extent that the federal Supreme Court does not, in usual circumstances, interpret and apply these instruments, whose final interpreters are the State supreme courts. Nonetheless, the State courts are of course influenced, when interpreting State constitutions, by the case law of the United States Supreme Court.

13 Beasley, Dorothy Toth, "Federalism and the Protection of Individual Rights: The American State Constitutional Perspective" in Ellis Katz and George Allan Tarr (eds.), *Federalism and Rights*, Lanham, Rowman & Littlefield Publishers, 1996, pp. 101-118; Howard, A. E. Dick, "Protecting Human Rights in a Federal System" in Mark V. Tushnet (ed.), *Comparative Constitutional Federalism: Europe and America*, New York, Greenwood Press, 1990, pp. 115-137.

effect). In a more general way, Canadian provinces and American States can experiment in the protection of human rights (as in any other area in which they have jurisdiction), with successful experimentation often adopted by other states or provinces and by the federal government. For example, Quebec was the first jurisdiction in Canada to prohibit discrimination based on sexual orientation, resulting in the eventual adoption of this initiative by the federal government and by the other provinces.

The role of provincial and state instruments in complementing national constitutional instruments is enhanced by the fact that the former can generally be modified much more easily than the latter, which makes them more adaptable to changing social problems and needs. In Canada, the provincial quasi-constitutional human rights instruments can be amended like ordinary legislation. In the United States, though the amendment of State constitutions requires a special procedure, it is still much easier than the modification of the Federal constitution[14]. The introduction of new rights by amendments to the Canadian or American Constitutions that have failed will sometimes succeed at the level of the state and provincial instruments. For example, after the failure of the *Equal Rights Amendment* (ERA) in the United States, which would have added to the Constitution a provision guaranteeing sex equality in a more specific way, a similar provision has been adopted by more than half the American States in their own constitutions.

Furthermore, if for any reason there appears a deficit in the protection of certain rights and freedoms at one level of government, this can be compensated for at the other level. Such a phenomenon (which has been designated the "New Judicial Federalis") occurred in the United States in the 1970s, when the American Supreme Court adopted a less favorable construction of the rights of those accused of criminal offences. State courts later developed a more robust defense of these rights under the State human rights instruments[15] [16].

---

14 May, Janice C., "Constitutional Amendment and Revision Revisited", *Publius: The Journal of Federalism*, vol. 17, nº 1, 1987, pp. 153-179.

15 Tarr, George Allan, "The Past and Future of the New Judicial Federalism", *Publius: The Journal of Federalism*, vol. 24, nº 2, 1994, pp. 63-79; D'Alemberte, Talbot, "Rights and Federalism: An Agenda to Advance the Vision of Justice Brennan" in Ellis Katz and George Allan Tarr, *Federalism and Rights*, Lanham, Rowman & Littlefield Publishers, 1996, pp. 123-138; Brennan, William, "State Constitutions and the Protection of Individual Right", *Harvard Law Review*, vol. 90, nº 3, 1997, pp. 489-504.

16 Of course, state level reforms are not necessarily uniformly progressive. For example, with respect to same-sex relationships, while some U.S. states provide some level of recognition for such relationships, the vast majority of the states have made efforts to prohibit the legal recognition of same-sex relationships. See Knauer Nancy J., "Same-Sex Marriage and Federalism", *Temple Journal of Political and Civil Rights Law Review*, vol. 17, nº 2, 2008, pp. 101-122.

It is inevitable that the existence of a double layer of national and State instruments will create some fragmentation in the benefits of rights and freedoms along state lines. Nevertheless, the federal Constitution guarantees a degree of homogeneity, since federal rights apply to the whole territory. Of course, the state or provincial instruments must be compatible with the federal Constitution, which in some cases means that they must provide at least the same protection in their particular field of application. For example, the *Alberta Human Rights Act*, which applies both in private relations and to state action but did not prohibit sexual orientation discrimination, has been declared contrary to the *Canadian Charter* that does prohibit that kind of discrimination but applies only to state action and not in private relations. Instead of striking down the provincial statute, the Supreme Court of Canada decided to "read in" the missing protection, which means that the federal Constitution was used to impose upon the Alberta legislature the obligation to protect homosexuals in private relations, a protection that the federal Constitution itself does not provide[17].

C. The Disadvantages of Federalism for the Protection of Rights: the Difficulties Arising in the Ratification and Implementation of Human Rights Treaties

Federalism does not only result in positive effects on the protection of rights and freedoms. The existence of a double layer of national and state or provincial human rights instruments provokes legal complexities that burden citizens as well as legal professionals (in particular when it involves an assessment of which of the several instruments is applicable). That same double layer exacerbates the *legalization* of politics that is probably the most regrettable consequence of the generalization of judicial review based on human rights. Social actors have a growing tendency to resort to constitutional provisions in order to formulate their political claims in terms of rights to be respected or won (i.e. they *legalize* the issue by formulating political claims in legal and constitutional terms). Many special interest groups now avoid democratic mechanisms, which they consider too unwieldy or costly, and find it easier to submit their requests to the courts by reformulating them in the language of rights and freedoms[18].

The most important disadvantage of federalism for the protection of human rights is that it seriously complicates the ratification and

---

17 *Vriend v. Alberta*, [1998] 1 S. C. R. 493.

18 Woehrling, José, "The *Canadian Charter of Rights and Freedoms* and its Consequences on Political and Democratic Life and the Federal System" in Alain-G. Gagnon (ed.), *Contemporary Canadian Federalism: Foundations, Traditions, Institutions*, Toronto, Toronto University Press, 2009, pp. 224-249.

implementation, by federal states, of international instruments for the protection of human rights. By its very nature, federalism divides powers between two levels of government. Conversely, international law presupposes the unity of state action in international relations and requires coherent and uniform conduct by the national government. Therefore, the risk is great that if the federation is granted all the needed authority to act effectively in the international area, the exercise of these powers will threaten to disrupt the internal division of responsibilities (by opening a channel for the national government to invade the states' jurisdictions). Most of the matters coming under the jurisdiction of the constituent states, in particular those involving human rights, are at the present time subject to international treaties.

These difficulties exist in almost all federations, irrespective of the particular solutions that have been adopted in regards to the relationship between international and domestic law, or to the division of powers between the federation and the constituent states in the matter of ratification and implementation of treaties. Canada, Belgium and the United States are good examples because these three federations cover a good part of all the possible situations. The United States and Belgium have adopted a monist system and recognize direct application of international conventions by domestic courts as well as a certain degree of supremacy of international law over domestic law. Canada, on the contrary, is a dualist country, where a treaty is only applicable by Canadian courts after it has been incorporated in domestic law and can have no higher authority than the incorporating statute. In the United States, the central government possesses all the powers necessary to ratify and to implement treaties, irrespective of their subject matter. In Belgium, the power to ratify as well as the power to implement treaties is divided between the federation and the constituent states along the internal division of powers. Finally, in Canada there is no such alignment between the power to ratify and the power to implement, as the federal executive holds the power to ratify any treaty, irrespective of the subject matter, while the power to implement, on the contrary, is divided between the federal parliament and the provincial legislatures along the internal division of powers.

In Canada, the absence of any power of the federal government to force provinces to implement a treaty which it has ratified, or to substitute for the provinces to this end, explains the risk that a duly ratified treaty will not be implemented, with such a situation engaging the international responsibility of the Canadian State. In rare cases, the Canadian government has simply abstained from ratifying a human rights treaty to avoid any complications likely to arise from an anticipated negative attitude of the provinces (this has been the case for the UNESCO *Convention Against Discrimination in Education*). But in most instances the federal government will conclude a federal-provincial agreement before the ratification, in which the provinces agree to fulfill their responsibility at the implementation stage. In return, provincial governments are associated in various ways in the negotiations. For example, such a procedure was followed in 1976 for the ratification and implementation of the two United Nations Human Rights Covenants. At that time, a more general federal-provincial agreement was also concluded, under which there is to be ongoing consultation and cooperation between the two levels of government, before as well as after the ratification of human rights conventions. Under this agreement, the provinces are able to prepare their specific part of the Canadian report to the monitoring agencies and are allowed, if they so wish, to have a representative on the Canadian delegation when the report is examined. Moreover, they can also defend their policies when these are attacked before an international body like the United Nations Human Rights Committee. However, some difficulties remain. If a province is found by the Committee to have adopted a policy contrary to the Pact and refuses to amend it, the federal government has no recourse to compel it to act or to substitute its own policy over that of the provincial authorities[19].

In Belgium, the power to ratify as well as the power to implement treaties has been divided between the federation and the constituent units along the internal division of powers. In the case of a "mixed" treaty, whose subject matter falls within the jurisdiction of both levels, agreement by both is necessary. Such a requirement will of course cause difficulties when the interests of the federated entities diverge, as is presently the case with the attempted ratification by Belgium of the *Framework Convention on the Protection of National Minorities* prepared by the Council of Europe. At the implementation stage, the Belgian Constitution provides for a power of temporary substitution of the constituent units by the federation when such an action is needed to implement a ratified treaty. However, in order to respect the units' autonomy, rigorous conditions have to be fulfilled before this power can be used. The Belgian situation thus illustrates the fact that the existence of a power of the federation to compel the constituent states to implement a treaty or to substitute for them does not remove all difficulties, nor does it dispense the two levels of government from the necessity to cooperate[20].

Finally, in the United States there appear to be no *legal* difficulties in the field of international treaty relations, since the Constitution, as

19 Hogg, Peter W., *Constitutional Law of Canada*, Scarborough, Thomson-Carswell, 2003, pp. 285 and ff.

20 Lejeune, Yves, "La conduite des relations internationales" in Francis Delpérée (ed.), *La Belgique fédérale*, Brussels, Bruylant, 1994, pp. 313-355.

interpreted by the Supreme Court, gives the federal authorities the power to ratify as well as to implement all treaties, irrespective of their subject matter. However, serious problems have appeared on a *political* level[21]. For many complex reasons, including the fear that the treaty power could be used by the federal government to invade the jurisdiction of the States, the Senate, whose approbation is necessary for the ratification of treaties by the President, has blocked or delayed the ratification of many important human rights conventions or has approved such a ratification only after having imposed reservations, understandings and declarations ("RUD's") that diminish considerably the importance of the treaty in its application to the United States. One of the most striking examples of such a situation has been the ratification of the *International Covenant on Civil and Political Rights*, for which the Senate has imposed a set of restrictive clauses, in particular a "federal understanding" under which the Covenant "shall be implemented by the Federal Government to the extent that it exercises legislative and judicial jurisdiction over the matters covered therein, and otherwise by the state and local governments, to the extent that state and local governments exercise jurisdiction over such matters [...]". Of course, this clause does not diminish the international obligations of the United States under the Covenant, but it conveys the concern that the exercise by the federal government of its treaty powers should not disturb the internal division of powers nor diminish the autonomy of the States in exercising their jurisdictions. It is striking to note that actual practice in Canada and the United States is comparable even if the legal situation is very different, partly because federalism concerns are the same in the two countries.

One can thus conclude that federalism inevitably entails some complications for the ratification and implementation of treaties in general and human rights treaties in particular. However, like other problems deriving from the division of powers in a federation, these difficulties can be overcome by negotiation and cooperation between the federation and the constituent states and, in any case, are not an excuse for not respecting the mutual autonomy of the two levels of government. Respect for human rights should not justify a lack of respect for federalism.

[21] Bradley, Curtis A. and Jack L. Goldsmith, "Treaties, Human Rights and Conditional Consent", *University of Pennsylvania Law Review*, vol. 149, nº 2, 2000, pp. 399-468; Henkin, Louis, "U.S. Ratification of Human Rights Conventions: The Ghost of Senator Bricker", *American Journal of International Law*, vol. 89, nº 2, 1995, pp. 341-350; Buergenthal, Thomas, "Modern Constitutions and Human Rights Treaties", *Columbia Journal of Transnational Law*, vol. 36, nº 1-2, 1997, pp. 211-223.

2. The Impact of the Protection of Rights on Federalism

Judicial review by federal courts under a national Charter of rights can lead to more *centralization* of powers as well as to more legal uniformity or *standardization*, with both contradicting some of the objectives pursued through federalism. Centralization consists in a transfer of powers from the federated states towards a federal body; it is antagonistic to the autonomy of the federated states. Standardization involves imposition, by the courts, of uniform values that limit the ability of the federated states to adopt differing policies; it compromises federal diversity.

A. Centralizing Effect of the Protection of Rights

The centralizing consequences of the protection of rights take three main forms.

1. Transfer of Some Decisional Power from Representative Bodies of the Federated States to Federal Judicial Bodies

Protection of rights by the federal courts implies a transfer of decision-making power over social, economic and political issues from representative provincial bodies to a federal judicial body. This implies a double deficit, first in terms of democracy, secondly in terms of federalism. As a federal body, the Supreme Court (or the Constitutional Court) is more sensitive to the priorities and concerns of the federal political class and elites than to those of the federated states. Natural and institutional links exist between the members of the Supreme Court and federal political office holders; they share the same political culture. This is even truer in Canada than in the United States and other federations. The Canadian federal executive has complete discretion to appoint members of the Supreme Court without any real input from the provincial governments. In contrast, in the United States as well as in most other federations, the federated states can exercise such influence through the Senate (or Federal Chamber), which participates in the appointment of members of the Supreme or Constitutional court. Studies show that in federated or regionalized states, Supreme and Constitutional Courts almost always exercise a centralizing influence, and foster a long-term increase in the political legitimacy and powers of the national government[22].

[22] Bzedra, André, "Comparative Analysis of Federal High Courts: A Political Theory of Judicial Review", *Canadian Journal of Political Science*, vol. 26, n° 1, 1993, pp. 3-29; Shapiro, Martin, *Courts: A Comparative and Political Analysis*, Chicago, University of Chicago Press, 1981, p. 20.

2. *Consolidation of National Identity to the Detriment of Regional Identities*

Protection of rights through the federal constitution and the federal courts helps to create and consolidate a shared national identity or, in other words, a feeling of common citizenship. Such nation-building is almost necessarily at the expense of identification with the regional community in the constituent state. Systems for the protection of rights through a national constitution and the federal courts are thus powerful tools for unifying mentalities and loyalties. This then facilitates the centralization of power. It is in this perspective that there is a relatively widely shared opinion that in 1982 one of the primary objectives of the *Canadian Charter* was nation-building: the establishment of an institution that would help to consolidate Canadian identity and the legitimacy of the central government, and thus foster centralization of power[23].

It is generally agreed that the *Canadian Charter* created new civic awareness, among Canadians, based on rights entitlement claims and expression of identity articulated at the national level rather than regionally or provincially[24]. This role of the federal constitution as an instrument of nation-building has also been noted in the United States, where it can be argued "that, rather than the American nation's creating the Constitution, the Constitution created the nation"[25].

3. *Economic and Social Rights as Justification for Federal Intervention in Jurisdictions of the Federated States*

In many federations, economic and social rights (i.e., primarily health care, social services and education rights) are used to justify federal intervention in areas under the jurisdiction of the federated states. Federal intervention is presented as necessary to redistribute resources among regions with different levels of wealth and to ensure a degree of uniformity in the way states deliver social services. Although economic and social rights are not formally guaranteed in many federal constitutions, like those of Canada and the United States, the need to implement such rights

23 Russell, Peter H., "The Political Purposes of the Canadian Charter of Rights and Freedoms", *Canadian Bar Review*, vol. 16, n° 1, 1983, pp. 30-54; Cairns, Alan C., *Charter versus Federalism*, Montreal and Kingston, McGill-Queen's University Press, 1992.

24 Morton, F. L., "The Effects of the Charter of Rights on Canadian Federalism", *Publius: The Journal of Federalism*, vol. 25, n° 3, 1995, pp. 173-188.

25 Howard, A. E. Dick, "Does Federalism Secure or Undermine Rights?" in Ellis Katz and George Allan Tarr, *Federalism and Rights*, Lanham, Rowman & Littlefield Publishers, 1996, pp. 11-28.

effectively and consistently is an argument used in political discourse to justify the redistributive, harmonizing role of federal authorities. In other words, individual rights discourse has been transposed into the domain of collective social rights and redistribution to provide legitimacy for federal intervention.

The vehicle for federal intervention is the spending power, which refers to the ability of federal authorities to employ financial resources for purposes under the exclusive jurisdiction of the federated states. The federal government has greater capacity than the states to raise and spend funds. By offering to provide all or part of the funding of programs under the jurisdiction of the states, and by attaching conditions on the receipt of such money, the federal government is able to intervene in areas under constitutionally exclusive provincial jurisdiction. Federal funding is generally conditional on compliance with certain national standards set by the central government. In many federations, like the United States and Canada, the federal spending power has thus been used to encourage constituent states to create or expand major shared-cost programs in the fields of education, health care and social assistance. On the positive side, the spending power has allowed the federal government to persuade the states or provinces to provide important services to the population and to secure nation-wide standards of health, education, income-security and other public services. On the negative side, the use of the spending power can be viewed as disturbing the priorities of the states or provinces and undermining their autonomy. An additional criticism of this system is that it creates confusion with respect to accountability for budgetary and political decisions: the real decisions are no longer made by the local political authorities who answer to their constituencies.

To summarize, in this area the problem stems from the opposition between protecting the autonomy of the federated states and the perceived necessity to establish or consolidate national social solidarity and protection programs.

B. Standardizing Effect of Constitutional Scrutiny Based on the Federal Constitution

One of the objectives of federalism is to promote legal, social and cultural diversity. In their areas of jurisdiction, federated states should be allowed to create different solutions to societal problems by taking into account the cultural values specific to each regional political community. Yet protecting rights through national constitutional instruments and the courts has standardizing effects that are obstacles to such diversity.

1. Why Rights Protection Results in Standardization: a Transcendental and Pre-Political Conception of Rights

The reason rights result in standardization is the way their philosophical nature is perceived: they are considered universal and transcendental (pre-political), particularly in the case of liberal individual rights. The very concept of "fundamental" rights implies that they have to apply to everyone in the same way, with no or very few exceptions. Construed in this way, all variations look like unacceptable forms of relativism[26]. Yet this vision corresponds to only one aspect of the real nature of human rights. In many respects, human rights necessarily result from weighing and balancing interests, which is a process that is largely contingent on context and can legitimately vary over time and from one country or regional context to the next. The logic of a fundamental right is partly dictated by the community's social, cultural and political values.

If we define rights as resulting from balancing interests through a democratic process in a concrete social and political situation, it seems advantageous to be able to adjust the solution to the specific context. Federalism promotes this kind of diversity. On the contrary, if we tend to define rights as intangible universals, they have to be applied in a uniform way by the courts. In this case, federalism is an obstacle because it necessarily results in different legal regimes and some fragmentation of the system of rights.

2. Legal and Political Aspects of Standardization Resulting From Rights Protection

On the legal level, the standardizing consequences of rights protection take well-known forms. The courts, in particular the Supreme or Constitutional Court, impose uniform norms and standards on the federated states, which limit their choices when exercising their constitutional jurisdictions. Every time a legislation of a federated state is declared unconstitutional, the same automatically applies to the other states. We can thus speak of *negative* standardization. Standardization can

---

26 "The idea of justice connotes consistency in the law, the notion that all citizens should envoy the same rights" (Howard, *ibid.*, p. 11). "Proponents of federalism who suppose that rights should be permitted to vary among the units of a federal system must be prepared to reckon with the power of this concept of justice" (Howard, *ibid.*, p. 23).

"What counts as fundamental rights may differ, and what is deemed the appropriate agent for enforcement of rights may also differ. But to the extent that our rights are portrayed in transcendent, universal terms, they demand a consistency that can only be satisfied by constitutional nationalism" (Jacobsohn, Gary Jeffrey, "Contemporary Constitutional Theory, Federalism, and the Protection of Rights" in Ellis Katz and George Allan Tarr, *Federalism and Rights*, Lanham, Rowman & Littlefield Publishers, 1996, p. 36).

also be more invasive. It is well known that Supreme and Constitutional Courts often hand down "constructive" decisions in which they set out in great detail how the legislature should amend legislation to make it consistent with the Constitution. Sometimes courts go so far as to write new legislation themselves by judicially rephrasing the impugned legislative provision (adding to it or deleting part of it). In such cases, the courts impose *positive* uniform standards, sometimes down to minute details, on all the federated states[27].

The standardizing consequences of rights protection can exist even without any court intervention, through state governments adjusting their policies to be compatible with rights and freedoms in an anticipated and preventive way. Observations in Canada show that, at the drafting stage, primary or delegated legislation is often modified or outright abandoned because it is considered as possibly incompatible with the *Canadian Charter of Rights and Freedoms*[28]. The same phenomenon has been observed in the United States[29]. This kind of internal constitutional scrutiny being subject to circulation and imitation among the federated states has also standardizing consequences.

3. Means of Attenuating the Standardizing Consequences of Rights Protection

Courts are aware of the potential standardizing effect of human rights protection and in some cases try to reduce those effects in order to protect the diversity goals pursued through federalism. For example, the Supreme Court of Canada has established that the very diversity of *provincial* legal regimes, originating from the fact that provinces exercise their constitutional powers in different ways, cannot be considered to be discrimination based on place of residence, unless the federal system is to be abandoned altogether. The Court also accepts geographical variations

---

27 A well-known illustration is to be found in *Roe v. Wade*, 410 U.S. 113 (1973), where the United States Supreme Court not only invalidated, directly or indirectly, the abortion statutes of a majority of states, but imposed upon all the states a very detailed judge-made regime. In this case, intervention by the Court had the effect of "federalizing" a problem that was traditionally legislated by the states (criminal law being a state responsibility in the United States). Conversely, in Canada the decision of the Supreme Court in *R. v. Morgentaler*, [1988] 1 R.C.S. 30, in striking down the abortion section of the federal Criminal Code (criminal law being a federal responsibility in Canada), had the effect of "provincializing" the field, which is now legislated by the provinces as relating to medical care.

28 Monahan, Patrick J. and Marie Finkelstein, "The Charter of Rights and Public Policy in Canada", *Osgoode Hall Law Journal*, vol. 30, n° 3, 1992, pp. 501-546.

29 Tushnet, Mark, "Policy Distortion and Democratic Debilitation: Comparative Illumination of the Countermajoritarian Difficulty", *Michigan Law Review*, vol. 94, n° 2, 1995, pp. 245-301.

in the application of *federal* laws, as long as these can be justified by the interaction between federal and provincial powers and the necessity for the federal Parliament to take into account the diversity of provincial legislation.

There are further ways to attenuate the standardizing consequences of rights and freedom protection. However, in order to use them, one has to be persuaded that a degree of relativism is acceptable in human rights.

First, adopting a less demanding interpretation of a right or freedom leaves greater leeway with respect to how the right is ensured. For example, it might be accepted that the principle of state religious neutrality could be complied with either by total absence of state support for religions or by perfectly equal support for all religions. If this interpretation were accepted, the federated states would have a choice between two policies that would both be equally in compliance with the Constitution; a degree of diversity would remain possible. However, if the neutrality principle were interpreted as requiring total absence of state support in all cases, only one solution would be possible and, consequently, standardization would be imposed on the constituent states. Thus some partisans of maximum protection for rights and freedoms distrust federalism because defence of diversity leads those in favour of federalism to request flexible application of rights and freedoms. The same consideration appears in the case law under the *European Convention on Human Rights*. The European Court recognizes a "margin of appreciation" to the member-states so as to allow a diversity of national solutions. Critics of this concept consider it to diminish the protection of rights[30].

Second, the standardizing effects of rights protection can be attenuated through the criteria applied when limitations to rights are examined for justification purposes. The primary criterion for justification is the concept of proportionality: a limitation is justifiable if it is proportional to important goals of social interest. Yet, the proportionality criterion is normally applied in a "context-dependent" way, in other words, by taking into account the variables of the specific spatial and temporal context. A limitation that would be unreasonable in a normal situation could appear reasonable under exceptional circumstances; a limit could be considered reasonable in circumstances specific to one federated state, but nowhere else in the federation. Thus, for example, the Supreme Court of Canada ruled in a well-known case that the vulnerability of the French language in Quebec justified some limitations on freedom of commercial expression[31]. Without saying so explicitly, it implied that the

30 Mahoney, Paul, "Marvellous Richness of Diversity or Invidious Cultural Relativism?", *Human Rights Law Journal*, vol. 19, 1998, pp. 5-6.

31 *Ford v. Québec* (A.G.) [1988], 2 S.C.R. 712.

same measures would not be justified with respect to English in the rest of Canada. This approach thus makes it possible for the scope of rights to vary in accordance with the limitations that can be imposed on them in certain specific contexts. Theoretically, this is a technique that could make it possible to reconcile a degree of universality in rights content with a degree of diversity in concrete application. However, it seems likely that the courts will accept variations in the scope of rights only in exceptional cases. This is because the implementation of criteria for justifying rights infringements inevitably results in a comparison between the challenged policy and policies adopted in the same area by other free and democratic societies. When the challenged policy is federal, the criteria for comparison will be sought mainly in comparative law and international human rights instruments, since they are considered a kind of synthesis of national rights protection systems. When the challenged policy is that of a federated state, the comparison will most often be with the law of other states in the federation. The greater the consistency among the various state legislations, the more difficult it will be to justify the challenged measure if it deviates from the common denominator among the states.

In summary, despite the fact that constitutional law contains a number of techniques that make it possible to introduce a degree of relativism into the scope of rights and freedoms, protection of such rights through the constitutional and judicial process will inevitably have standardizing results. The universal, individualistic logic of rights is too powerful for concerns related to federalism and diversity to be able to oppose it effectively.

Conclusion

Federalism's greatest merit is that it promotes community values. Yet, just as community values regress before individualism and personal autonomy, federalism loses strength when faced with individual rights. The "rights consumer" takes the place of the deliberating citizen. When rights are seen as resulting from a process in which interests are weighed and opposing claims adjusted in a democratic manner, federalism is an advantage because it promotes participation and thus rights can be expressed, made concrete and adjusted in accordance with the political communities sharing a geographic area. However, when rights are seen as resulting from restriction of the democratic process through anti-majority mechanisms, federalism appears threatening in some respects, for it is at the local level that majorities seem most dangerous. Moreover, if rights are pre-political and transcendental, they will be by definition universal and it will be very difficult for them to vary from one jurisdiction to another.

CHAPTER 7

Rights Beyond the State

The European Union and the European Court of Human Rights

Ascensión ELVIRA

Professor of Constitutional Law, Carlos III University of Madrid, Madrid

Introduction

In internal law, Spain has two catalogues of rights: one derived from the Spanish Constitution and the other from various "*Estatutos de Autonomía*"[1]. The Constitution defines rights as "fundamental rights", whereas rights in the "Estatutos" are not referred to as fundamental. However, among the seventeen Autonomous Communities, only those that have amended their "Estatutos" over the last few years have actually formulated such a category of rights. Like other Member States of the European Union, Spain is also subject to a single international system for the protection of rights – the European Convention for the protection of Human Rights (ECHR) – as well as supranational protection represented by European Union legislation[2].

The ECHR is an international instrument, which was created to protect human rights in European democratic states following World War II; it differs from other international instruments due to its judicial arm – the

1 The "*Estatutos de Autonomía*" outline the "basic institutional rule" of each Autonomous Community (Art. 147.1 Spanish Constitution). These rules hold a unique position in the hierarchy of legal sources, due to their role in implementing constitutional provisions, with the formal particularity of combining both the will of the State, manifested through approval by Parliament, and the will of the Assembly of each Autonomous Community, with the possibility of consulting the local population in certain cases.

2 There is abundant bibliography on the European Convention and European Union rights, including the bibliographical references made herein. See also Elvira Perales, Ascensión, "Los relaciones entre Tribunales en la Unión Europea", in F. Javier Matia Portilla (ed.), *Pluralidad territorial, nuevos derechos y garantias*, Granada Comores, 2012, pp. 57-78.

European Court of Human Rights (ECtHR) – which acts as a guarantee against the state's breach of individual human rights[3]. Despite its minimal content, the ECHR has been complemented with various Protocols and, most importantly, with the ECtHR's judgments. This case law has not only provided protection for individuals against a State's infringement of rights, but has also served to reinterpret many rights.

All Member States undertake to abide by the final judgment of the Court in any litigation involving them, and the Committee of Ministers ensures enforcement (Art. 46 ECHR)[4]. The ECtHR's decisions have a double effect: a direct one, where the State in breach must repair the damage and adopt the necessary measures to avoid future infringements in similar cases; and a general hermeneutic effect, which is valid for the States and the EU (see below).

Spain ratified the Convention in 1979 soon after the democratic Constitution of 1978 was approved, consolidating Spain's status as a democratic State that guaranteed the rule of law. By the year 2009, 78 cases had been decided by the ECtHR (5,603 cases were declared inadmissible) and the State was found guilty in 50 cases, most of them related to Article 6 (due process of law), as used to be the case in many Western European countries. A positive balance may be concluded from the foregoing.

The European Union represents the other supranational system. At the time Spain joined the European Community (January 1986)[5], the Court of Justice had developed a long-standing practice of establishing fundamental rights as a general principle of Community law, based on

---

3 "The Strasbourg Regime, as construed by the ECtHR, constitutes the most advanced and effective regional human rights regime in the world" (Harpaz, Guy, "The European Court of Justice and its relations with the European Court of Human Rights: The quest for enhanced reliance, coherence and legitimacy", *Common Market Law Review*, vol. 46, 2009, p. 106).

4 Protocol number 14 aimed at achieving better enforceability: "3. If the Committee of Ministers considers that the supervision of the execution of a final judgment is hindered by a problem of interpretation of the judgment, it may refer the matter to the Court for a ruling on the question of interpretation. A referral decision shall require a majority vote of two thirds of the representatives entitled to sit on the Committee. 4. If the Committee of Ministers considers that a High Contracting Party refuses to abide by a final judgment in a case to which it is a party, it may, after serving formal notice on that Party and by decision adopted by a majority vote of two thirds of the representatives entitled to sit on the Committee, refer to the Court the question whether that Party has failed to fulfil its obligation under paragraph 1. 5. If the Court finds an infringement of paragraph 1, it shall refer the case to the Committee of Ministers for consideration of the measures to be taken. If the Court finds no infringement of paragraph 1, it shall refer the case to the Committee of Ministers, which shall close its examination of the case."

5 *Act of Adhesion of Spain and Portugal* (August 1985).

the common constitutional traditions of the Member States. Right after, it established protection under the ECHR, to which all the Member States of the European Community were signatories. It is a well-known fact that the original European Treaties omitted a catalogue of human rights, due to their prevailing economic purpose and the difficulties in reaching a consensus. Nevertheless, between the late 1960s and early 1970s (*Stauder*, 1969; *Internationale Handelsgesellschaft*, 1970; *Nold*, 1974), the European Court of Justice (ECJ) began to uphold the rights involved in these cases, mainly as a way of preserving the primacy of Community law (one of the principles, together with the principle of direct effect, created by the Court of Luxembourg as one of the grounds of European law). It would have been difficult to preserve the supremacy of European law before domestic courts (particularly the Constitutional Courts[6] or Supreme Courts) without upholding the human rights already protected by internal laws. By the time Spain had joined the European Community the Court had guaranteed various rights, some of which seemed unrelated to the purpose of European law: property rights or non-discrimination, though also including due process of law, freedom of expression, religious rights, etc[7].

The Treaty on the European Union (TEU 1992, Art. 6) enshrined the European Union's commitment to human rights, albeit with a generic reference, but expressly recognised the protection granted by the Court of Justice. The TEU also created European citizenship and its inherent rights: freedom of movement and residence, etc., suggesting the creation of a new class of rights for the nationals of Member States. This reference

---

6 The Italian Constitutional Court (183/76 and 232/94) and German Constitutional Court had proclaimed the supremacy of internal law in relation to the protection of fundamental rights. Of significance are the German Constitutional Court's decisions in the *Solange I* (1974) and *II* (1986) cases, *Maastricht* (1993), *Banana* (2000) and *Lisbon* (2009), indicating the limits or conformity of German law with EU Law and the protection of rights granted by the ECJ. All these decisions indicated the discussions being held between EU Member States. For a good analysis of the relationship between the ECJ and Constitutional or Supreme Courts, see Mayer, Franz C., "Multilevel Constitutional Jurisdiction" in Armin von Bogdandy and Jürgen Bast (eds.), *Principles of European Constitutional Law* (2nd ed.), Oxford, München, Hart Publishing, Verlag C.H. Beck, 2010, pp. 399-439; Baquero Cruz, Julio, "Cooperación, competencia, deferencia: La interacción entre el Tribunal de Justicia y los Tribunales constitucionales en el ámbito de los derechos fundamentales" in José María Beneyto Pérez (ed.), *Tratado de Derecho y Políticas de la Unión Europea. Tomo II. Derechos Fundamentales*, Aranzadi-Thomson Reuters, Cizur Minor, 2009, pp. 119-160.

7 Property: *Nold*, C-4/73, J. 14 May 1974; *Hauer*, C-44/79, J. 13 December 1979; *Wachauf*, C-5/88, J. 13 July 1989; non-discrimination: *Defrenne*, C-149/77, J. 15 June 1977; *Hayes*, C-323/94, J. 20 March 1997; due process: *Johnston*, C-222/1984, J. 15 May 1986; freedom of expression: *Familiapress*, C-368/95, J. 26 July 1997; freedom of religion: *Prais*, C-130/75, J. 27 October 1976.

to guaranteed rights was followed by the Amsterdam and Nice Treaties[8]. In December 2000, during the summit of Nice, the European Charter of Rights was solemnly proclaimed, a European catalogue of rights drawn up by a "Convention" consisting of representatives from European and State institutions[9]. Although the Charter was not binding, it would eventually become a reference for European Institutions. Some authors have even indicated that since 2000 the ECJ has taken a more serious approach towards fundamental rights[10]. Advocate General Kokott pointed out that "[w]hile the Charter still does not produce binding legal effects comparable to primary law, it does, as a material legal source, shed light on the fundamental rights which are protected by the Community legal order"[11]. The Advocates General were the ones who first referred to the Charter, then came the First Instance Court and, finally, the Court of Justice itself[12]. The Charter has also served as a reference for state

8 The current wording of Art. 6 TEU provides as follows:

"1. The Union recognises the rights, freedoms and principles set out in the Charter of Fundamental Rights of the European Union of 7 December 2000, as adapted at Strasbourg, on 12 December 2007, which shall have the same legal value as the Treaties.

The provisions of the Charter shall not extend in any way the competences of the Union as defined in the Treaties.

The rights, freedoms and principles in the Charter shall be interpreted in accordance with the general provisions in Title VII of the Charter governing its interpretation and application and with due regard to the explanations referred to in the Charter, that set out the sources of those provisions.

2. The Union shall accede to the European Convention for the Protection of Human Rights and Fundamental Freedoms. Such accession shall not affect the Union's competences as defined in the Treaties.

3. Fundamental rights, as guaranteed by the European Convention for the Protection of Human Rights and Fundamental Freedoms and as they result from the constitutional traditions common to the Member States, shall constitute general principles of the Union's law."

9 Two issues are usually highlighted with respect to the Convention: (i) the significant participation of members of both the European and national parliaments, reinforcing its democratic nature; and (ii) the transparent nature of its activity, permanently updated on a website, and feedback meetings with individuals or NGOs.

10 Cartabia, Marta, "'Taking Dialogue Seriously'. The Renewed Need for a Judicial Dialogue at the Time of Constitutional Activism in the European Union", *Jean Monnet Working Paper*, 12/07, pp. 13-14.

11 Advocate General Kokott in case C-540/03, para. 108.

12 GA Tizzano, Bectu, C-173/99; GA Jacobs, *Unión de Pequeños Agricultores (UPA)*, C-50/00. CFI: *max.mobil Telekommunikation/Commission*, 30 January 2002, T-54/99; Jégo Quere, J. 3 May 2002, T-177/01; ECJ: *Parlement/Conseil*, J. 27 June 2006, C-540/03; Unibet C-432/05, J. 13 March 2005, right of judicial appeal; *Advocate voor de Wereld*, J. 3 May 2007, C-303/05, rule of law and principle of non-discrimination; *Laval un Partneri*, J. 18 December 2007, C-341/05, collective bargaining agreement.

institutions. In Spain, the Charter was invoked by the Constitutional Court (even before its proclamation[13]) and by ordinary courts[14].

The Treaty of Lisbon[15], which came into force on 1 December 2009, turned the Charter into a binding instrument. In this new scenario, only a conjecture is possible. The Charter "provides the Court with both a more solid and complete fundamental rights framework and a reinforced legitimacy in addressing the action of the Council"[16] and it becomes "a basic element from the body of Union 'primary' norms, meaning Union constitutional norms"[17]. We agree with Cartabia, when she states that the Charter is "undoubtedly a turning point"[18], despite the fact that, in terms of its content, the Charter merely collects rights already protected by the case-law further to the constitutional traditions shared by Member States and principles of Community law. In turn, the new Charter entails "a substantial upgrade in the status of human rights in Union law. If Art. 47 of the Charter is taken seriously, it will be much more difficult to tolerate gaps in the EU system of protection of any rights, including human rights"[19].

The Charter does not attribute any new competences to the European Union. The States have been reassured that the Charter is not an indirect measure towards Union federalization, nor does it enable the Court of Justice to assume more power or to become a supra-constitutional Court. Nevertheless, the Court of Justice can strengthen its role as a rights guarantor.

The Charter affects European institutions, bodies and their agents, and State authorities and their agents, in the application of European law.

13 Constitutional Court Judgment 292/2000, of 30 November.

14 Andrés Sáenz de Santa María, Paz, "La Carta Europea de los Derechos Fundamentales en la Práctica Española", *Revista de Derecho de la Unión Europea*, nº 15, 2008, pp. 233-254; Alonso García, Ricardo and Daniel Sarmiento, *La Carta de los derechos fundamentales de la Unión Europea*, Thomson-Civitas, Cizur Minor, 2006.

15 The current version of the Charter reflects the update that followed the Treaty of Lisbon. Charter of Fundamental Rights of the European Union, 2007, OJ C303/1. Reissued in 2010, OJ C/83/2.

16 Poiares Maduro, Miguel, "The double constitutional life of the Charter or Fundamental Rights" in Natividad Fernández Sola, *Unión Europea y derechos fundamentales en perspectiva constitucional*, Madrid, Dykinson, 2004, p. 303.

17 Grossot, Xavier and Laurent Pech, "La protection des droits fondamentaux dans l'Union européenne après le traité de Lisbonne", *Questions d'Europe*, Fondation Robert Schuman, nº 173, p. 4.

18 Cartabia, *op. cit.*, p. 6.

19 Leczykiewicz, Dorota, "Effective judicial protection of human rights after Lisbon: Should national courts be empowered to review EU secondary Law?", *European Law Review*, vol. 35, 2010, p. 334.

The Charter is a comprehensive instrument[20]: it contains the standard rights of a modern catalogue, albeit closely related to the European Union's purposes and freedoms (e.g. freedom of property, circulation and residence), including others that can potentially be affected by European law or institutions (e.g. freedom of expression, due process of law, etc. et). However, it also contains rights that are apparently far removed from the scope of European Union action, such as the prohibition of the death penalty or inhumane punishment. There are two reasons why these rights have been introduced: (i) to prohibit this type of punishment or to protect the relevant rights when the States apply European law; and (ii) the Charter will act as a parameter for the obligatory fulfilment of European rights, and any non-fulfilment may trigger the mechanism foreseen in Art. 7 TEU[21].

Nevertheless, please note that Art. 6 TEU does not merely endow the Charter with legal value but continues to refer to constitutional traditions, shared by Member States, that are treated as general principles of Union

---

20 Rights are divided into six chapters: Dignity, Freedoms, Equality, Solidarity, Citizen's rights and Justice

21 1. On a reasoned proposal by one third of the Member States, by the European Parliament or by the European Commission, the Council, acting by a majority of four fifths of its members after obtaining the consent of the European Parliament, may determine that there is a clear risk of a serious breach by a Member State of the values referred to in Article 2. Before making such a determination, the Council shall hear the Member State in question and may address recommendations to it, acting in accordance with the same procedure.

The Council shall regularly verify that the grounds on which such a determination was made continue to apply.

2. The European Council, acting by unanimity on a proposal by one third of the Member States or by the Commission and after obtaining the consent of the European Parliament, may determine the existence of a serious and persistent breach by a Member State of the values referred to in Article 2, after inviting the Member State in question to submit its observations.

3. Where a determination under paragraph 2 has been made, the Council, acting by a qualified majority, may decide to suspend certain of the rights deriving from the application of the Treaties to the Member State in question, including the voting rights of the representative of the government of that Member State in the Council. In doing so, the Council shall take into account the possible consequences of such a suspension on the rights and obligations of natural and legal persons.

The obligations of the Member State in question under this Treaty shall in any case continue to be binding on that State.

4. The Council, acting by a qualified majority, may decide subsequently to vary or revoke measures taken under paragraph 3 in response to changes in the situation which led to their being imposed.

5. The voting arrangements applying to the European Parliament, the European Council and the Council for the purposes of this Article are laid down in Article 354 of the Treaty on the Functioning of the European Union.

law. Although these references are given a mere interpretative value[22], now that the Charter is considered to hold "primary" status as opposed to the subsidiary nature of general legal principles, the latter may be used to cover potential gaps in the Charter[23] and also as a way of recognising other rights or allowing a broader interpretation of already existing rights[24].

As in nearly all catalogues of rights, the rights do not actually represent the entire content; there are also principles that are not directly enforceable, without prejudice to their informative value and the obligations imposed on EU and national public powers. On the other hand, throughout the TEU and TFEU specific references are made to certain rights also included in the Charter, such as rights related to European citizenship (Art. 20 and ff.), personal data protection (Art. 16 TFEU and Art. 39 TEU) or various manifestations of the principle of equality (Arts. 18, 19 and 45 TFEU[25]).

The qualitative jump triggered by the implementation of the Treaty of Lisbon, with the consequent attribution of legal value to the Charter of rights, has been immediate, making the enforcement of rights a standard procedure and encouraging the ECJ to give these rights the same status as other rights under primary EU law. This rapid acceptance of the full validity of Charter rights is a logical consequence of the evolution of EU rights[26]. The recognition of the Charter's full legal value is merely a further step towards this evolution, whilst we await the next step (the European Union's adhesion of the ECHR, the significance and scope of which are still undetermined).

After the Charter was endowed with new meaning, many different rights have been invoked in all types of cases, e.g. principle of non-discrimination on the grounds of age (*Kücükdeveci*, ECJ (Grand Chamber), Judgment 19 January 2010, C-555/2007); freedom of movement for persons and right of permanent residence as fundamental rights (*Lassal*, J. 7 October 1010, C-162/09); right of access to documents of the institutions (*Kingdom of Sweden* and *Association de la presse*

22 According to Art. 52.4 of the Charter: "Insofar as this Charter recognises fundamental rights as they result from the constitutional traditions common to the Member States, those rights shall be interpreted in harmony with those traditions".

23 See Groussot and Pech, *op. cit.*, p. 6.

24 As is the case with extensive ECtHR doctrine regarding certain rights, such as the right to private family life (see below).

25 Although TEU or TFEU rights would be treated as special law, the ECJ tends to widen the scope of these rights due to their inclusion in the Charter, as will be seen in this article.

26 Despite the significance of the Charter, its full recognition represents a smaller step for Spain than, for instance, the approval of the Spanish Constitution in 1978, with a catalogue and guarantee of rights, which forced all legal operators to conform to this new direct recognition of fundamental rights.

internationale ASBL (API) ECJ – Grand Chamber – J. 21 September 2010, Appeals C-514/07 P, C-528/07 P and C-532/07 P)[27]; linguistic pluralism (*Spain v. Commission* case, GC J. 13 September 2010, T-156/07 and T-232/07); ensuring judicial protection (*Winner Wetten GMBH* case, J. 8 September 2010, C-409/06[28]); fundamental rights of children (*Doris Povse* and *Mauro Alpag* case, J. 1 July 2010, C-211/10 PPU[29]); and protection of human health related to the freedom of establishment (*Blasco Pérez* and *Chao Gómez* case, ECJ (Grand Chamber) J. 1 July 2010, C-570/07 and C-571/07).

The meaning of the Charter has already been made clear in the interpretation of European citizenship-based rights. In fact, the Treaty of Maastricht created the idea of a European citizenship for the nationals of Member States, and a series of derivative rights (freedom of circulation and residence; right to vote for the European Parliament and at municipal elections in the country of residence; right to diplomatic and consular protection; as well as the right of access to the European Ombudsman and, later on, the right to address EU institutions), albeit linked to traditional Community freedoms (freedom of movement for workers and suppliers or recipients of services and freedom of establishment). In any case, further to this citizenship, the ECJ interpreted the rights in question in a much more favourable manner[30]. Due to the full applicability of the Charter, some of these rights, particularly the freedom of circulation and residence, have been acknowledged as such, without any association to the traditional freedom of circulation for workers and the limitations it imposed (see, for example, the *Lassal* case cited above[31]). The arguments provided by Advocate General Sharpston in the *Ruiz Zambrano* case are clear:

> from the moment that the Member States decided to add, to existing concepts of nationality, a new and complementary status of 'citizen of the Union', it became impossible to regard such individuals as mere economic factors of production. Citizens are not 'resources' employed to produce goods and

27 The ECJ was examining the right of access to procedural documents. The claim was rejected on the grounds that it was not a generally accepted right, although this was in fact so in some EU States. Furthermore, although the right is foreseen in relation to documentation presented to the ECtHR, it is excluded in ECJ proceedings; moreover, the reasons alleged by the parties were insufficient to justify the distribution of the disputed documents.

28 "According to reiterated case law, the principle of effective court protection is a general principle of EU Law, derived from constitutional traditions shared by the Member States".

29 The case examined the issue of judicial cooperation in civil matters related to parental responsibility and the illegal transfer of a minor.

30 *Czerlick*, *Bidar* or *Martínez Sala* cases.

31 Although the foregoing decisions were along these lines, it was the *Lassal* case where the ECJ make a clear pronouncement.

services, but individuals bound to a political community and protected by fundamental rights (para. 127)[32].

Finally, we should refer to the exceptions foreseen for the ECJ's control: Arts. 275 and 276 TFEU. The first provides an exception in relation to foreign policy and common security, the former "second pillar" created by the Treaty of Maastricht, still contained in the TEU following the amendments brought by the Treaty of Lisbon and of a strongly intergovernmental nature[33]. Nevertheless, of interest is the fact that in this field control has already been applied when upholding fundamental rights, in a series of decisions that began with the *Kadi*[34] case and which discussed EU[35] regulations further to Resolution 1267 (1999) of the UN Security Council, highlighting the ECJ's strong wish to defend human rights. In the *Kadi* case, the ECJ stated that "the review by the Court of the validity of any Community measure in the light of fundamental rights must be considered to be the expression, in a community based on the rule of law, of a constitutional guarantee stemming from the EC Treaty as an autonomous legal system"(para. 316).

Specifically, Art. 276 TFEU provides that "In exercising its powers regarding the provisions of Chapters 4 and 5 of Title V of Part Three relating to the area of freedom, security and justice, the Court of Justice of the European Union shall have no jurisdiction to review the validity

---

32 Opinion of Advocate General Sharpston, delivered on 30 September 2010, Case C-34/09, *Gerardo Ruiz Zambrano*. J. 8 March 2011 stated that "Article 20 TFEU is to be interpreted as meaning that it precludes a Member State from refusing a third country national upon whom his minor children, who are European Union citizens, are dependent, a right of residence in the Member State of residence and nationality of those children, and from refusing to grant a work permit to that third country national, in so far as such decisions deprive those children of the genuine enjoyment of the substance of the rights attaching to the status of European Union citizen" (para. 45).

33 Art. 275:

The Court of Justice of the European Union shall not have jurisdiction with respect to the provisions relating to the common foreign and security policy nor with respect to acts adopted on the basis of those provisions.

However, the Court shall have jurisdiction to monitor compliance with Article 40 of the Treaty on European Union and to rule on proceedings, brought in accordance with the conditions laid down in the fourth paragraph of Article 263 of this Treaty, reviewing the legality of decisions providing for restrictive measures against natural or legal persons adopted by the Council on the basis of Chapter 2 of Title V of the Treaty on European Union.

34 C-402 and 415/05, Judgment 3 September 2008.

35 Common Position 1999/727/CFSP concerning restrictive measures against the Taliban (OJ 1999 L 294, at 1), whose Article 2 prescribes the freezing of funds and other financial resources held abroad by the Taliban under the conditions set out in Security Council Resolution 1267 (1999).

or proportionality of operations carried out by the police or other law-enforcement services of a Member State or the exercise of the responsibilities incumbent upon Member States with regard to the maintenance of law and order and the safeguarding of internal security". Consequently, in these matters, internal jurisdictional bodies will be the ones in charge of ensuring that rights are upheld, and the ECtHR will be addressed if necessary. Nevertheless, it would be possible for the ECJ to ascertain their compliance with European law, particularly with respect to the values enshrined in Art. 2 TEU and respect for the rights of Art. 6 TEU (in the same way as the ECJ pronounced itself in relation to the traditional "third pillar" in the *Pupino* case[36]).

It is clear that ongoing developments in the European Union and European law are changing the way rights and rights competences are handled throughout the EU. This chapter will thus examine the interaction of rights competences between Spain's internal courts and autonomous communities and those of the regimes of the ECJ and ECtHR, in addition to tracing the evolution of EU rights and discussing the potential changes a binding Charter might bring.

2. Spain: EU Law and the ECtHR

In Spain, Art. 10.2 of the Spanish Constitution (SC) establishes that: "Provisions related to fundamental rights and liberties recognized by the Constitution shall be construed in conformity with the Universal Declaration of Human Rights and international treaties and agreements thereon ratified by Spain".

As such, the institutions and particularly the courts are subject to this obligation. One of the main international treaties on human rights is the ECHR, with its significant provisions and protocols, as well as the case-law laid down by the ECtHR, given that the Spanish Constitution, amongst others, contains a longer and more protective list of rights than the ECHR. The decisions adopted by the ECtHR have contributed a new meaning to traditional rights: an example is Art. 8 ECHR, with its equivalent in Art. 18.1 SC – respect for privacy and family life –, which imposes a prohibition on the emission of foul smells or loud noise[37] and is interpreted more broadly than its original definition. Furthermore, the ECtHR has also defended certain rights more strictly, in cases that directly

36 *Maria Pupino* case, C-105/2003, Judgment 16 June 2005.

37 *López Ostra* (Judgment 9 December 1994) and *Moreno Gómez* (Judgment 16 November 2004) cases.

affected Spain[38], and other times because it was a way of consolidating case-law that improved or upheld internal doctrine[39].

There is also an outstanding problem with regard to the ECHR: the Parliament has not yet adopted a mechanism to allow the direct enforceability of ECtHR judgments in cases where there is a final judgment from an internal court. It would be appropriate to have a system to resolve these issues, as other European countries have done, in order to allow for a review of these cases by internal courts[40].

In any case, of significance is the fact that Spain has received very few sanctions from the ECJ, especially when compared to neighbouring countries. This clearly confirms Spain's commitment to respect the parameters of the protection of rights guaranteed by the Convention[41].

It is a different issue when we consider EU law; in this case there is a double binding effect: one, the obligation to directly apply EU law, as internal law, even in a prevailing manner; two, the obligation to interpret internal human rights according EU law, further to Art. 10.2 SC. Both Spain's ordinary courts and Constitutional Court[42] apply EU law in both ways; this has been useful, for example, in relation to the principle of equal treatment, basically as regards reverse discrimination. We could challenge the foregoing on the grounds that occasionally the courts

---

38 *Valenzuela Contreras* (30 July 1998) or *Prado Bugallo* (Judgment 18 February 2003) cases in relation to the secrecy of communications; *Castillo Algar* (28 October 1998) or *Perote Pellón* (5 July 2002) cases in relation to the right to an impartial hearing.

39 Queralt, Argelia, *La interpretación de los derechos: del Tribunal de Estrasburgo al Tribunal Constitucional*, Madrid, CEPC, 2008; Elvira, Ascensión, "Tribunal Constitucional y Tribunal Europeo de Derechos Humanos" in Pablo Pérez Tremps (ed.), *La reforma del Tribunal Constitucional*, Valencia, Tirant lo blanch, 2007, pp. 513-524.

40 *El informe del Consejo de Estado sobre la inserción del Derecho europeo en el ordenamiento español*, Consejo de Estado-Centro de Estudios Políticos y Constitucionales, Madrid, 2008.

41 As stated, the total number of judgments in which Spain was the defendant State, until 2009, was 78; in 50 of these cases the infringement of a right was upheld, whereas in 24 no such violation was found. For a comparative table of the various Member States, see [Online]: http://www.echr.coe.int/NR/rdonlyres/E26094FC-46E7-41F4-91D2-32B1EC143721/0/Tableau_de_violations_19592009_ENG.pdf.

Only in relation to 2009, there were 17 judgments in which Spain was the defendant, entailing 11 sanctions, and 6 cases in which the absence of the infringement alleged was declared. These figures may be compared with France which, in the same period, was the object of 33 judgments and 20 sanctions; or Italy, with 69 judgments and 67 sanctions. [Online]: http://www.echr.coe.int/NR/rdonlyres/C25277F5-BCAE-4401-BC9B-F58D015E4D54/0/Annual_Report_2009_Final.pdf.

42 Elvira, Ascensión, "Tribunal Constitucional y Derecho Comunitario en los recursos de amparo" in Miguel Revenga Sánchez *et al.*, *50 años de Corte Constitucional italiana. 25 años de Tribunal Constitucional español*, Madrid, Ministerio de Justicia, 2007, pp. 487-502.

fail to use preliminary rulings, when they should do so, or when this would be useful. The Constitutional Court has refused to acknowledge any obligation to apply for a preliminary ruling, as its task is restricted to interpreting the Constitution or deciding on the constitutionality of internal rules. Nevertheless, the Constitutional Court did recognise an infringement of the right to due process, on the grounds that the ordinary court had failed to apply for a preliminary ruling before the ECJ[43].

In other matters, the Constitutional Court issued its decision on certain provisions of the Treaty establishing a constitution for Europe[44]. One of the matters presented to the Constitutional Court was the government's doubt as regards "the compatibility with the Constitution of a system of rights which, further to the reference contained in Art. 10.2 SC, would become, after its integration, a determining parameter in the configuration of rights and freedoms, not only within the scope of European law itself, but also in purely internal terms, due to its inherent capacity for growth". The Constitutional Court considered that it could not deliver an abstract decision in an anticipatory manner, and that solutions had to be found on a case-by-case basis according to established procedures. It also pointed out that an interpretation of the European Charter in light of Art. 10.2 SC would entail no further issues than those raised by the ECHR, particularly as both the Charter and the Spanish Constitution "ultimately designate the case-law of the ECtHR as a common denominator to establish common interpretation criteria of a minimum content"[45]. Consequently, the Constitutional Court

43 Constitutional Court Judgments 58/2004, 194/2006 and 78/2010.

44 Declaration 1/2004, of 13 December, further to the Government's application for a pronouncement on a potential conflict between certain provisions of Treaty establishing a constitution for Europe and the Spanish Constitution. Please note that this Treaty was not eventually applied following the negative outcomes of the referendums respectively held in France and Holland (in addition to the reluctance of other States). Finally, the Treaty of Lisbon was applied, which gathers a large part of the content of the so-called European Constitution, removing or restricting the most controversial issues, such as a reference to the primacy of Union Law or including the Charter of Rights in the Treaty provisions. The Treaty of Lisbon continues with this division in two treaties: the Treaty of the European Union and the Treaty on the Functioning of the European Union (former European Community Treaty). When the Treaty of Lisbon was approved, an opinion was not requested from the Constitutional Court.

45 Spain has not undergone any constitutional reform, unlike most other European countries, as a result of amendments implemented by European Treaties following the Treaty of Maastricht (1992). Only on this occasion was an amendment introduced in the Spanish Constitution to include the right of foreigners to stand for election, in addition to the right to vote in municipal elections that was initially established (Art. 13.2 SC). Both the ratification that enabled Spain's adhesion at the time to the European Communities (1985), and the ratification of subsequent treaties of amendment, are a result of Art. 93 SC, which allows the assignment of "the exercise of rights to an international organization, with the sole requirement of obtaining its approval in an organic act, i.e. with the absolute majority of the lower house of Parliament ("*Congreso de los Diputados*").

finds it difficult to handle conflicts involving rights, precisely due to this interpretative uniformity.

3. Autonomous Community Rights and European Rights

The relationship between internal fundamental rights and European protection not only involves constitutional (State) fundamental rights[46], but also autonomous community rights or principles[47]. Generally speaking, these cases will require a regulatory implementation in autonomous community laws. The issue is whether or not these rights are connected to European guarantees.

When the Autonomous Communities implement European law, they must guarantee the Charter (and Europe's values for the protection of rights) and implement these rights further to European law.

On the other hand, when autonomous community rights have an equivalent in the ECHR, they are still entitled to address the ECtHR if internal protection has failed and internal procedures have been exhausted.

---

[46] Rights acknowledged in "*Estatutos de Autonomía*", defined by the Constitution as a basic institutional rule of each Autonomous Community (Art. 147 SC); these "Estatutos" require an approval both from the Autonomous Community Assembly and the upper house of Parliament ("*Cortes Generales*"). The possibility of including rights in the "Estatutos" was disputed and eventually settled by Constitutional Court Judgment 31/2010, of 28 June, which resolved one of the appeals lodged against the Catalonian "Estatuto"; before then, the issue was anticipated, albeit in more restricted terms, in Constitutional Court Judgment 247/2007, of 12 December, in relation to reform of the "Estatuto" of the Autonomous Community of Valencia. Nevertheless, Constitutional Court Judgment 31/2010 reaffirms that *fundamental* rights will only be those that the Constitution acknowledges as such. Regarding the debate as to whether "Estatutos" may or may not acknowledge rights, see, amongst others: Díez-Picazo, Luis María, "¿Pueden los Estatutos de Autonomía declarar derechos, deberes y principios?, *Revista Española de Derecho Constitucional*, nº 78, 2006, pp. 63-75; Caamaño, Francisco, "Sí, pueden (Declaraciones de derechos y Estatutos de Autonomía)", *Revista Española de Derecho Constitucional*, nº 79, 2007, pp. 33-46; Díez-Picazo, Luis Maria, "De nuevo sobre las declaraciones estatutarias de derechos", *Revista Española de Derecho Constitucional*, nº 81, 2007, pp. 63-70; Ferreres Comella, Víctor, "Derechos, deberes y principios en el nuevo Estatuto de autonomía de Cataluña", in the book of the same title published by CEPC, Madrid, 2006; Ortega Álvarez, Luis, "Los derechos de los ciudadanos en los nuevos estatutos de autonomía", *Estado compuesto y derechos de los ciudadanos*, Barcelona, Institut d'Estudis Autonómics, 2007, pp. 55-81. Although Constitutional Court Judgment 31/2010 effectively upholds the constitutionality of these catalogues of rights, this does not settle the doubts of legal scholars regarding their suitability and scope.

[47] Said Constitutional Court Judgment 31/2010 states that, in general, rights are in fact "orders to act entrusted to public powers, whether expressly referred to as "governing principles" or literally defined as rights that the autonomous legislator must materialize and all other autonomous public powers must uphold" (para. 16).

In relation to jurisdictional guarantees and to what is required to file a claim before the ECtHR, the judicial system is national, there are no autonomous courts separate from national courts. Each and every judge and court belong to the State judiciary, although its structure is linked to the Autonomous Communities ("The principle of jurisdictional unity is the basis of the organization and operation of the courts") (Art. 117.5 SC), and "The Supreme Court, with jurisdiction over the whole of Spain, is the highest judicial body in all branches of justice, except with regard to provisions concerning constitutional guarantees" (Art. 123 SC); although "A High Court of Justice, without prejudice to the jurisdiction of the Supreme Court, shall be the head of the Judiciary in the territory of a self-governing Community" (Art. 152.1 SC)[48].

As a result, in most cases, proceedings will eventually reach the High Courts of Justice of the Autonomous Communities. Subsequently, the European Court of Human Rights could examine the claim if the right in breach is protected by the Convention[49].

The problem we would face in these cases is similar to the one encountered in relation to the application of European Union law by the Member States. In fact, in this case, a breach would be attributed to the State regardless of the internal party responsible for the breach (the State, Autonomous Communities or municipalities). A similar situation would arise with respect to the ECHR: if the ECtHR were to affirm the existence of a breach, it would be attributed to the State, irrespective of whether the right was infringed by a body or agent belonging to an Autonomous Community.

A potential breach of fundamental rights by Autonomous Communities and the subsequent liability of the State are not new. Although fundamental rights, to a large extent, were a competence of the state[50] before the reform of the "*estatutos de autonomía*", there were already precedents that indicated a breach of a right on the part of Autonomous

---

48 Constitutional Court Judgment 31/2010 has reaffirmed this principle.

49 If the right in question, in turn, is linked to any fundamental rights that are constitutionally recognised and protected by the "*recurso de amparo*", the Constitutional Court must first be addressed. As an example, the infringement of an autonomous community right may entail a breach of the principle of equal treatment.

50 Please note that some Autonomous Communities had already assumed competences in relation to rights without involving their strict implementation. Such is the case of the right of association, for which the Basque Country and Catalonia assumed competence and led to the necessary regulatory implementation. After the applicable laws were challenged, the Constitutional Court defined the boundaries of these competences. See Constitutional Court Judgments 173/1998, of 23 July, and 133 to 135/2006, of 27 April. For comments on these judgments, see Elvira, Ascensión, "A vueltas con el derecho de asociación", *Revista española de Derecho Constitucional*, 2008, n° 83, pp. 301-323.

Community bodies or agents. Occasionally, the issue has even entailed an appeal before the ECtHR, as in the *Riera Blume et al. vs. Spain* case[51], where the appellants (members of a sect) were led to a hotel and kept there for ten days as part of a "de-programming" treatment, against their will. According to the ECtHR: "While it is true that it was the applicants' families and the *Pro Juventud* association that bore the direct and immediate responsibility for the supervision of the applicants during their ten days' loss of liberty, it is equally true that without the active cooperation of the Catalan authorities the deprivation of liberty could not have taken place", given that the autonomous police force was the one that led the appellants to the hotel and interrogated them in the course of their deprivation of liberty. As a result of the conduct of the Catalonian authorities, Spain was found guilty.

This possibility would likewise arise with respect to the European Union in cases where Autonomous Community bodies or agents were to breach EU rights, thus rendering mandatory the devices for cooperation and supervision in relations between the State and Autonomous Communities[52]. Thus, the State should provide the necessary devices to avoid a potential breach.

The issue in either case is rendered more complex when handling autonomous community rights, as this will not involve competences that formerly belonged to the State and were attributed to the Autonomous Community but, rather, competences that the Autonomous Community has directly assumed through its "Estatuto". It would therefore be difficult to apply devices that are in fact useful in other situations, such as the State's vicarious liability[53].

Nevertheless, there is often not a total separation between constitutional and autonomous community rights, as they are interrelated to a certain extent.

Occasionally competences are distributed between the State and Autonomous Communities, e.g. the right of association, a fundamental right under Section 1, Chapter 2, Title 1 of the Constitution; this right would enjoy the maximum protection[54] and would require its implementation by

---

51 Judgment of the ECtHR of 14 October 1999.

52 Cooperation between Autonomous Communities and the State has been disclosed as one of the flaws of Spain's "*Estado de las Autonomías*" [State of Autonomous Communities].

53 See Constitutional Court Judgments 79/92, 28 May 1992; 80/93, 8 March 1993, or 148/98, 2 July 1998.

54 Art. 53 Spanish Constitution:

1. The rights and freedoms recognized in Chapter 2 of the present Part are binding on all public authorities. Only by an act which in any case must respect their essential

the autonomous community as part of its competences (an issue excluded from the scope of organic regulations).

In other cases, autonomous community rights are linked to constitutional rights: most autonomous community rights implement the "right to life" (Art. 15 SC), the right to privacy (Art. 18 SC), child protection (Art. 39 SC) or many "principles" foreseen in Chapter III, Title I, of the Spanish Constitution[55]. Many autonomous community rights are a development of these "principles", though obviously these social claims depend on political decisions and the availability of resources, as opposed to fundamental rights, whose essential content is guaranteed regardless of economic and social circumstances.

And finally, there are cases which could be indirectly linked to constitutional rights, e.g. the principle of equal treatment or non-discrimination, as a way of protecting other rights.

Also significant is Art. 149.1.1 SC: "The regulation of basic conditions guaranteeing the equal treatment of Spanish citizens in the exercise of their rights and when fulfilling their constitutional duties". This means that the State can establish the grounds of various rights (without interfering with autonomous community competences) as a way of guaranteeing a common regime.

In either case, it must be highlighted that the national jurisdictional bodies are in charge of remedying any infringed rights, involving both the ordinary jurisdictional bodies and the Constitutional Court, as the case may be[56]. This is clear in the case of national rights, whether of a state or autonomous community nature. With respect to European Union law, the national jurisdictional bodies are also in charge of ensuring that these

---

content, could the exercise of such rights and freedoms be regulated, which shall be protected in accordance with the provisions of section 161(1) a).

2. Any citizen may assert a claim to protect the freedoms and rights recognized in section 14 and in division 1 of Chapter 2, by means of a preferential and summary procedure before the ordinary courts and, when appropriate, by lodging an individual appeal for protection ("recurso de amparo") to the Constitutional Court. This latter procedure shall be applicable to conscientious objection as recognized in section 30.

[55] Art. 53.3 Spanish Constitution:

Recognition, respect and protection of the principles recognized in Chapter 3 shall guide legislation, judicial practice and actions by the public authorities. They may only be invoked before the ordinary courts in accordance with the legal provisions implementing them.

[56] Please note that the proceedings surrounding a "*recurso de amparo*", introduced through an amendment of Organic Act 6/2007 by the Organic Act on the Constitutional Court, have strengthened the role of the ordinary courts by reducing the number of matters that may be forwarded to the Constitutional Court. It is to be seen whether this will entail a lesser internal control and, consequently, a greater number of matters eventually reaching the ECtHR.

rights are upheld, without prejudice to the possibility of a preliminary ruling and the interpretation and control conducted by the ECJ.

We may thus affirm that the protection of rights, regardless of the reason for their breach, will be entrusted to national jurisdictional bodies. Consequently, an appeal to the ECtHR will only possible in those cases where ordinary protection (and the "recurso de amparo", if applicable) has failed, whereas an appeal to the ECJ, in most cases, will usually follow a preliminary ruling[57]. Therefore, although the ECJ's assistance is very valuable, effective protection of the right in question will still be entrusted to the national courts. An exception would arise in those cases where European law is directly questioned, in which case the ECJ would issue a decision on the validity of the challenged rule[58].

Clearly, all of this requires a strengthening of internal protective devices, which will depend on the level of knowledge and application of European regulations by national jurisdictional bodies. Consequently, not only would infringements be avoided due to a non-application or misapplication of European law, but also those classified as "convenient", i.e. when a more favourable interpretation is possible or future doubts may be cleared, particularly if these doubts arise from the particularities of internal law *vis-à-vis* European law or the ECJ's interpretations as regards other jurisdictions[59].

---

57 Although the interpretation given by the ECJ refers to European Union law, it is in fact also pronouncing itself on the compatibility of internal and European Union law and on any interpretations of internal regulations that are compatible with European law. We will not examine the issues raised by the obligation to "cleanse" an internal legal system further to a breach of European law, which is a matter excluded from the object of this article.

58 This challenge could also arise from a preliminary ruling (Art. 267 TFEU), an action for annulment (Art. 263 TFEU) or an exception of illegality. Nevertheless, an action for annulment brought by individuals is restricted to those cases where they are the object of the challenged act "or are directly or individually affected, and against any regulatory acts with a direct effect, excluding measures of enforcement". Although the new wording brought by the Treaty of Lisbon is more open-ended, it does not generally attribute standing to individuals. This limitation has been occasionally considered to hinder the ECJ in exercising a full protection of rights. See, for example, Marciali, Sébastien, "Les rapports entre les systèmes européennes de protection de droits fondamentaux" in Joel Rideau (ed.), *Les droits fondamentaux dans l'Union européenne*. Bruylant, 2009, pp. 345-377. On the scope of individual standing, see Alonso, Ricardo, *Sistema jurídico de la Unión Europea* (2nd ed.), Cizur Menor, Civitas-Thomson Reuters, 2010, pp. 182 and ff.; Craig, Paul, *The Lisbon Treaty*. Oxford, Oxford University Press, 2010, pp 129-132.

59 We are aware of how complex this task is and of the workload it would involve for the courts.

4. The ECJ and ECtHR

Over the last few years, the co-existence of the ECJ and ECtHR has been the focus of much inquiry, even though the latter's supervision of EU law is not new. Control of the EU is not possible in law, but the ECtHR has devices to control state conduct when executing EU law (e.g. *Hornsby v. Greece*[60]; *Dangeville S.A. v. France*[61]; *Aristimuño v. France*[62]), and claims brought against Member States are also a way of controlling EU law (e.g. *Matthews v. United Kingdom*[63]). At other times, EU law has been treated as a parameter to examine the legitimacy of an expulsion order (*Maslov v. Austria*[64]). The European Charter and ECJ case-law has became a usual parameter as we can see e.g. in VilhoEskelinen[65], Demir and Baykara[66], Aigner[67], or Schalk and Kopf[68] cases.

This relationship, not only with EU law but with the ECJ itself, was examined in the *Bosphorus v. Ireland*[69] case, in which the ECtHR declared its approval of the ECJ's protection of rights. It could be said that this judgment represents the mutual respect held by both courts and a recognition of the efforts made by the ECJ to defend fundamental rights.

Under EU law, given that EU Member States are bound by the ECHR, the ECJ had to apply it when resolving a case that involved a human right protected by the ECHR. Ultimately, it resorted both to general principles of (European) law and constitutional traditions common to the Member States.

The ECJ must use the ECHR as a parameter in its defence of human rights. Use of the ECHR dates back to the mid 1970s, after France ratified

---

60 Judgment 19 March 1997.

61 Judgment 4 April 2002.

62 Judgment 13 December 2005.

63 Judgment 18 February 1999.

64 Judgment 23 June 2008. The ECtHR took EU law into account, although the facts of the case referred to a period (late 1990s and early 2000s) when Bulgaria (of which Mr. Maslov was a national) was not yet a member of the European Union. It recalled two Community Directives (Directive 2003/109/EC of 25 November 2003, concerning the status of third-country nationals who are long-term residents, and Directive 2004/38/EC of the European Parliament and of the Council of 29 April 2004, on the right of citizens of the Union and their family members to move and reside freely within the territory of Member States) and ECJ case law (*Orfanopoulos and Oliveri*; *Commision v. Spain*) in order to examine to what extent the expulsion measure decreed against the applicant was in line with EU law.

65 Judgment 19 April 2007.

66 Judgment 12 November 2008.

67 Judgment 10 May 2012.

68 Judgment 24 June 2010.

69 Judgment 30 June 2005.

the Convention (1974). The ECJ had to prove its strong defence of human rights in order to uphold the primacy of EU Law, even in this sphere, as a way of avoiding the national constitutional courts' invocation of their own constitutions against EU law that offered no protection of human rights[70]. The first time the ECJ expressly invoked the ECHR was in the Rutili case (1975)[71].

Thereafter, from the *Wachauf* (1989)[72] case onwards, the ECJ declared that Member States were obliged to uphold human rights as protected by European law. This protection was required in any application of European law, e.g. when implementing a Directive or when assisting the Commission in the execution of administrative procedures, and also if a Member State invoked its exemption from European law[73].

The ECJ has used case-law on the ECtHR as an interpretative tool, with an increased influence in its own right. Nevertheless, legal scholars have suggested that ECJ case-law occasionally exceeds the ECtHR's protection of certain rights (e.g. the rights of transsexuals (*P. v. S.*[74]/*Goodwin*[75] case) and at other times it is the ECtHR which offers better protection (e.g. limitation on a company's registered address (*Hoechst*[76]/*Niemietz*[77])). The influence of Strasbourg case-law continues after Lisbon Treaty as we can appreciate with Aladzhov[78], N.S. and M.E. and others[79], or McCarthy and Dereci and others cases[80].

However, both Courts have very different tasks. Of interest is the fact that, once internal resources are exhausted, anybody may bring a claim before the ECtHR, specifically entrusted with the defence of human rights.

---

70 *Supra* note 6.

71 Case 36/75.

72 Case 5/88, J. 13 July 1989. See also *Bostock*, C-2/92, Judgment 24 March 1994; *Booker Aquaculture and Hydro Seafood*, C-20/00 and C-64/00, J. 10 July 2003; *Rodríguez Caballero*, C-442/00, J. 12 December 2002.

73 C-260/89, *ERT*, and C-62/90, *Commission v. Germany*.

74 *P. v. S. and Cornwall County Council*, Judgment 30 April 1996.

75 *Christine Goodwin v. U.K.*, 11 July 2002, which cited the ECJ's decision in *P. v. S.*, and Art. 9 European Charter.

76 C-46/87 and C-227/88, Judgment 21 September 1989.

77 Judgment 16 December 1992. For some examples of various possible relationships between both European Courts see Ripol Carulla, Santiago, "Las interacciones entre el sistema europeo de protección de los derechos humanos y el sistema comunitario de protección de los derechos fundamentales", in José María Beneyto Pérez (ed.), *Tratado de Derecho y Políticas de la Unión Europea. Tomo II. Derechos Fundamentales*. Aranzadi-Thomson Reuters, Cizur Minor, 2009, pp. 59-118.

78 C-434/10, J. 17 November 2011, para 17.

79 J. 21 December 2011, cases N.S. C-411/10, and M.E. and others C-493/10.

80 McCarthy, C-434/09, J. 5 May 2011: Dereci and others C-256/11, J. 15 November.

Nevertheless, the possibility of an individual reaching the ECJ is small[81] and most cases brought by individuals involve "preliminary rulings" as regards interpretation[82]. This guarantees a uniform interpretation throughout the EU and implements the European legal order: the ECJ interprets EU law, or shows how internal law must be interpreted according to EU law. The ECJ does not hold an independent duty to defend human rights. It may only do so in the execution of its tasks (although domestic courts have the last word).

Some authors have suggested the possibility of creating an appeal before the ECJ to defend human rights, similar to Spain's "*recurso de amparo*" or Germany's "*Verfassungsbeschwerde*"[83]. We do not believe that this is an adequate option, at least for the moment, given that the ECJ only handles human rights on an incidental basis. Furthermore, the existence of a special remedy could in fact transform the role of the ECJ[84]. In addition, depending on the matter at hand, States have the necessary devices to protect rights, albeit provisionally and, on the other hand, there is already a preference as regards the ECJ to examine preliminary issues affecting individual freedoms (Art. 267 TFEU).

---

81 *Supra* note 57.

82 Preliminary rulings ensure that there is an authoritative source of interpretation, guaranteeing the supremacy of European law (see Article 267 TEU (ex Article 234 TEC)): "The Court of Justice of the European Union shall have jurisdiction to give preliminary rulings concerning:

(a) the interpretation of the Treaties;

(b) the validity and interpretation of acts of the institutions, bodies, offices or agencies of the Union;

Where such a question is raised before any court or tribunal of a Member State, that court or tribunal may, if it considers that a decision on the question is necessary to enable it to give judgment, request the Court to give a ruling thereon.

Where any such question is raised in a case pending before a court or tribunal of a Member State against whose decisions there is no judicial remedy under national law, that court or tribunal shall bring the matter before the Court.

If such a question is raised in a case pending before a court or tribunal of a Member State with regard to a person in custody, the Court of Justice of the European Union shall act with the minimum of delay".

83 Andriantsimbazovina, Joël, "À qui appartient le contrôle des droits fondamentaux en Europe?" in Bertrand Favreau (ed.), *La Charte des Droits Fondamentaux de l'Union Européenne après le Traité de Lisbonne*, Bruxelles, Bruylant, 2010, p. 59; Craig, Paul, *The Lisbon Treaty*. Oxford, Oxford, University Press, 2010, p. 242; Kokott, Juliane and Christoph Sobotta, *The Charter of Fundamental Rights of European Union after Lisbon*. EUI Working Paper AEL 2010/6, p. 11, [Online]: http://cadmus.eui.eu/bitstream/handle/1814/15208/AEL_WP_2010_06.pdf?sequence=3.

84 Nevertheless, according to Craig, the greater relevance of the European Parliament in decision-making including, in particular, ordinary legislative proceedings, raises the issues already manifested in various countries in relation to the legitimacy of judicial review. Craig, *op. cit.*, pp. 244-245.

The relationship between the ECJ and ECtHR may change when the EU adheres to the ECHR[85]. Art. 59 ECHR, as changed by Protocol 14, provides that "2. The European Union may accede to this Convention". And Art. 6.2 TEU says: "The Union shall accede to the European Convention for the Protection of Human Rights and Fundamental Freedoms"[86]. Nevertheless, the ECJ has not only used ECtHR case-law as a parameter in its own doctrine, but has also recognized the value of its judgments: in *Spain v. United Kingdom*, the ECJ upheld the obligation to enforce the decision reached in the *Matthews*[87] case.

The adhesion will enable a better integration between both systems of rights protection, as well as between European and national protection, both in formal and material terms.

5. Who Will Be the Supreme Interpreter of Human Rights?

This issue is not incipient: background dialogue between the courts has increased over recent years and is expected to progress.

But who will be the supreme guardian of fundamental rights? This will depend on each particular case. Surely, in the event of a breach, the last resort would be an application to the ECtHR. In ordinary circumstances,

---

85 On 7 July 2010, on the basis of a mandate from the Council, The Commission initiated negotiations with the Council of Europe for this purpose. See *General Report on the activities of the European Union 2010*, [Online]: http://europa.eu/generalreport/index_en.htm. The first document: CDDH(2011)009, Strasbourg, 14 October 2011 can be found on http://www.coe.int/t/dghl/standardsetting/hrpolicy/CDDH-UE/CDDH-UE_documents_en.asp. The «Explanatory report»: http://www.coe.int/t/dghl/standardsetting/hrpolicy/CDDH-UE/CDDH-UE_MeetingReports/CDDH_2011_009_en.pdf. For a commentary, see Groussot, Xavier, Tobias Lock and Laurent Pech, "Adhésion de l'Union européenne à la Convention européenne des droits de l'Homme: analyse juridique du projet d'accord d'adhésion du 14 octobre 2011" in *Question d'Europe*, n° 218, Fondation Robert Schuman, 7 novembre 2011. http://www.robert-schuman.eu/question_europe.

Also "Joint communication from the Presidents of the European Court of Human Rights and the Court of Justice of the European Union, further to the meeting between the two courts in January 2011" (http://curia.europa.eu/jcms/upload/docs/application/pdf/2011-02/cedh_cjue_english.pdf). Recently, http://www.coe.int/t/dghl/standardsetting/hrpolicy/Accession/Working_documents/47_1%282013%29002_Draft_Explanatory_report_rev_EN.pdf

86 This possibility was rejected by the ECJ-Rapport 2/94 because it exceeded EU competences and was not contemplated in the Treaties.

87 *Spain v. United Kingdom*, C-145/04, Judgment 12 September 2006; *Matthews v. United Kingdom*, ECtHR Judgment 18 February 1999. In this case, Mrs. Matthews alleged that the United Kingdom had denied her right to vote in the European Parliament elections because she resided in Gibraltar (a small territory within Spain under United Kingdom's control).

rights would be upheld by the internal courts or by the ECJ, if possible in procedural terms. And, in any case, the best and most effective guarantee for citizens is the one that is most easily available[88].

Moreover, the ECJ "is not, as such, a 'human rights court'", but, "[a]s the supreme interpreter of EU law, the Court nevertheless has a permanent responsibility to ensure respect for such rights within the sphere of the Union's competence"[89].

A reply would be easier to find if we first decide who provides a general interpretation of fundamental rights. This will depend on the task in question, and on the type and degree of protection. There are cases where constitutional fundamental rights have not been protected by a "recurso de amparo" but are in fact protected by the ECHR (e.g. right to private property: Charter, Art. 33, and 1st Protocol, Art. 1). Other rights have taken on a more comprehensive meaning through the ECtHR's interpretation (namely, the right to family life, Art. 8 ECHR), and new rights or new meanings have been created by the European Charter (e.g. biomedicine, Art. 3). Furthermore, some rights seem out of the competences interpreted by the ECJ (the right to life or ban of torture). Certainly, some rights may be interpreted by the ECJ and others by the ECtHR, but the increase of European Union competences will allow many rights to enter its sphere, subject to the fact that "The Charter does not extend the field of application of Union law beyond the powers of the Union or establish any new power or task for the Union, or modify powers and tasks as defined in the Treaties" (Art. 51.2).

The provisions of the Charter will not resolve these issues. According to Art. 52:

> 3. Insofar as this Charter contains rights which correspond to rights guaranteed by the Convention for the Protection of Human Rights and Fundamental Freedoms, the meaning and scope of those rights shall be the same as those laid down by the said Convention. This provision shall not prevent Union law providing more extensive protection.
>
> 4. Insofar as this Charter recognises fundamental rights as they result from the constitutional traditions common to the Member States, those rights shall be interpreted in harmony with those traditions.

Paragraph 3 in fact reaffirms the usual practice of the ECJ since the 1970s. However, until now the ECJ only had indirect tools (the ECHR) to defend human rights, but now it has a proper tool, a full catalogue of

88 Art. 51.1: "The provisions of this Charter are addressed to the institutions, bodies, offices and agencies of the Union with due regard for the principle of subsidiarity".

89 Opinion of Advocate General Sharpston, delivered on 30 September 2010, Case C-34/09, *Gerardo Ruiz Zambrano*, para. 155.

rights, more specific and updated than the ECHR; this tool is the outcome of a convention involving the participation of representatives (though not direct representatives of the people), approved by the Member States, and with the same binding power as European Treaties. So it could be said that the ECJ now has a better, closer, master tool. The ECJ has to count on the ECtHR's experience and expertise, but fundamental rights in the EU are no longer "stone guests". Furthermore, there are indications of the ECJ defending fundamental rights even stronger than the classical Community freedoms[90] (see the well-known *Omega* or *Schmidberger*[91] cases).

The Charter specifies that greater protection of rights will be encouraged, but this may raise difficulties in cases where Union law imposes an obligation that may be contrary to national protection of rights. Situations of this kind have been previously raised, including a significant one involving the European arrest warrant (EAW[92]), which obliges a country to hand over individuals found guilty in another country, even in breach of the guarantees existing in the country where the individual surrendered, which gave rise to various constitutional disputes[93]. Specifically in relation to Spain, the ordinary courts allowed the EAW in cases where the individual had been judged without a hearing, contrary to the interpretation of the right to effective judicial protection, upheld and confirmed by the Constitutional Court[94]. The system was actually based on what was known until the Treaty of Lisbon as the "third pillar" (cooperation in criminal matters), governed by framework decisions, which request regulatory implementation by the State and are not effective until implemented, but which nonetheless prevent a State from adopting measures to the contrary[95]. This type of dispute could also

90 Free movement of persons, services, goods and capital.

91 *Omega*, C-36/02, Judgment 14 October 2004. *Schmidberger*, C-112/00, Judgment 12 June 2003.

92 Framework Decision 2002/584/JHA, 13 June, and Framework Decision 2009/299/JHA, 26 February, aimed at reinforcing individual procedural rights and to encourage the application of a principle of mutual recognition of resolutions, issued in response to trials held without a hearing of the accused party. The second Decision was in fact aimed at resolving disputes raised by the greater protection offered by Member States.

93 One case, amongst others, is the Judgment issued by the Federal Constitutional Court in Germany on 18 July 2005. Regarding the European Arrest Warrant and the issues involved, see Guild, Elspeth (ed.), *Constitutional Challenges to the European Arrest Warrant*, Nijmegen, Wolf Legal Publishers, 2006.

94 Judgments 177/2006, of 5 May, and 199/2009, of 28 September. Later, on the same subject the Constitutional Court raised a preliminary ruling by Auto 86/2011, 9 June 2011 (C-399/11).

95 Regarding this issue, see Izquierdo Sans, Cristina, "Conflictos entre la jurisdicción comunitaria y la jurisdicción constitucional española (en materia de derechos fundamentales)" *Revista Española de Derecho Europeo*, nº 34, 2010, pp. 193-233.

arise in the future with respect to other types of provisions; if so, there would probably be an obligation to apply for a preliminary ruling to clarify the scope and interpretation of European law in relation to each Member State's jurisdiction, and the ECJ's interpretation would bind the national courts.

The State Council stated its opinion in the Report on the incorporation of European law into the Spanish legal system; given a potential contradiction between a Directive and the Convention, it stated that: "In any case and unless there is a blatant contradiction between one and the other, national rules will in principle follow Community law, without prejudice to the fact that, if a breach of the European Convention is alleged, the former may be cleansed by the national judge or, through an application for a preliminary ruling, by the Court of Justice in Luxembourg. The constant case-law of this Court has reiterated that "the rights and freedoms acknowledged in said Convention are part of the general principles of Community law""[96].

If a breach of a right is alleged, due to an interpretation made by the national courts, and once the relevant internal remedies are exhausted[97], an action may be brought before the ECtHR, as long as the right is covered by the ECHR. A decision from the ECtHR could end the dispute and the affected State (and the European Union, if applicable) would have to adopt the relevant measures. It could also happen that the ECtHR, as is often the case, may decide to grant the State a margin of discretion and, even if the conflict is resolved, the maximum protection of the disputed right would not be guaranteed.

Furthermore, the last word in resolving a conflict does not mean that the right will be fully protected. Consequently, we will wait and see how the ECtHR interprets EU law in relation to the law of Member States and to the Convention itself.

Another issue, despite the leading role acquired by the Charter, is the fact that the EU has another instrument to defend fundamental rights: "the common constitutional traditions to the Member States". This was the initial force and argumentation to defend human rights within the EU, but Europe at the time was more homogenous – with just 27 States it was easier to protect rights with a single instrument. However, it is a

---

96 Rubio Llorente, Francisco, *El Informe del Consejo de Estado sobre la inserción del Derecho Europeo en el ordenamiento español. Texto del informe, estudios y ponencias*. Consejo de Estado-Centro de Estudios Políticos y Constitucionales, Madrid, 2008, p. 246.

97 With respect to the exhaustion of the remedies available, once the European Union ratifies the ECHR the ECtHR may also require, if advisable in each case, that a preliminary reference be made to the ECJ.

difficult task to keep a balance between European law, as a *jus commune europium*, and the particularities of State Constitutions, and between the ECJ's interpretation and the one made by each State's constitutional and domestic courts. The role played by the ECJ will be crucial here, particularly its decision to apply either self-restraint or adopt a more pro-active role, for which it is often criticised. Although Member States share common values and principles, they still have many particularities[98] and, at least theoretically, a margin of discretion.

In this complicated mesh and regardless of how wide the scope of European Union rights, they play a limited role in EU activity. Consequently, although the Union and Member States have to purge traditional economical criteria in favour of accepting a new scenario (frequently referred to as "moving on from a merchant Europe to a Europe of rights"), Europe is not a federal state; Union competences are attributed or assigned by the Member States in order to enable the achievement of common objectives. With the Treaty of Lisbon these competences were determined according to a list, following standard techniques for the

[98] Some States have tried to guarantee their individuality through protocols attached to the Treaties, such as the case of Ireland (Protocol nº 35: "Nothing in the Treaties, or in the Treaty establishing the European Atomic Energy Community, or in the Treaties or Acts modifying or supplementing those Treaties, shall affect the application in Ireland of Article 40.3.3 of the Constitution of Ireland", Article which bans abortion), or the "opting-out" of the United Kingdom, Poland and the Czech Republic as certain provisions of the Charter (Protocol nº 30):

"Article 1

1. The Charter does not extend the ability of the Court of Justice of the European Union, or any court or tribunal of Poland or of the United Kingdom, to find that the laws, regulations or administrative provisions, practices or action of Poland or of the United Kingdom are inconsistent with the fundamental rights, freedoms and principles that it reaffirms.
2. In particular, and for the avoidance of doubt, nothing in Title IV of the Charter creates justifiable rights applicable to Poland or the United Kingdom except in so far as Poland or the United Kingdom has provided for such rights in its national law".

"Article 2:

To the extent that a provision of the Charter refers to national laws and practices, it shall only apply to Poland or the United Kingdom to the extent that the rights or principles that it contains are recognised in the law or practices of Poland or of the United Kingdom)".

Kühling considers that "Apart from the undermining of fundamental rights in the Charter itself, this shall ensure that case law does not create any protection exceeding the national *status quo*" ("Fundamental Rights" in Armin von Bogdandy and Jürgen Bast, *Principles of European Constitutional Law* (2nd ed.), Oxford, München, Hart Publishing, Verlag C.H. Beck, 2010, p. 488).

distribution of competences[99]. It is further to these competences that the EU must protect fundamental rights; in all other fields, the protection of rights will still be entrusted to the States (with a possibility of ultimately addressing the ECtHR). Of interest in this respect are the conclusions reached by Advocate General Sharpston:

> The desire to promote appropriate protection of fundamental rights must not lead to usurpation of competence. As long as the European Union's powers remain based on the principle of conferral, EU fundamental rights must respect the limits of that conferral.
>
> Transparency and clarity require that one be able to identify with certainty what 'the scope of Union law' means for the purposes of EU fundamental rights protection. It seems to me that, in the long run, the clearest rule would be one that made the availability of EU fundamental rights protection dependent neither on whether a Treaty provision was directly applicable nor on whether secondary legislation had been enacted, but rather on the existence and scope of a material EU competence. To put the point another way: the rule would be that, provided that the EU had competence (whether exclusive or shared) in a particular area of law, EU fundamental rights should protect the citizen of the EU even if such competence has not yet been exercised[100].

This adequate proposal could in fact clarify the limits of the ECJ's activity in order to avoid the Union's federalization, one of the fears maintained by the States that voted against the Charter and claimed a guarantee of their national independence. This clarification is even more necessary now, when fundamental rights are becoming commonplace in almost every case brought before the ECJ.

In the relationship between internal courts and the ECJ, it would be better to have more fluent communications between Constitutional or Supreme Courts and the ECJ, through references for preliminary rulings. Historically, both Constitutional and Supreme Courts in Member States have been very reluctant to encourage preliminary rulings from the ECJ, at times claiming that it was not their role (which was limited to the application and interpretation of internal law and the Constitution), and other times upholding the "*acte clair*"[101] theory as a way of avoiding the

---

99 Also, Art. 352 TFEU allows competences to be extended if necessary to fulfil the objectives pursued. Nevertheless, the method used to achieve this (Council unanimity and prior approval from the European Parliament) represents a guarantee against the Union's *ultra vires* conduct.

100 Opinion of Advocate General Sharpston, delivered on 30 September 2010, Case C-34/09, *Gerardo Ruiz Zambrano*, paras. 162-163.

101 "The correct application of Community law may be so obvious as to leave no scope for any reasonable doubt as to the manner in which the question raised is to be resolved. Before it comes to the conclusion that such is the case, the national court or tribunal must be convinced that the matter is equally obvious to the courts of the other member

reference. In most cases, this merely indicated their wish to assert their independence and supremacy within the State[102].

In other cases, the conflict arises from the duality between an issue of unconstitutionality and a preliminary ruling, and what instrument should be used by internal jurisdictional bodies (or which has priority) in the event of a conflict between internal and European law[103]. However, a dialogue or relationship between the Courts is currently more important in order to secure a common understanding about the interpretation of rights, whilst preserving individual constitutional traditions; a more comprehensive common interpretation is provided, but some deeply-rooted constitutional traditions may be swept away: "Only over time, as more conversations take place, will it be possible to reach a broad consensus. Dialogue cannot determine the substantive outcome in advance. It will always depend on the particular community in which it takes place"[104].

Occasionally these traditions have been interpreted as remains of former prejudices, with European law being contemplated as a way of overcoming this[105]; at other times, national peculiarities are interpreted differently and may reaffirm the protection of rights or, at least, an alternative approach[106]. The enforcement by the ECJ must surpass any "margin of appreciation" (also claimed by the ECHR and the Strasbourg Court) and not consist of a "concession" to Member States. Rather, it should be used to create a common instrument for the protection of rights,

states and to the Court of Justice. Only if those conditions are satisfied may the national court or tribunal refrain from submitting the question to the Court of Justice and take upon itself the responsibility for resolving it" (para. 16, *Cilfit*, Judgment 6 October 1982, C-283/81).

102 *Supra* note 5 and Cartabia, *op. cit.*, where it was accurately pointed out that "the constitutional courts are under the influence of the European Court of Justice even though they refuse to ask for preliminary rulings" (p. 29).

103 The primacy of EU law or the nature of the doubt does not prevent a conflict from arising. The ECJ's position on the matter is made clear in the *Melki* case (C-188/10 and C-189/10, Judgment 22 June 2010), which resolved an application for a preliminary ruling filed by the *Cour de Cassation* (France), when the question of constitutionality (*question prioritaire de constitutionnalité*) was still new, before the Constitutional Council. In particular, see paras. 45, 49 and 57. Spanish Constitutional Court Judgments 58/2004, 194/2006 and 78/2010 also examined the unconstitutionality-preliminary ruling duality.

104 Torres Pérez, Aida, *Conflicts of rights in the European Union*. Oxford, Oxford University Press, 2009, p. 111. The ECJ counts on many sources to find out various opinions and legal systems: General Advocate opinions, national courts, European institutions, Member States, parties to the suit (all of whom may file references to the ECJ), as well as its own research service (*Ibid.*, pp. 162 and ff).

105 *Kreil*, C-285/98, Judgment 11 January 2000; *Richards*, C-423/04, Judgment 27 April 2006.

106 *Omega* case.

though allowing other points of view and diversity, insofar as not contrary to European law and common values.

Furthermore, not only may a catalogue of rights and its specific protective devices affect the relationship between various forms of protection, but of consideration also is the country's judicial structure itself. Of relevance here are the already stated "confrontations" between constitutional courts and the ECJ – in which there is a greater tendency to raise a conflict in the case of constitutional courts, due to their presumed role as guarantors of constitutionally recognised rights and their protection – but there is also a wish for a better integration of European law or more fluent relations between internal courts and the ECJ[107]. A fluent relationship between the various parties would, in turn, enable a more comprehensive interpretation of fundamental rights.

As illustrated above, we know how the ECJ and ECtHR interact. However, we have to wait and see what role will now be played by the ECJ with a binding Charter and the entitlement that this Charter would offer the Court. It is likely that the ECJ will become more active and try and avoid the European Union receiving a sanction from the ECtHR.

In the case of Spain, the Charter will not entail any significant change since the Spanish Constitution already includes a long catalogue of rights and has proven to provide sufficient internal protection. However, it may offer more security in the implementation of EU law and, perhaps, a harmonization or reaffirmation of certain fundamental rights. In any case, it would be useful to procure a more active role by the ordinary courts and the Spanish Constitutional Court, by using preliminary references as a way of allowing the ECJ to have a better understanding of how Spain protects its fundamental rights and establishing a true dialogue between the courts.

[107] The number of preliminary rulings varies considerably between one State and another and, within a State, between one jurisdictional body and another. Of interest is the possibility of bringing an action due to a breach on the part of the State, if the breach is caused by internal jurisdictional bodies (see *Commission v. Italy*, C-129/00, Judgment 9 December 2003).

CHAPTER 8

On the (Human) Rights to Self-Determination and National Conflicts

Eduardo J. Ruiz VIEYTEZ

Professor of Constitutional Law and Director of Pedro Arrupe Institute of Human Rights, University of Deusto (Bilbao)

Introduction: Aim and Subject

This paper focuses on controversial aspects of the right to self-determination. Its context is a general debate on the dialectic between internal and external self-determination within a framework of plurality and identity management. With this in mind, the paper seeks to provide insight into the basic theoretical aspects of the right to self-determination while also considering the political implications of these challenges.

The right to self-determination is an important topic when reflecting on the nature and legal accommodations of pluralist societies. Following the fall of the Berlin Wall in 1989, collective identities and national conflicts re-emerged in different parts of the European continent. References to self-determination in several of these situations have varied from rhetorical to substantial. The main hypothesis of this paper is that prevailing theories on self-determination lack a significant degree of consistency, particularly in terms of the characterisation of self-determination as a human right.

Such a topic cannot be studied solely from a juridical standpoint; it is an area in which politics and the law are interdependent. It is obvious that collective identities revealed through political choices, opinions and strategies are closely related not only to ideologies but also to a sense of belonging and subjective identification. In this context, law must be approached from a global perspective, with contributions from the fields of politics, anthropology, sociology, history and geography. As Falk noted, the right to self-determination has matured along three distinct but often overlapping and sometimes uneven and confusing paths: morality, politics and law[1].

Furthermore, any discussion of the idea of self-determination is not only complex, but also extremely sensitive. Even when discussed within academic and intellectual realms, there is a high level of sensitivity to any political or legal debate related to collective identities, deep fears and perceived threats. One of the most difficult aspects of reflecting on this topic is that it may challenge the assumptions of the status quo. It may also create a deep sense of insecurity and instability, which appears incompatible with the essence of law[2]. The rational management of these emotional reactions appears to be a difficult task, but it is a necessary step in the process of creating a more democratic culture.

The goal of this study is to identify the concrete aspects of the theory and practice of self-determination that may be challenged and to offer possible criteria for interpretation. This study does not refer to particular cases where a reference to self-determination is at the centre of the debate; rather, it seeks a more coherent (and, consequently, more useful) approach to this right. The establishment of some general criteria may aid in eliminating the fears and threats that arise in particular debates. Identifying the problematic aspects of this right that need further reflection makes sense from the perspective of self-determination as a legal and political instrument of conflict prevention and management aiming to foster peaceful and democratic solutions for today's governance.

1. The Right to Self-determination as a Human Right

The right to self-determination means the right of peoples to determine "in full freedom when and as they wish, their internal and external political status, without external interference, and to pursue as they wish their political, economic, social and cultural development"[3]. As a right, it can be understood formally as a legally protected interest.

1 Falk, Richard, "Self-Determination under International Law: The Coherence of Doctrine Versus the Incoherence of Experience" in Wolfgang Danspeckgruber (ed.), *The Self-Determination of Peoples. Community, Nation and State in an Interdependent World*, London, Lynne Rienner Publishers, 2002, p. 42.

2 Again, following Falk, "what makes the right to self-determination so difficult to clarify is that its exercise involves a clash of fundamental world order principles. On the one side is the basic geopolitical norm that the existing array of states is close to the maximum that can be accommodated within existing diplomatic frameworks. […] On the other side of self-determination is the sense that peoples should be treated equally and that since some peoples have the benefit of statehood, others should be entitled as well" (*Ibid.*, p. 31).

3 *Final Act of the Conference on Security and Co-operation in Europe* (Helsinki Final Act), 14 *ILM* 1292, Part VIII.

From a material point of view, however, it is obvious that the context determines the effective degree of liberty with which this right can be exerted by its holder. In practice, no collective entity may enjoy an unlimited right to decide its own status. Nevertheless, the fact that a formal reading of the right does not correspond to the material or real capacity of its exercise is not exclusive of this particular right, nor of any other human right.

The human right of peoples to self-determination is firmly established in contemporary international law. Using a diachronic perspective, Obieta distinguishes four steps in the evolution of self-determination in international law. The idea of self-determination was already consolidated in the first decades of the twentieth century, evolving partially from the previous principle of nationalities. During the interwar period, self-determination was not incorporated into the Covenant of the League of Nations, although it was partially implemented and was regarded as a political principle, not a rule of international law[4]. The second phase began in 1945 with the approval of the Charter of the United Nations, in which self-determination is expressly mentioned in articles 1, 2 and 55. Thus, it can already be seen as a legal principle and not merely as a political idea. The third significant step was taken when the General Assembly approved Resolution 1514 in 1960[5]. In this document, self-determination was considered not only as a legal principle, but also as a right of colonised peoples. Finally, the signing in 1966 of the International Covenants on Civil and Political Rights and on Economic, Social and Cultural Rights, and the enforcement of these ten years later, represented the final step toward recognising the right to self-determination for all peoples[6].

Thus, from its beginning as a political principle, self-determination evolved in a short period of time to the much higher rank of a human right, providing this idea with a completely different understanding in international law. The right has been incorporated into the most prominent instruments protecting human rights and, through these, into various domestic legal systems. Furthermore, attaining the status of a human right elevates the importance of this inalienable right[7]. Its nature

---

4 The League of Nations Commission of Jurists did not consider the relevant practice sufficient to consider the principle of self-determination a positive rule of the Law of Nations (League of Nations *Official Journal*, Special Supplement nº 3, 1920, p. 5).

5 UN General Assembly's *Declaration on the Granting of Colonial Countries and Peoples*, GA Res. 1514 (XV), 14 December 1960.

6 Obieta Chalbaud, Jose Antonio, *El derecho humano de la autodeterminación de los pueblos*, Madrid, Tecnos, 1985, pp. 103-104.

7 Vienna Declaration and Programme of Action, UN Document A/CONF.157/23, 12 July 1993, section I.2.

is clearly collective because its holder (all peoples) must be a collective entity. In fact, it is probably the only right for which its collective nature can be defended with no possible challenge. This collective element, however, when compared to individual human rights, implies that its legal application will be much more challenging to enforce.

Theoretically, as a human right, self-determination did not even need to be incorporated into the Covenants to become legally binding for all actors. However, its placement as the first article of both Covenants reinforces its importance in the system of human protection. Self-determination has thus been defined as an integral component of human dignity. According to the United Nations Human Rights Committee,

> Its realization is an essential condition for the effective guarantee and observance of individual human rights and for the promotion and strengthening of those rights. It is for that reason that States set forth the right of self-determination in a provision of positive law in both Covenants and placed this provision as article 1 apart from and before all of the other rights in the two Covenants[8].

The United Nations Committee on the Elimination of Racial Discrimination reaffirms that "the right to self-determination of peoples is a fundamental principle of international law"[9]. Furthermore, the human right to self-determination of all peoples is part of the so-called *ius cogens* in international law. This means that it cannot be disposed of by the States. At the same time, this right generates obligations *erga omnes*, as the International Court of Justice has stated[10]. Of course, this creates obligations for the members of the international community. Thus, States have the duty to "promote the right to self-determination of peoples", and the promotion of self-determination "requires every State to promote, through joint and separate action, universal respect for and observance of human rights and fundamental freedoms in accordance with the Charter of the United Nations"[11]. States are also obliged to report on this active promotion to the Human Rights Committee through constitutional and political processes[12] because "the realization of and respect for the right of self-determination of peoples contributes to the establishment of

8 United Nations Human Rights Committee, *General Comment N° 12, The right to self-determination of peoples (Art. 1)*, 13 March 1984, para. 1.

9 United Nations Committee on the Elimination of Racial Discrimination (CERD), *General Recommendation N° 21, Right to self-determination*, 23 August 1996, Doc. A/51/18, para. 2.

10 International Court of Justice, *East Timor* (Portugal v. Australia), judgement of 30-06-1995, *ICJ Reports* (1995), p. 102.

11 UN CERD, *op. cit.*, para. 3.

12 UN Human Rights Committee, *op. cit.*, para. 4.

friendly relations and cooperation between States and to strengthening international peace and understanding"[13].

While the existence and validity of the (human) right to self-determination have been established in international law, bitter debates arise when it is used as a means of legitimating different (or even contradictory) political aspirations. International practice in recent decades has shown that the decolonisation process was not the final point of territorial distribution of political entities. Although the international community tends to reject any further aspirations to statehood, through self-determination or any other means, the generous recognition of this (human) right carries within it seeds for radical – and even revolutionary – change. The main concern regarding self-determination is, of course, that it can lead to the erosion, division or fragmentation of existing states. Nevertheless, as a human right, self-determination should be fundamentally regarded as an instrument for conflict prevention and for the democratic management of diversity. This leads the discussion of self-determination to a focus on the concrete elements of the right.

As the African Commission on Human and Peoples' Rights states, "All peoples have the right to self-determination. There may, however, be controversy as to the definition of peoples and the content of the right"[14]. Indeed, the entitlement of the right and its scope are the two elements on which the current debates on self-determination are focused. These controversies about the definition of peoples and the content of the right will be dealt with in the subsequent subchapters.

2. Questions about the Holder of the Right

Article 1 of both international covenants on human rights is clear in outlining that all peoples possess the right to self-determination. However, the legal notion of peoples' actual entitlement to self-determination is ambiguous. To date, the practice of States has been to avoid conclusively defining the notion of a people[15], and the same can be said with respect to international organisations. Therefore, we lack a legal definition of people, just as we lack definitions of a (national) minority, ethnic group, nationality, nation and other related concepts. The contemporary reality

13 UN Human Rights Committee, *ibid.*, para. 8.

14 African Commission on Human and People`s Rights, *Katangese People's Congress v. Zaire* (communication 75/92), document ACHPR/RPT/8th Annex VI (1995), para. 3 (hereinafter Kantangese People case).

15 International Court of Justice, Accordance with International Law of the Unilateral Declaration of Independence by the Provisional Institutions of Self-Government of Kosovo (Request for Advisory opinion), Written Statement addressed to the International Court of Justice by the Swiss Confederation, p. 18, para. 70.

of these entities may be too complicated to be shaped into a satisfactory literary definition. This results in uncertainty as to who is not entitled to this particular human right. This problem derives from the collective nature of this right as we do not face the same question with respect to individual human rights.

The concept of *people* is variable and contested in scope. The sociological use of the term is imprecise and not always consistent; thus, we hear references to the "Scottish people", the "Andalusian people" or the "Roma people". The term "people" can thus correspond to an ethno-cultural conception of people or can merely refer to an administrative idea. At the same time, expressions such as "Spanish people" or "the people of Belgium" are also commonly used without clarifying whether they refer to the cultural or the legal (civic) definition of those peoples. Indeed, as is the case with the controversial concept of *nations*, either approach can be defended: a legal (civic) approach in which the people correspond to the entire population of a (democratic) state or a cultural approach in which several peoples live within the same state[16].

In any case, state practices are not consistent, nor are the practices of international organisations. For instance, the United Nations Committee on the Elimination of Racial Discrimination, when commenting on the right to self-determination, included ambiguous references to other related entities, such as nationality or ethnicity, religious and linguistic minorities, and ethnic or linguistic groups[17]. Related cases like those of Bangladesh, Eritrea, Katanga or Biafra have led to different solutions by the United Nations General Assembly.

In fact, the differentiated sets of rights that the International Covenant on Civil and Political Rights assigns to peoples (art. 1) and minorities (art. 27) would play in favour of a legal interpretation of the term *peoples*. This was, for instance, the position defended by New Zealand in the Apirana Mahuika case, arguing that "the rights in Article 1 attach to "peoples" of a state in their entirety, not to minorities, whether indigenous or not, within

16 The Parliamentary Assembly of the Council of Europe has acknowledged the plural meaning of the concept of "nation" as it is used by European legal and political documents, recognising above all the two classic civic and cultural approaches. See *Parliamentary Assembly, Recommendation 1735 (2006), The concept of "nation"*, adopted by the Assembly on 26 January 2006 (7th Sitting). See Aurescu, Bogdan, "Cultural Nation versus Civic Nation: Which Concept for the Future Europe? A Critical Analysis of the Parliamentary Assembly's Recommendation 1735 (2006) on The Concept of Nation", *European Yearbook of Minority Issues*, Leiden-Boston, ECMI-Eurac Research, Martinus Nijhoff publishers, 2005/6, vol. 5, pp. 147-159.

17 UN CERD, *op. cit.*, paras. 3 and 5.

the borders of an independent and democratic state"[18]. This position has also been held by countries such as Serbia, Argentina or Russia[19] in the proceedings of the International Court of Justice in relation to the legality of the unilateral declaration of independence for Kosovo. Thus, the whole population of a State constitutes a people, as does the whole population of each non-autonomous territory (i.e., colony), as defined in conformity with the principles enshrined in the United Nations General Assembly Resolution 1541. According to Pentassuglia, in general terms, this "whole people approach" is the dominant position[20] and provides a high degree of certainty[21].

In contrast, Obieta maintains that there has been a progressive and intentional confusion of the concepts of *people* and *population* in the international community. The latter corresponds to the group of persons who are subject to the personal jurisdiction of the state, while the former refers to any ethnic group having a territorial reference where the majority of its constituents live[22]. Obviously, the problem with this alternative approach to the idea of peoples is its uncertainty and the difficulties of delimiting the different possible peoples that may live in the same state. In any case, there may be other arguments in favour of this second position.

One argument may be based on the correspondence between the object of the right (self-determination) and its holder. Thus, because self-determination is characterised as a human right, it follows that when the process of self-determination is recognised and protected through law, the holders of such a right must be categorised as a people. In other words, no other holders of the right may exist. As Crawford notes, "At the root, the question of defining people concerns identifying the categories of territory to which the principle of self-determination applies as a matter of right"[23]. This reasoning suggests that European minorities (i.e., those not corresponding to the whole population of a state) enjoying an explicit or implicit right to self-determination must be recognised as peoples. This would be the case for Northern Ireland, according to the Good Friday

---

18 UN Human Rights Committee, *Apirana Mahuika et al. v. New Zealand* (Communication N° 547/1993), decision of 25-7-2001; Doc. CCPR/C/72/D/884/1999, para. 7.6.

19 Although the Russian position leaves the door open for other interpretations.

20 Pentassuglia, Gaetano, *Minorities in International Law*, Strasbourg, Council of Europe, 2002, p. 163.

21 International Court of Justice, Accordance with International Law of the Unilateral Declaration of Independence by the Provisional Institutions of Self-Government of Kosovo (Request for Advisory opinion), Written Statement addressed to the International Court of Justice by the Russian Federation, 16 April 2009, para. 81.

22 Obieta Chalbaud, *op. cit.*, p. 47.

23 Crawford, James, *The Creation of States in International Law* (2nd ed.), Oxford, Oxford University Press, 2006, p. 126.

Agreement of 1998, or for the Gagauzian people in Moldova. More implicit formulations of this right could be appreciated in cases like the Faroe Islands, the Aland Islands, South Tyrol or Quebec.

A second argument in favour of the pluralist solution is the fact that some (European) legal systems recognise, in different terms and through relevant constitutional dispositions, the presence of peoples not corresponding to the whole population of the respective State. The point can be challenged in those cases where plurality is admitted for the concept of *nation* and not for the concept of *people*. For instance, the national plurality of the United Kingdom is widely accepted ("one country, four nations"), the Parliament of Canada has recognised Quebec as a distinct nation (within a united Canada), and the Russian Constitution enshrines the sovereignty of the "multinational people" of the Russian Federation (art. 1). Clearer legal recognitions of the existence of various peoples within the same State can be found in other legal documents, such as the Constitutions of the Russian Federation (arts. 68 and 69), Ukraine (art. 11), Bosnia-Herzegovina (Preamble), Norway (art. 110a) and Finland (art. 17). This is also the case in some relevant subnational constitutions and acts delineating autonomy, like the Autonomy Act of the Aland Islands of 1991, the Act on the Home Rule of the Faroe Islands of 1948 and some acts on autonomy (*estatutos*) of different Spanish regions, particularly the Basque Country and Valencia[24] (in line with the reference to the "peoples of Spain" included in the Preamble of the 1978 Constitution).

Insofar as these countries have not made any reservation or interpretation of the international covenants on human rights, the legal recognition of different peoples can easily be linked with the same term, as included in Article 1 of both international covenants[25]. Obviously, we could add to the list constitutional or legal references to the presence of indigenous peoples in other non-European countries.

In addition to the cases that may fit into the two previous arguments, the pluralist solution to the definition of *people* seems to have gained

24 The mention of a particular people is also included in the Acts on Autonomy of Aragón, the Canary Islands and Andalusia.

25 The Netherlands opposes reservations or declarations formulated in response to the 1966 Covenants with the aim of limiting the scope of the right to self-determination: "The Kingdom of the Netherlands has objected to such reservations or declarations, pointing out that any attempt to limit the scope of this right or to attach conditions not provided for in the relevant instruments undermines the concept of SD itself and thereby seriously weakens its universally acceptable character. Other States have entered similar objections". International Court of Justice, Accordance with International Law of the Unilateral Declaration of Independence by the Provisional Institutions of Self-Government of Kosovo (Request for Advisory opinion), Written Statement of the Kingdom of the Netherlands, 17 April 2009, p. 12, para. 3.18.

much ground. Thus, in its general recommendation on the right to self-determination, the United Nations Committee on the Elimination of Racial Discrimination refers to "all peoples within a State", reflecting a position that clearly goes against the whole people approach[26]. Similarly, in the *Katangese People's Congress v. Zaire*, the African Commission on Human and Peoples' Rights states that there is a people of Katanga entitled to self-determination (although it is obliged to exercise it in a way compatible with the sovereignty and territorial integrity of Zaire[27]). Furthermore, the Supreme Court in Canada's well-known Quebec case recognised that "as the right to self-determination has developed by virtue of a combination of international agreements and conventions coupled with state practice, with little formal elaboration of the definition of 'peoples', the result has been that the precise meaning of the term 'people' remains somewhat uncertain"[28]. However, the Court concludes, "It is clear that 'a people' may include only a portion of the population of an existing state [...]. The reference to 'people' does not necessarily mean the entirety of a state's population"[29]. Moreover, the Court refers to "a common language and culture" as "characteristics that would be considered in determining whether a specific group is a 'people'"[30].

Finally, the statement submitted by the Swiss government to the International Court of Justice in relation to Kosovo's independence is noteworthy:

> The right to self-determination applies to a collective that goes beyond a mere group of individuals. What binds a people is a shared consciousness or a common political will. This results from the exact nature of the right of peoples to self-determination which is a fundamental standard of the democratic State. Thus any effort to define the notion of a people entitled to self-determination in a conclusive, objective and scientifically observable manner is intrinsically contradictory[31].

---

26 UN CERD, *op. cit.*, para. 5.

27 Kantangese People case, para. 6.

28 Supreme Court of Canada, *Reference re Secession of Quebec*, (1998), 2 SCR 217 (Can), para.123 (hereinafter Quebec case).

29 *Ibid.*, para. 124.

30 *Ibid.*, para. 125.

31 International Court of Justice, Accordance with International Law of the Unilateral Declaration of Independence by the Provisional Institutions of Self-Government of Kosovo (Request for Advisory opinion), Written Statement addressed to the International Court of Justice by the Swiss Confederation, p. 19, para. 71.

3. Questions about the Scope of the Right: Internal and External Aspects

The extent of the right to self-determination also remains a matter of dispute. As in the case of the issue of rights holders, this may be due to the lack of peaceful theoretical development regarding the exercise of this right, which has been subjected to excessive political debate and contradictory aspirations.

The Final Act of the Conference on Security and Co-operation in Europe, held in Helsinki in 1975, recognised the right of peoples to self-determination. It explained its content as the right of peoples to determine, when and as they wish, in full freedom, "their *internal and external political status*, without *external* interference, and to pursue as they wish their political, economic, social and cultural development"[32] (emphasis added).

This reference to the external and internal aspects of the right is common within international references pertaining to the scope of this controversial right, although the descriptions of these aspects are not homogenous. Thus, the United Nations Committee on the Elimination of Racial Discrimination maintains:

> The right to self-determination of peoples has an internal aspect, that is to say, the rights of all peoples to pursue freely their economic, social and cultural development without outside interference. In that respect there exists a link with the right of every citizen to take part in the conduct of public affairs at any level, as referred to in article 5 (c) of the International Convention on the Elimination of All Forms of Racial Discrimination. In consequence, Governments are to represent the whole population without distinction as to race, colour, descent or national or ethnic origin.

On the other hand, "the external aspect of self-determination implies that all peoples have the right to determine freely their political status and their place in the international community based upon the principle of equal rights and exemplified by the liberation of peoples from colonialism and by the prohibition to subject peoples to alien subjugation, domination and exploitation"[33].

In the European institutional framework, the Venice Commission also distinguishes between internal and external aspects of self-determination. According to this advisory body, "[t]he internal aspect defines the right of peoples freely to determine their political status and to pursue their cultural, social and economic development. The external status refers to

[32] Final Act of the Conference on Security and Co-operation in Europe, *op. cit.*

[33] UN CERD, *op. cit.*, para. 4.

the right of peoples freely to determine their place in the international community of states"[34].

The Supreme Court of Canada also referred to this division in its Quebec case, defining internal self-determination as "a people's pursuit of its political, economic, social and cultural development within the framework of an existing state" and external self-determination as "the establishment of a sovereign and independent State, the free association or integration with an independent State or the emergence into any other political status freely determined by a people"[35].

In fact, this last reference reflects the possibilities foreseen in United Nations General Assembly Resolution 2625[36] as possible outcomes of the exercise of self-determination[37], although the resolution does not establish whether they correspond to the external or internal elements of the right. Similarly, the African Commission on Human and Peoples' Rights asserts: "Self-determination can be exercised giving path to different results like independence, self-government, local government, federalism, confederalism, unitarism or any other form of relations that accords with the wishes of the people (but fully cognizant of other recognized principles such as sovereignty and territorial integrity)"[38].

The distinction between an internal and an external aspect of the right to self-determination is also present in many analyses of doctrine. The most exhaustive description of the content of the right to self-determination is the one offered by Obieta some decades ago. Following this author[39], the self-determination right includes the following faculties or aspects:

1. Self-affirmation or self-qualification: the group expresses itself as a people.
2. Self-definition, or a personal element: the people determines who its members are.

---

34 European Commission for Democracy through Law (Venice Commission), "Self-determination and secession on constitutional law", 10-11 December 1999, Doc. CDL-INF (2000) 2.

35 Quebec case, para. 126.

36 UN General Assembly's *Declaration on Principles of International Law concerning Friendly Relations and Co-operation among States in accordance with the Charter of the United Nations*, GA Res. 2625 (XXV), 24 October 1970 (*Declaration on Friendly Relations*).

37 These three possibilities had already been included in the previous UN General Assembly's *Principles which should guide members in determining whether or not an obligation exists to transmit the information called for under article 73e of the Charter*, GA Res. 1541 (XV), 15 December 1960, but restricted to the decolonization process.

38 Kantangese People case, para. 4.

39 Obieta Chalbaud, *op. cit.*, pp. 64-78.

3. Self-delimitation, or a territorial element: the people determines the limits of its own territory, if necessary, through referenda.
4. Self-disposition, or a formal element: the political power of the people. It has two sides corresponding to its internal organisation and its relations with the outside world:
   a. Internal: the ability to provide the people with the government it desires.
   b. External: the ability to determine the people's status in relation to other peoples. According to General Assembly Resolution 2625, in international law this can lead to three possible outcomes:
      i. Integration within an existing State.
      ii. Association/union with other peoples to create a common State.
      iii. Secession to create a new independent State.

When describing the content of the right to self-determination, most analysts focus on what Obieta calls "self-disposition". There seems to be a consensus on the possibility of distinguishing an internal and an external element within the right of self-determination. However, it cannot be said that there is consensus about the meaning of this division.

For most authors, the distinction between internal and external self-determination refers to the outcome of the exercise of this right. In this sense, Raic states, "[e]xternal self-determination is a mode of implementation of the right to self-determination through the formation of an independent state, the integration in or association with a third state [...] It is this feature of external self-determination which forms an important distinction with respect to internal self-determination"[40].

Cassese also refers to secession as "the most radical form of external self-determination"[41], which implies that there may be other forms of external self-determination that differ from secession. However, in other cases, the external aspect of self-determination seems to be restricted to access to independence. Hannum makes a distinction between the possibility of achieving freedom from a former colonial power (external self-determination) and the independence of the whole state's population from foreign intervention or influence (internal self-determination)[42].

40 Raic, David, *Statehood and the Law of Self-Determination*, The Hague, Kluwer Law international, 2002, p. 289.

41 Cassese, Antonio, *Self Determination of Peoples: A Legal Reappraisal*, Cambridge, Cambridge University Press, 1995, p. 120.

42 Hannum, Hurst, *Autonomy, Sovereignty, and Self-Determination: the Accommodation of Conflicting Rights*, revised edition, Philadelphia, University of Pennsylvania Press, 1996, p. 49.

This also seems to be the opinion of Beaufort, for whom internal self-determination is the right of a nation, already constituted as a state, to choose its own form of government and to determine according to its own views the course of its policies without interference by others. However, for this author, external self-determination means the right of a group that considers itself a nation to form a state on its own. A third possibility is cited by Roethof: regional self-determination, the right of a nation in a multinational state or part of a nation to obtain an autonomous status within that state. According to this tripartite division, both the internal and external aspects constitute international relations and would be regulated by international law, whereas regional self-determination is a matter of domestic affairs regulated by constitutional law[43].

In other cases, the scope or focus of the internal/external distinction is not clearly linked with the outcomes of the exercise of the right. Pentassuglia emphasises, "The internal dimension to self-determination is concerned with the relationship between a people and its own state or government"[44]. Rosas contends that the internal aspect is composed of three layers:

1. The right of the people to constitute its own political system (constituent power).
2. The right of the people to have a say in amending the Constitution, including the right to resistance against tyranny and oppression.
3. The right of the people to govern and to take part in the conduct of public affairs, including participation in elections, referenda and so on.

Moreover, for Rosas, "The idea of internal self-determination as a principle of public international law is a challenge to the traditional inter-state paradigm, as it may imply a collective human right enjoyed by the population of a state against the sovereign state"[45].

This division between the internal and external aspects of self-determination has also been challenged. Jamilah Koné criticises Cassese's assertion that the problem of territorial integrity comes into play only in cases of "external" self-determination, whereas disputes over "internal" self-determination merely threaten public order. According to Koné, "The difference between the two types of self-determination may not

43 Belfort and Roethof as quoted in Haro F. Van Panhuys (ed.), *International Law in The Netherlands*, vol. 3, The Hague, Sijthoff and Noordhoff Oceana, 1980, pp. 151-152.

44 Pentassuglia, *op. cit.*, p. 161.

45 Rosas, Allan, "Internal self-determination" in Christian Tomuschat (ed.), *Modern Law of Self-Determination*, Dordrecht, Boston, Martinus Nijhoff Publishers, 1993, p. 227.

be as clear-cut as Cassese seems to believe"[46]. Another critical author is James Anaya, who challenges this internal/external distinction because it is based in a Western conception of the international community as a Westphalian order of exclusive domains. Anaya prefers to speak of a "constitutive element" of self-determination, referring to the moments at which the institutions of a people are constituted or modified, and an "ongoing element", which refers to the shape and function of these institutions[47].

In any case, the internal/external dichotomy has failed to achieve enduring and consistent success. During the 1980s, the idea of limiting self-determination to its internal aspect to exclude the possibility of changing internationally established borders gained support. However, this does not mean that the international community has adopted proactive policies in favour of internal self-determination processes or a clear definition of other possible outcomes of this right.

As Falk recognises, "There is no assured or necessary link between exercising the right to self-determination and a particular outcome"[48]. If the idea is to divide the content of the right to exclude the possibility of secession as a legitimate outcome (at least under "normal" circumstances), then it would be necessary to link any other political solution to internal self-determination. However, some analyses include other options (such as integration or free association) within the external aspect because they focus on the exercise and not on the outcome.

This reflects a duality in the criteria used to construct the two dimensions of self-determination. On the one hand, the division can refer to what Obieta calls "self-disposition", in other words, the level of political relations (*ad intra* or *ad extra*) effected on each side. On the other hand, it can refer to the outcome of the right in terms of international versus domestic consequences. Thus, if a given people exercises its right to self-determination by freely deciding on its integration (e.g., permanence) in the State through a territorial autonomy system, those following the first criterion would consider this a manifestation of the external element (i.e., the relation between the people holding the right and other peoples living in the same state). In contrast, those following the criterion of the outcome would see the result as an example of internal self-determination.

---

46 Jamilah Kone, Elizabeth, "The Right of Self-Determination in the Angolan Enclave of Cabinda", Paper presented at the Sixth Annual African Studies Consortium Workshop, October 1998, [Online]: http://www.africa.upenn.edu/Workshop/kone98.html.

47 Anaya, James, *Indigenous Peoples in International Law*, New York, Oxford University Press, 2000, pp. 78-81.

48 Falk, *op cit.*, p. 50.

In summary, it is necessary to clarify the meaning and legitimacy of the distinction between internal and external self-determination. From the point of view of the final political outcome of a self-determination process, it may be relevant to differentiate between the exercise of the right in a manner that preserves international boundaries and those cases that involve a change of international boundaries. However, from another perspective, a given right should be structured based on its object or its constituting faculties. Seen from this perspective, the internal aspect can only refer to the way a given community organises itself *ad intra* and among its members. On the contrary, the ability to decide its political status in relation to other peoples composes the external element of the right, regardless of the particular outcome chosen in each case (integration, limited autonomy or secession, among others). In the first perspective, there is a risk of confusing the content of the right with a de facto situation derived from its exercise, particularly if no progress is made in defining standards of internal self-determination. For this reason, the second option can be seen as more correct from a methodological perspective.

4. Prevailing Interpretations and Problematic Issues

It is not surprising that the most sensitive aspect of the right to self-determination is the possible effect on the territorial integrity of the state, including the hypothetical redefinition of borders. The main concern for many states, and consequently for international organisations, is to limit secession as a legitimate outcome of the right to self-determination. Potential cases of secession and the redefinition of boundaries are normally regarded as elements affecting the necessary stability of the international order. This is the main argument raised by international documents and qualified opinions in favour of severely reducing the likelihood of these outcomes. Once self-determination is internationally recognised as a human right of all peoples, this aim may be achieved in two different ways: on the one hand, by restricting the definition of people to exclude as much as possible this condition of "less-than-total-population-of-the-state groups"; on the other hand, by restricting the content of the right by limiting its exercise or the possible outcomes of its exercise.

In this context, a general but diffuse approach to the right to self-determination prevails, in which there are certain restrictive conditions that may legitimate the external aspect of the exercise of self-determination and even more restrictive conditions to justify secession as a legitimate outcome. In parallel, the people, as the holder of this right, are normally restricted to the total population of the state, the remaining colonised peoples and a very limited number of specific situations. Nevertheless, the existing interpretations of the right to self-determination are not consistent, even among those provided by European states. Therefore, further clarification of the different aspects of self-determination remains necessary to move toward a more solid theory of this collective human right. This paper will try to identify some of these controversies using a systematic approach.

4.1. Issues concerning the Holder of the Right

4.1.1. The "Whole People" Approach

The first option considered holds that only the total population of an existing state may qualify as a people under international law. It is well established in international law that colonised units, defined in conformity with the principles enshrined in General Assembly Resolution 1541, constitute peoples and holders of the right to self-determination. This complements the whole people approach. Given the fact that almost all formerly colonised peoples have gained independence, in practical terms, this affirms the argument that only the population of an independent state can be considered a people in the sense of the International Covenants on Human Rights[49].

However, this position contradicts other logical stands. First, it means denying the legal existence of indigenous peoples, who would be treated, at best, as indigenous populations; this is a tendency that is not consistent with the latest developments in this field. Second, this position would make it easy to identify the list of peoples existing at a given moment because it would be equivalent to a list of states or colonised territories. In this case, it would not make sense to distinguish the content of the right to self-determination depending on the outcome of its exercise. Those who restrict external self-determination to particular circumstances would find no cause to deny this possibility because all holders would already be independent or would be entitled to independence following General Assembly Resolutions 1514, 1541 and 2625. This would make the right to self-determination duplicative and superfluous.

Finally, if a remedial consideration of the exercise of self-determination (see below) for groups that do not correspond to the total population of the state is considered, it must be clarified that the entitlement to a human right cannot be determined by the violation of the same right or other human rights. This means that the condition of people as a holder of a

49 This narrow sense of the term *people* in international law is defended by the Republic of Argentina: International Court of Justice, Accordance with International Law of the Unilateral Declaration of Independence by the Provisional Institutions of Self-Government of Kosovo (Request for Advisory opinion), Written Comments of the Argentine Republic, 17 July 2009, p. 27, para. 61.

human right cannot "appear and disappear" depending on the behaviour of external actors. Human rights must be held continuously as long as the holder of the right exists. In other words, the exercise of a human right does not create the right or the holder of the right. Even if we favour the remedial approach, it cannot be defended logically that a particular kind of people arises suddenly when massive human rights violations take place against such an entity[50]. By the same logic, the existence of that people would disappear upon reaching a satisfactory situation. As this does not happen in other human rights categories, when taking a remedial approach, the holder of the right(s) must be previously defined and recognised.

The strict "whole people" approach does not convincingly address these objections and therefore must be rejected at the current stage. There is a growing consensus that "the right to self-determination does not apply exclusively in the context of decolonization"[51]. In accordance with the correspondence between the right and its holder, this implies that there are holders other than colonised peoples and state populations. As the Supreme Court of Canada state:

> It is clear that "a people" may include only a portion of the population of an existing state. [...] The reference to "people" does not necessarily mean the entirety of a state's population. To restrict the definition of the term to the population of existing states would render the granting of a right to self-determination largely duplicative [...] and would frustrate its remedial purpose[52].

4.1.2. The "Plurality of Peoples" Approach

If the previous position is shown to be contradictory for the current state of international law, then it is necessary to invoke the opposite opinion: that it is possible to find different kinds of peoples in the international community apart from the existing states' populations and colonised peoples. First, it must be admitted that in several cases the

---

50 In this respect, the position expressed by the Argentine Republic in the Kosovo consultative opinion makes sense when it states, "Argentina has asserted that [...] grave violations of human rights do not transform a group of individuals into a people entitled to self-determination, although other important rights are granted to minorities and other groups", International Court of Justice, Accordance with International Law of the Unilateral Declaration of Independence by the Provisional Institutions of Self-Government of Kosovo (Request for Advisory opinion), Written Comments of the Argentine Republic, 17 July 2009, p. 26, para. 59.

51 International Court of Justice, *Legal Consequences of the Construction of a Wall in the Occupied Palestinian Territory* (Advisory Opinion of 9-7-2004); Separate Opinion of Judge Higgings, *ICJ reports 2004*, at 214, paras. 29-30.

52 Quebec case paras. 113 and 124.

legal system, either international or domestic, recognises the existence of differentiated peoples within a given state. Indigenous peoples can be added to the list of generally recognised groups without much difficulty under the plurality of peoples approach.

Problems arise, however, because these previously enumerated groups do not represent the entirety of possible peoples existing in the international community. This ambiguity makes it difficult to establish guiding principles to aid in identifying additional peoples. International and constitutional comparative law should attempt to define these criteria along democratic lines. I will return to this point later when reflecting on the concept of "national conflicts".

At this point, it is appropriate to move forward in the critical analysis of the positions expressed by different actors, specifically addressing the correspondence between the consideration of a people and the entitlement to, or exercise of, the right in itself. In this respect, the following possible opinions arise:

A) The right to self-determination only corresponds to some peoples, and excludes others. In other words, only some peoples (i.e., those corresponding to the total population of the state or to colonised units) are entitled to the right to self-determination.

This position must be discouraged from the very beginning because it is in manifest violation of Article 1 of both Covenants on Human Rights, which clearly refer to "all peoples". Including the term "all" in the article eliminates any possibility of developing an interpretation by which only some peoples should enjoy that right. The same can be said regarding the creation of different categories of peoples with respect to the entitlement to this (human) right. Any contrary position would constitute a violation of the covenants and of a basic principle of international law. Once the existence of a people is recognised, the human nature of this right requires that all holders of this right be considered equal. This position is backed by the Swiss government's statement, "The right to self-determination is closely linked with the principle of equality. All peoples possess this right to the same extent. It cannot be granted to one people but denied to another in a selective manner on subjective grounds"[53].

Nevertheless, an international legal document, the International Labour Organization Convention n° 169 concerning Indigenous and Tribal Peoples in Independent Countries, subscribes to this position when it states in

53 International Court of Justice, Accordance with International Law of the Unilateral Declaration of Independence by the Provisional Institutions of Self-Government of Kosovo (Request for Advisory opinion), Written Statement addressed to the International Court of Justice by the Swiss Confederation, p. 19, para. 71.1.

Article 1.3, "The use of the term peoples in this Convention shall not be construed as having any implications as regards the rights which may attach to the term under international law". The clause is intended to avoid any implications with respect to the right to self-determination, but, as has been said, it is logically inconsistent and contrary to the law in force, since in any legal system, the use of a technical term having legal implications and the simultaneous denial of these same implications should be avoided. In addition to being confusing, this creates a legal problem. In any case, having characterised self-determination as a human right, the clause can also be considered void insofar as these rights are inalienable and not subject to disposition. Finally, it must be argued that with respect to indigenous peoples, this clause must be considered outdated by the approval of Article 3 of the United Nations Declaration on the Rights of Indigenous Peoples, which was adopted in September 2007.

B) The right to self-determination only corresponds to some peoples according to particular circumstances. This position entails a remedial consideration of the right to self-determination in the case of some categories of peoples.

In fact, this position is similar to the previous one. It adds the possibility of recognising new holders of the right given some particular circumstances. Unlike case 1.1., this implies a recognition that the holders of the rights existed as recognised peoples before the violations occurred. Nevertheless, refusal to extend the right of self-determination to all peoples again violates Article 1 of the Human Rights Covenants, as in the previous hypothesis.

C) The right to self-determination attaches to all peoples, but its content may be different for different categories of peoples according to particular circumstances; or its exercise may be limited for peoples in particular contexts.

In a general overview of the institutional and academic positions on the right to self-determination, this is the most commonly defended position. The main concern about self-determination is the potential political consequences of the exercise of this right. We know that "the right to self-determination is sufficiently broad to include a multitude of choices, including but not limited to independence, depending on the particular circumstances of each case"[54]. According to United Nations General Assembly Resolutions 1541 and 2625, the possible outcomes of self-determination are emergence as a sovereign independent State; the free association of a people with an independent State; or the integration of

54 International Court of Justice, Western Sahara (Advisory Opinion of 16-10-1975), *ICJ Reports* 1975, at 33.

the people with an independent State. Similarly, the African Commission on Human and People's Rights points out that self-determination can lead to "independence, self-government, local government, federalism, confederalism, unitarism or any other form of relations that accords with the wishes of the people"[55].

However, there are many opinions in agreement on limiting some of these possible outcomes for specific holders and concrete circumstances. In very general terms, this prevailing position suggests that the possibility of secession (which some positions fully identify with external self-determination) is an option limited to the peoples of former colonies, peoples submitted to foreign occupation or oppressed peoples who are denied meaningful access to government to pursue their political, economic, social and cultural development[56].

Indeed, during the 1980s, the idea of limiting self-determination to internal outcomes and thus excluding the possibility of secession gained support. This has been broadly identified with the distinction between internal and external elements of the right to self-determination. However, the dichotomy focuses on the consequences of its exercise more than on the real elements of the right itself, distinguishing those affecting previous international boundaries from other solutions at the domestic level. In any case, this "internal" interpretation of self-determination prevails[57], although others state that this approach cannot be considered fully accepted[58]. This prevailing approach must be analysed from the point of view of the content of the right to self-determination rather than from the point of view of the entitlement of this right.

4.2. Issues concerning the Content or Exercise of the Right

4.2.1. "All-Possible-Outcomes" Self-Determination Cases

For some categories of holders of the right to self-determination, all possible outcomes are legitimately recognised. These holders enjoy what could be considered a "full" or "unlimited" right to self-determination.

---

55 Kantangese People case, para. 4.

56 See, for instance, Quebec case, para. 138.

57 Narrow interpretation according to Cardenas, Emilio and Maria Fernanda Cañas, "The Limits of Self-Determination" in Wolfgang Danspeckgruber (ed.), *The Self-Determination of Peoples. Community, Nation and State in an Interdependent World*, London, Lynne Rienner Publishers, 2002, p. 111.

58 Tomuschat, Christian, "Democratic Pluralism: the Right to Political Opposition" in Allan Rosas and Jan Hegelsen (eds.), *The Strength of Diversity: Human Rights and Pluralist Democracy*, Dordrecht, Martinus Nijhoff Publishers, 1992, p. 39.

A) Peoples corresponding to the total population of the State

Peoples that already have their own independent and internationally recognised state enjoy their right to self-determination with no restrictions. Doubts may arise concerning the peoples of states that are not widely recognised, such as Kosovo, Abkhazia, Northern Cyprus and South Ossetia, among others.

B) Peoples for whom the right to self-determination is expressly recognised

No problem arises when the right to self-determination is legally recognised without clear restrictions on other peoples. This possibility can be foreseen in international treaties or in domestic legal documents. It implies the consent of the states concerned. Thus, for instance, the United Nations Committee on the Elimination of Racial Discrimination established that discouraging any self-determination outcome that may "dismember or impair, totally or in part, the territorial integrity or political unity of sovereign and independent States [...] does not, however, exclude the possibility of arrangements reached by free agreements of all parties concerned"[59]. Cases like Northern Ireland, Gagauzia, New Caledonia or the different Ethiopian peoples would fit into this category.

C) Peoples under colonial domination

Colonised peoples, as defined in conformity with the principles of General Assembly Resolution 1541, are recognised as having the right to self-determination, including all possible outcomes foreseen in Resolution 2625. In fact, it must be admitted that it was decolonisation that enshrined the right to self-determination in international law because, based on the strict version of the whole people approach, the formulation of self-determination could have been regarded as duplicative.

However, it must also be clarified that decolonisation and self-determination do not correspond to one another in all cases. On the one hand, self-determination is not the only way that decolonisation may proceed; territorial retrocession is another option that applies in specific circumstances. On the other hand, the exercise of self-determination cannot be restricted to the colonial context[60]. As Obieta argues, reducing self-determination to the colonial liberation process denaturalises this right, transforming it from a right of the people to freely decide their political status to a right of the states to their own territory[61].

59 UN CERD, *op. cit.*, para. 6.

60 Vienna Declaration and Programme of Action, UN Document A/CONF.157/23, 12 July 1993; Spilipoulou Akermark, Athanasia, *Justification of Minority Protection in International Law*, The Hague, Kluwer Law International, 1997, p. 30.

61 Obieta Chalbaud, *op. cit., p.* 56.

D) Occupied peoples or peoples subjected to alien domination

People subjected to alien domination are entitled to exercise self-determination, including all of its possible outcomes, with the aim of removing the illegitimate domination. As the Supreme Court of Canada says, "The other clear case where a right to external self-determination accrues is where a people is subject to alien subjugation, domination or exploitation outside a colonial context. This recognition finds its roots in the Declaration on Friendly Relations" (United Nations General Assembly Resolution 2625)[62].

This category implicitly refers to peoples subjected to alien domination (excluding those under colonial domination, who fit into the previous category). Similarly, we do not include here peoples subjugated by the same state where they have traditionally lived, as this group comprises the majority of the following category.

E) Oppressed or unrepresented peoples

Justices Wildhaber and Ryssdal from the European Court of Human Rights stated:

> Until recently in international practice the right to self-determination was in practical terms identical to, and indeed restricted to, a right to decolonization. In recent years a consensus has seemed to emerge that peoples may also exercise a right to self-determination if their human rights are consistently and flagrantly violated or if they are without representation at all or are massively under-represented in an undemocratic and discriminatory way. If this description is correct, then the right to self-determination is a tool which may be used to re-establish international standards of human rights and democracy[63].

This position is also expressed in a different way by Crawford, who recognises an additional category of people with the right to self-determination: "Entities part of a metropolitan State but that have been governed in such a way as to make them in effect non-self-governing territories", expressly quoting the cases of Bangladesh, Kosovo and Eritrea[64].

In the aforementioned opinions, the right to self-determination is attached to peoples in these particular circumstances. This makes self-determination in itself a remedial right, something that is difficult to admit from a human rights perspective. The prevailing position today is that

---

62 Quebec case, para. 133.

63 European Court of Human Rights, *Loizidou v. Turkey* (judgement of 18-12-1996), Concurring Opinion of Judge Wildhaber, joined by Judge Ryssdal.

64 Crawford, James, *The Creation of States in International Law* (2nd ed.), Oxford, Oxford University Press, 2006, p. 126.

peoples living in a context of oppression within their states may exercise their right to self-determination with no restriction in terms of possible outcomes. The Supreme Court of Canada reflects this widely accepted opinion when it states, "[t]he right to self-determination generates, at best, a right to external self-determination (i.e., independence) in situations [...] where a definable group is denied meaningful access to government to pursue their political, economic, social and cultural development"[65].

In this sense, the remedial element is not the right to self-determination, but a part of its content, or, even less than that, some possible outcomes of the external self-disposition. Those who identify external self-determination with modification of international boundaries will consider this external aspect the remedial element. In attempting to gain a broader understanding of the external dimension of the right, we could restrict this remedial content to secession. The general formulation would be that "the right to self-determination does not amount to a general rule legitimising secession from an independent State. However, under exceptional circumstances, the right to self-determination gives rise to secession"[66]. However, it is true that the international community is not always consistent in dealing with the situations of peoples that may fit into this category. The cases of Bangladesh, Katanga, Biafra, Tibet, Kosovo and Chechnya have led to different considerations and solutions.

Finally, it should be clarified whether we are really admitting a full right to self-determination in favour of repressed peoples or, from another perspective, only a remedial right to secession arising in these critical situations[67]. The first option would imply the recognition of a human right in its entirety and, obviously, the recognition of a holder of this right. The second option would use secession as a remedy for specific political circumstances without linking it to a self-determination process. Although practical outcomes in particular cases may coincide with both possibilities, other kinds of consequences may diverge considerably.

F) Peoples belonging to a dismembering state

In the case of the disintegration of a state, the peoples living within the boundaries of that state may exercise their right to self-determination

---

65 Quebec case, para. 138.

66 Musgrave, Thomas D., *Self-Determination and National Minorities*, Oxford, Clarendon Press, 1998, p. 76. Also, International Court of Justice, Accordance with International Law of the Unilateral Declaration of Independence by the Provisional Institutions of Self-Government of Kosovo (Request for Advisory opinion), Reply of the Government of the Republic of Albania, July 2009, p. 31, para. 55.

67 Okafor, Obiora Chinedu., "Entitlement, Process, and Legitimacy in the Emergent International Law of Secession", *International Journal on Minority and Group Rights*, vol. 9, nº 1, 2002, pp. 60 and ff.

without restriction, leading to independence if that is the wish of the respective population. This rule may be derived from the recent experiences of the disintegration of the Soviet Union, Yugoslavia and Czechoslovakia. However, it is not clear if this rule can be applied to any country as the three given examples adopted a federal structure and included clearly established federated units.

It may also be disputed that, unlike secession, integration into another state may be a legitimate option in a dismembering state. From international practice, it seems clear that only previously adopted internal boundaries of federal units are admitted as new international boundaries. The application to the case of the principle of *uti possidetis iuris* makes it doubtful that one of the federal units could join a neighbour state instead of gaining independence. The Arbitration Commission of the Conference on Yugoslavia (Badinter Commission) found that "it is well established that, whatever the circumstances, the right to self-determination must not involve changes to existing frontiers at the time of independence (*uti possidetis iuris*) except where the States concerned agree otherwise"[68]. From that perspective, not all possible external outcomes would be admitted.

International practice has shown reluctance to admit any alteration of the boundaries of the former federated units. It is also reluctant to extend this solution to other peoples living within second-level administrative units. This restrictive solution can be challenged because the former units accede to the first internal territorial level once the federated entity has gained independence, as the Kosovo case clearly shows[69].

4.2.2. Limited Self-Determination Cases

According to the prevailing opinion, in the case of other peoples not included in the previous categories, the right to self-determination cannot be exercised in a manner that leads to secession or that affects international boundaries. This seems to be the dominant opinion in current international law, although there is still a significant degree of confusion around the problem of identifying the holder of the right and its material scope. Furthermore, there may be confusion between the right to self-determination and a hypothetical remedial right to secession.

In any case, accepting the prevailing opinion as it has been described, a different set of theoretical and practical questions arise. To progressively build a solid and consistent theory of the human right to

68 Arbitration Commission of the Conference on Yugoslavia (Badinter Commission), Opinion No.2 of 11 January 1992, 31 *ILM*, 1992, p. 1497.

69 Falk, *op. cit.*, p. 35.

self-determination, it would be necessary to seek a higher degree of legal certainty by addressing the following three remaining issues:

1. The justification of the distinction between unlimited and limited self-determination.
2. The identification of peoples entitled to (limited) self-determination.
3. The (substantial) content of the limited version of the right.

4.3. The Justification of the Distinction between Unlimited and Limited Self-Determination

The idea of limiting the possible outcomes of the exercise of self-determination in some cases is widely assumed in the international community. It is true that Article 1 of both Covenants establishes no restriction in this respect, but it is not unprecedented to fix limits and conditions for the exercise of a human right. Obviously, the exercise of self-determination can be limited, restricted or reduced to a given number of possible outcomes or options, but as with any other human right, this decision will consider the global context of the holder of the right. This does not mean that external self-determination is erased from the content of the right, but only that its exercise comes to be qualified. However, in the case of human rights, these limits or conditions should be clearly prescribed by law and justified as necessary to achieve a legitimate aim in a democratic society. In this respect, some countries have made reservations or declarations with regards to the 1966 Covenants with the aim of limiting the scope and holders of the right to self-determination. However, as the government of The Netherlands stated, "Any attempt to limit the scope of this right or to attach conditions not provided for in the relevant instruments undermines the concept of self-determination itself and thereby seriously weakens its universally acceptable character"[70].

The main basis on which to justify the restriction of what some authors call "external self-determination" is respect for other principles of international law, such as the territorial integrity and political unity of independent states. This idea is contained in the so-called safeguard clause of General Assembly Resolution 2625, which states "Nothing in the foregoing paragraphs shall be construed as authorizing or encouraging any action which would dismember or impair, totally or in part, the territorial integrity or political unity of sovereign and independent states conducting themselves in compliance with the principle of equal rights

70 International Court of Justice, Accordance with International Law of the Unilateral Declaration of Independence by the Provisional Institutions of Self-Government of Kosovo (Request for Advisory opinion), Written Statement of the Kingdom of the Netherlands, 17 April 2009, p. 12, para. 3.18.

and self-determination of peoples as described above and thus possessed of a government representing the whole people belonging to the territory without distinction as to race, creed or colour"[71].

The main justification for denying the possibility of affecting international borders in the exercise of the right to self-determination is the need for stability in the international order, which relates to the conservative nature of international law. From this viewpoint, any secession process (or even a partial modification of international borders) is regarded as an *ultima ratio* solution to problematic circumstances affecting other human rights or the right to self-determination. Thus, it is submitted that "the separation of a minority from the State of which it forms a part and its incorporation in another State can only be considered as an altogether exceptional solution, a last resort when the State lacks either the will or the power to enact and apply just and effective guarantees"[72]. This last resort approach would also mean that external consequences of self-determination may be accrued only after "the exhaustion of all possible avenues aiming to restore a situation in which human rights are respected, including the right to internal self-determination"[73]. To defend a consistent position, it must be understood that it is not the right itself, or even the substantial content of the right, that is in question, but the way this right may be exercised by peoples living in circumstances other than those specified in the previous chapter.

4.4. The Identification of Peoples Entitled to (Limited) Self-Determination

This second question is far more problematic than the previous one. Consistent with the previous findings, the concept of *people* in current international law corresponds to the total population of an independent state. However, clearly established criteria for a legal identification of other peoples are still lacking. If other peoples are entitled to self-determination in addition to indigenous peoples, it is necessary to establish a set of criteria or elements of interpretation to facilitate their identification. The idea of drafting commonly accepted criteria for identification of other

71 Similar provisions were also foreseen in the World Conference on Human Rights, Vienna Declaration and Programme of Action, 25 June 1993 (A/CONF.157/23, article I.2) and the United Nations Declaration on the Rights of Indigenous peoples, General Assembly Resolution 61/295, 13 September 2007, article 46(1).

72 Commission of Rapporteurs, League of Nations Doc. B.7.21/68/106 (1921), *Official Journal*, 1921, Suppl. nº 5, at 24.

73 International Court of Justice, Accordance with International Law of the Unilateral Declaration of Independence by the Provisional Institutions of Self-Government of Kosovo (Request for Advisory opinion), Written Comments addressed to the International Court of Justice by the Swiss Confederation, at 2, para. 7.

peoples, similar to the attempt by General Assembly Resolution 1541 to identify colonised units, would clarify and facilitate the search for a more stable understanding of self-determination.

Furthermore, whether the concept of *people* should be static or dynamic must be determined. The possibility also exists that peoples may overlap in their composition and that the contemporary postmodern world may give rise to identities comprising multiple peoples.

4.5. The Scope of the Limited Version of the Right

We have already concluded that the exercise of the right by a self-determination unit usually does not include the creation of a new State[74]. The African Commission on Human and Peoples' Rights, in its case on Katanga, established that "in the absence of concrete evidence of violations of human rights [...], the Commission holds the view that Katanga is obliged to exercise a variant of self-determination that is compatible with the sovereignty and territorial integrity of Zaire"[75]. The government of the Swiss Confederation noted, "The right to self-determination cannot be exercised externally until after the exhaustion of all possible avenues aiming to restore a situation in which human rights are respected, including *the right to internal self-determination*"[76] (emphasis added). The subsequent question is about the content or scope of this limited version of the right. For those who identify secession with external self-determination, the question pertains to the content of internal self-determination. For those who use a different criterion for distinction, the question is simply about the remaining possible outcomes of the right and the ways it can be exercised by its holder.

The United Nations Declaration on the Rights of Indigenous Peoples, adopted by the General Assembly in September 2007, develops the right to self-determination of indigenous peoples (recognised in Article 3). It states that indigenous peoples, "in exercising their right to self-determination, have the right to autonomy or self-government in matters relating to their internal and local affairs, as well as ways and means for financing their autonomous functions"[77]. However, there are no other

74 International Court of Justice, Accordance with International Law of the Unilateral Declaration of Independence by the Provisional Institutions of Self-Government of Kosovo (Request for Advisory opinion), Further Written Contribution of the Republic of Kosovo, 17 July 2009, at 78.

75 Kantangese People case, para. 6.

76 International Court of Justice, Accordance with International Law of the Unilateral Declaration of Independence by the Provisional Institutions of Self-Government of Kosovo (Request for Advisory opinion), Written Comments addressed to the International Court of Justice by the Swiss Confederation, at 2, para. 7.

77 United Nations Declaration on the Rights of Indigenous Peoples, Adopted by General Assembly Resolution 61/295 on 13 September 2007, art. 4.

legal or political references clarifying the content of the "internal aspects" of self-determination or the minimum content of the right, even when secession is out of consideration.

Precisely because secession is considered a last resort in the exercise of self-determination, it is necessary to establish alternative ways for other peoples to exercise this right. The lack of development in this respect shows that self-determination has been avoided due to its identification with secession. The Declaration on the Rights of Indigenous Peoples' statement on autonomy or self-government may be considered a guideline in this respect, but it is far from a hallmark in the description of the content of the right to self-determination of other peoples. Other statements refer to additional possible outcomes of the right, such as integration, free association, "local government, federalism, confederalism, unitarism or any other form of relations that accords with the wishes of the people"[78]. However, apart from an open list of possible outcomes, we lack a systematic description of the content of this human right before reaching the *ultima ratio* solution.

Some approaches to the idea of internal self-determination refer solely to the democratic political organisation of a given people. However, this *ad intra* element can be distinguished from the external outcomes of the right regardless of whether all or only some are considered external self-determination. Thus, recognition of the right to political participation by all members of the people and subsequent democratic representation of all members of the political community in the government bodies of the state does not exhaust the right to self-determination, as can be easily understood from a reading of the International Covenant on Civil and Political Rights. The right to political participation is not part of the content of the right to self-determination but a specific individual human right enshrined in Article 25 of the Covenant and therefore different in terms of holder and content. The latter must show content intrinsically different from the participatory one, which may be exercised by the collective holder of the right and not only by its individual members.

On the contrary, developments of territorial or personal autonomy, local or national self-government, or other possible constitutional arrangements may complete the content of the right to self-determination of those peoples whose conditions do not justify access to the *ultima ratio* solutions.

An important issue arises at this point in the discussion: the question of the substantial content of the right that should be respected and

78 Kantangese People case, para. 4.

guaranteed in every case. As mentioned previously, it is not incompatible with human rights theory to admit restrictions in the exercise of the rights or limitations according to legal proceedings in previously defined circumstances. However, these limitations by no means diminish the substantial content of any human right such that the right becomes unrecognisable. For instance, in the Spanish legal system, the expression "essential content" is used in Article 53 of the Constitution as a limit that cannot be unheeded by the legislator when regulating constitutionally recognised rights. In terms of internationally recognised human rights, a parallel theory can be defended to secure the substantial content of this right and establish its minimum parameters.

A relevant question is whether, in the case of peoples showing a clear political will to secede from their current state (either to constitute their own state or to join another independent state), the restriction of some external outcomes of the right to self-determination undermines this substantial content of a collective human right. In this respect, Seymour proposes an extremely interesting distinction between three levels or degrees of the political dimension of internal self-determination: "weak", "canonical" and "strong"[79]. This question requires further research and clarification as it seems to reside on the border between law, politics and philosophy.

5. Self-Determination and Democratic Management of National Conflicts

The right to self-determination must be regarded not only as a human right, but also as a useful instrument to prevent conflicts and pave the way for democratic solutions in conflict situations. These situations set up what I call "national conflicts", contexts where further clarification of the right to self-determination may be beneficial in reducing unnecessary tensions. A more robust theory of the right to self-determination, including identification of its potential holders and means of implementation, would facilitate a less dramatic approach to this right by states and would provide more legal certainty.

It is obvious that the main concern over the implementation of this particular right in the context of some national conflicts is that it may affect the territorial integrity of the state or the relations between two or more states. However, it is necessary at the outset to address fears of

79 The French words used by Seymour are "faible", "canonique" and "robuste". Seymour, Michel, "L'autodétermination interne du Québec dans la fédération canadienne", Paper presented at the international seminar "Le féderalisme multinational en perspective: un modèle viable?", held at the Université de Québec à Montréal, on 25-26-27 September 2009, pp. 4-5.

a stronger regulation of this right by emphasising that there are a very limited number of real cases where self-determination implies major political consequences. The number of national conflicts in Europe, where secession is the aspiration of a significant sector of the population involved, is extremely low. In fact, most States are not affected by these types of conflicts. Therefore, fears of creating general anarchical chaos by recognising self-determination in generous terms do not seem proportionate to the real state of affairs. Only a very limited number of states face specific problems of accommodating national or ethnic diversity to this extent.

In any case, when sovereignty is the issue at stake, debating the legitimacy of self-determination has limited effects because the whole issue tends to be located in the political arena instead of in the legal sphere. In some cases, the role played by international law is that of recognising the new factual situation[80]. As the government of the United Kingdom recognises:

> The constitutional authority of the seceding entity to proclaim independence within the predecessor State is not determinative as a matter of international law. In most if not all the cases, provincial or regional authorities will lack the constitutional authority to secede. The act of secession is not thereby excluded. Moreover, representative institutions may legitimately act, and seek to reflect the views of their constituents, beyond the scope of already conferred power […][81].
>
> Of course attempts at secession may well (as already noted) be contrary to the municipal law of the State concerned. The Declaration of Independence of 4 July 1776 was at the time considered an act of treason under British law. But from the standpoint of international law there was, and is, no prohibition per se of secession[82].

It would be beneficial to build a more precise theory of the right to self-determination that could be applied to different situations, including contexts in which a national conflict arises. *National conflict* implies a situation in which a minority group (as defined, for instance, in the Council of Europe's Parliamentary Assembly Recommendation 1201 (1993)) expresses, more or less directly, its aspiration to enjoy a certain level of self-government that may significantly affect the sovereignty

---

80 Pentassuglia, Gaetano, "State Sovereignty, Minorities and Self-Determination: A Comprehensive Legal View", *International Journal on Minority and Group Rights*, vol. 9, nº 4, 2002, p. 312.

81 International Court of Justice, Request for an Advisory opinion of the International Court of Justice on the question "Is the Unilateral Declaration of Independence by the Provisional Institutions of Self-Government of Kosovo in accordance with international law?", Written Statement of the United Kingdom, 17 April 2009, at 86 para. 5.7 and at 87 para. 5.13.

82 *Ibid.*, at 87, para. 5.13.

of the host state. These situations raise the issue not only of democratic management of different types of diversity (religious, linguistic, ethnic, cultural or national) but also of potential conflict regarding the distribution of political power. From this perspective, national conflicts can be considered part of the more general concept of diversity conflicts[83].

A problematic aspect of national conflicts is defining them in relation to other less problematic cases. Kymlicka refers to protagonist collectives as "national minorities" (an overly broad name when it is used in the European legal context). Others have proposed the term "minority nations"[84]. These groups may correspond to other possible peoples in legal terms, and therefore they may be entitled to claim a right to self-determination. The determination of these cases must be made methodologically based on empirical data and not on subjective perceptions.

How can these cases be differentiated from other minority contexts? Following Requejo's proposal, I suggest taking into consideration the following facts:

a) The existence of a significant degree of affiliation to those political or social entities that claim a substantial modification of the legal order in the name of the corresponding minority (people). Fifteen percent of the total census in the territory concerned can be considered a significant level of affiliation.

b) The fact that "pro-sovereignty" political forces (those calling for a significant modification of the legal status quo) obtain a relevant percentage of votes in elections held in the territory concerned. A "significant percentage" in this respect can be considered 20% of all valid votes cast in that territorial scope.

c) The fact that the legal order in force has a significantly lower degree of democratic legitimation in comparison with other parts of the state. This element may be observed, for instance, in the refusal of a particular territory to ratify the national constitution or in a significantly different result obtained in referenda held to legitimate or adopt the constitutional order. In this respect, a significant difference can be appreciated when the social support differs by more than 25% from that of the state as a whole.

These empirical data may serve as guidelines to identify the existence of a "minority nation" or a potentially different self-determination unit.

83 Ruiz Vieytez, Eduardo, "Estudio comparado de otros conflictos nacionales" in Xabier Etxeberria Mauleon *et al.*, *Derecho de autodeterminación y realidad vasca*, Vitoria-Gasteiz, Gobierno Vasco, 2002, pp. 193-210.

84 Requejo, Ferran, "Justicia cosmopolita y minorías nacionales", *Claves de la razón práctica*, nº 171, 2007, p. 36.

Obviously, the criteria must be consistent in the sense that they must be maintained for a minimum period of time. In any case, they must be evaluated case by case by all parties concerned (including the state authorities) in good faith. Guiding principles like those mentioned may be useful in determining other possible holders of the right to self-determination without prejudicing the conditions for the exercise of this right.

It is clear that a minimum territorial basis is required to determine the territorial scope in which these principles must be analysed[85]. Following the spirit of the *uti possidetis iuris* principle, internally existing administrative or political divisions must be taken into consideration as the territorial references through which peoples may be identified[86]. The need to consider a minimum extent of this territorial basis leads us to exclude the local-level divisions. However, units like provinces, departments, cantons, regions or other similar territorial units can serve as the reference framework for the analysis of electoral or political data.

When any of the previously mentioned elements is certified as consistent in territorial and temporal terms, we can admit the existence of a national conflict and of a self-determination unit. Thus, the recognition of different peoples cannot take place according to subjective or voluntary criteria but must be based on existing political expressions that reflect the existence of a collective will in a particular territory. Obviously, this can be supplemented with additional evidence, but the correspondence between democratic expression and entitlement to self-determination must be clearly stated. Thus, as the Swiss government states, "The fact that close ties exist between the right of peoples to self-determination and the fundamental rights of a democratic society sets at the same time the condition that the demand for self-determination can only be considered if the majority of the population within the territory concerned declare that they are in favour of self-determination"[87].

85 International Court of Justice, Accordance with International Law of the Unilateral Declaration of Independence by the Provisional Institutions of Self-Government of Kosovo (Request for Advisory opinion), Written Statement addressed to the International Court of Justice by the Swiss Confederation, at 19, para. 71.

86 "To what unit does the concept of self-determination apply? If the international order is not to be reduced to a fragmented chaos, then some answer must be provided to this question [...]. Self determination refers to the right of the majority within a generally accepted political unit to the exercise of power: It is necessary to start with stable boundaries and to permit political change within them" (Higgins, Rosalyn, *The Development of International Law through the Political Organs of the UNO*, London, 1963, at 104 (para. 72)).

87 International Court of Justice, Accordance with International Law of the Unilateral Declaration of Independence by the Provisional Institutions of Self-Government of Kosovo (Request for Advisory opinion), Written Statement addressed to the International Court of Justice by the Swiss Confederation, at 20, para. 78.

When this kind of internal conflict appears, the reference to self-determination usually leads to bitter debates between those in favour and those opposed to recognising the rights of the "minority nation". Frequently, the debate focuses on an inaccurate idea of what self-determination may mean, with a tendency to identify this right with the possible outcome of secession.

It would be beneficial to establish a set of commonly accepted standards to manage these (potentially conflictive) situations in a more democratic and inclusive way. In a previous work, I suggested dealing with these sensitive contexts using a set of basic ideas:

1. It is necessary to admit national conflicts as inherent to political and social life. It is not the conflict in itself that is positive or negative, but its management. In this sense, the worst possible management of a national conflict is refusal to recognise the conflict or denial of political or ethical legitimacy to the unofficial or alternative aspirants. It is necessary to assume the differences and the legitimacy of conflicting political aspirations and to focus the debate in the political or legal arena instead of the moral arena.
2. Any potential distribution of political power in personal or territorial terms is contingent, and it cannot be considered intrinsically illegitimate without adopting a dogmatic approach. In any democratic framework where individual human rights are the basis for all political projects, any hope of totally or partially modifying the set of holders entitled to sovereignty is as legitimate as those willing to maintain the status quo.
3. Any political and legal system, to a greater or lesser degree, is based on elements of identity that work as (dominant) references for the construction or regulation of the public space or the legal order. Linguistic, religious, cultural, ethnic or national identity references may be more or less expansive in each case, but so far it has not been possible to build a neutral political community in terms of identity. It is necessary to recognise this factor to debate the political accommodation of different nations or peoples. Any alternative solution relevant to political sovereignty will be based, to some extent, in particular identity elements, as is already the case with the status quo.
4. Due to the regular process of law making, so-called national conflicts tend to be unbalanced from a political perspective. In general terms, those proponents of maintaining the status quo are in favour of the system and may be tempted to deny the existence of a conflict or a new subjectivity. Nevertheless, in this kind of conflict, the status quo is one of the dividing factors.

5. It must be admitted that in some situations, there may be no common solution acceptable to all parties involved. When political aspirations are contradictory, it is best to look for the most comprehensive and inclusive resolution while acknowledging its enactment will not always be possible. In this respect, to suspend basic political decisions by asking qualified majorities for their revision may lead to the use of a veto power by those sectors that are satisfied with the status quo. This would not be encouraged in the interest of facilitating a negotiated alternative solution.
6. As has been mentioned, the very nature of this kind of conflict is more political than legal. Law must be an instrument to facilitate democratic solutions, give legal force to political consensus or pave the way to democratic processes. Nevertheless, a basic assumption of any democratic solution must be that a people cannot legitimately be governed without that people's consent. Law cannot become an obstacle when seeking a democratic solution in controversial situations. Constitutional law must be reread in terms of a continuously evolving system of basic agreements. It must be an open framework of political consensus that continues to be updated as long as the political community evolves in its composition and in its aspirations. Pluralist societies require a more flexible understanding of constitutional law that can admit new realities through participatory proceedings and democratic expressions.

With these guidelines as a procedural reference, the so-called national conflicts may be dealt with through a more democratic perspective using the right to self-determination as a useful tool for conflict prevention. Once we have provided some interpretive elements by which to recognise other possible holders of the right, it is necessary to develop a more consistent theory on the content of the right and the exercisable elements of that right, thus eventually putting an end to such conflicts.

In this sense, the exercise of the right to self-determination is conditioned according to the particular circumstances of the case, leading the way to a set of possible outcomes related to self-government, political collective participation, recognition of identity elements, or constitutional accommodations like consociationalism, federal arrangements, free association and other possible intermediate solutions[88]. In this respect, the Lund Recommendations drafted by the High Commissioner for National

[88] I offer a systematization of political and legal accommodation of minority realities following the criteria in Ruiz Vieytez, Eduardo, *Minorías, inmigración y democracia en Europa. Una lectura multicultural de los derechos humanos*, Valencia, Tirant lo blanch, 2006, Chapter 3.

Minorities of the OSCE, although directed toward national minorities (and not necessarily toward peoples), offer interesting guidelines[89].

Nevertheless, a final issue has yet to be resolved. When a people, defined in conformity with the aforementioned criteria, expresses its will to accede to the last resort outcome of the right to self-determination (i.e., secession), should that possibility be legally denied unless there is a pattern of human rights violations? In other words, may this concrete aspiration only be invoked as a remedy and not as a legitimate aspiration in the case of peoples who do not correspond to the whole state? Obviously, if the host state agrees to that possibility (e.g., Northern Ireland, Gagauzia), no problem would arise. However, when the state is reluctant to agree to that possibility and the democratic will of the people is clearly and repeatedly manifested in favour of secession, it is doubtful that a total denial of those outcomes is in accordance with the right to self-determination.

According to the current development of international law, it seems that the possibility of secession is excluded in non-colonial and non-remedial cases. However, following the path opened by the Quebec case, it seems reasonable that when a majority of an interested people democratically expresses a desire for secession, then their desire should be politically considered. If this is not currently part of the content of the right, the normal evolution from a democratic perspective should proceed in the direction of incorporating this option according to empirical criteria. The discussion can also be linked to a recognition that the substantial content of any human right must be ensured, probably on a case-by-case basis. As the Quebec case shows, such a political situation may not be in accordance with current law but cannot be ignored politically. From this perspective, it is reasonable to consider the possibility of adapting the substantial content of the right to each concrete situation. Thus, consistently repeated political expressions of a majority of interested voters could be incorporated into the substantial options of a self-determination process.

Conclusion

The need for stability and security at both the internal and international levels presides over and conditions the development of the right to self-determination as understood by the international community. Because the issue is extremely sensitive and potentially affects the sovereignty of States, the debate on the nature of self-determination as a human right is

[89] Lund Recommendations on the Effective Participation of National Minorities in Public Life, adopted in September 1999, text available at [Online]: http://www.osce.org/documents/hcnm/1999/09/2929_en.pdf.

complex. In fact, legal and political aspects of self-determination interact on an uneven playing field. The consequence is a significant degree of inconsistency in the definition and exercise of the right. Nevertheless, from a human rights perspective, a coherent interpretation must be achieved and shared through a possible reformulation of some legal and political concepts.

To put it briefly, self-determination is not only a human right, but also an instrument to prevent conflict and enhance democracy. This instrument can be reinforced if a wider but more concrete recognition and implementation of this important right is agreed upon. In today's pluralist societies, the democratic management of political (and national) diversity requires a new constitutional theory that understands law as a dynamic and evolving product based on an inclusive political consensus. The stability of the legal system can only be realised through legal flexibility. There is still significant work to be done, from an academic perspective, to transform the right to self-determination from a source of conflict into a possible solution.

Part IV

Politics of Diversity: Multiculturalism and Interculturalism

CHAPTER 9

What Is Interculturalism?

Gérard BOUCHARD

Professor, Department of Humanities and Canada Research Chair in the Comparative Study of Collective Imaginations, Université du Québec à Chicoutimi

Introduction

The responsible management of ethnocultural diversity is an unprecedented challenge for most democratic nations. The debate in Quebec on this subject is an old one, marked by its dynamism and originality – we should celebrate that. As it does elsewhere, for the majority culture the debate stems largely from an insecurity over the future of the identity and heritage from which it draws its strength. Inevitably, emotionalism and symbolism occupy a large part of the debate, as do divergent visions and, quite often, incompatible aspirations. All this makes for difficult arbitration based on a delicate balance between competing imperatives, requiring all the precautions and all the modesty that must accompany the search for a general model of integration.

Keeping these concerns in mind, I would like to use this essay primarily to present my vision of interculturalism as a model for integration and the management of ethnocultural diversity. I draw inspiration for this goal from the path taken by Quebec since the 1960s and 1970s[1], but also from personal reflection and from experiments conducted in Europe, where interculturalism, as a formula for coexistence in the context of diversity,

1 For an excellent reconstruction of the approach in Quebec, see Rocher, François *et al.*, “Le concept d’interculturalisme en contexte québécois: généalogie d’un néologisme”, Report presented to the Commission de consultation sur les pratiques d’accommodements reliées aux différences culturelles (CCPARDC), Montreal, 21 December 2007.

has significant roots[2]. In Quebec itself, interculturalism currently benefits from widespread popular support (as the public hearings of the Bouchard-Taylor Commission demonstrated)[3], but it is also the object of significant criticism. It is certain that there is significant work left to do in terms of clarification, promotion, and applications for this model.

A second goal is to repudiate a number of the misunderstandings and distortions that have entered the public debate, especially in Quebec. I plan to show or remind that:

1. collective integration is a global process affecting all the citizens and constituents of a society, not simply immigrants;
2. interculturalism is not a disguised (or "underhanded", as has been said) form of multiculturalism[4];
3. integration is based on a principle of reciprocity – newcomers and members of the host society share an important responsibility;
4. when applied with discretion and rigour, pluralism (an attitude advocating respect for diversity) and especially the principle of recognition, do not lead to fragmentation (or "communitarianism") and do not put the basic values of the host society into question;
5. pluralism is a general option with various applications corresponding to as many models, including multiculturalism – it is thus inaccurate to establish an exclusive relationship between these two concepts and to present them as synonymous;
6. the type of pluralism advocated by interculturalism could be described as integrational in that it takes into account the context and future of the majority culture;

2 The interculturalist approach found strong sites for promotion and study in Europe, particularly within the European Union and the Council of Europe. A complete review of this past history would require another paper.

3 This refers to the Consultation Commission on Accommodation Practices Related to Cultural Differences (CCAPRCD), created in February 2007 by the government of Quebec. This committee was co-chaired by the philosopher Charles Taylor and myself. The report was made public in May 2008. See Bouchard, Gérard and Charles Taylor, *Building the Future: A Time for Reconciliation*, Report of the Consultation Commission on Accommodation Practices Related to Cultural Differences, Québec, Gouvernement du Québec, 2008. The vast majority of the memoranda and testimonies submitted to the committee favoured interculturalism as the path for Quebec, even if the definitions they proposed were generally rather brief. Three elements of consensus recurred throughout – the rejection of Canadian multiculturalism, the rejection of assimilation, and the importance of integration on the basis of the fundamental values of Quebec society (gender equality, secularism, and the French language).

4 This last model, for reasons that will be discussed later on, has received very negative press in Québec.

7. accommodations (or concerted adjustments) are not privileges, they are not designed solely for immigrants and they should not give free rein to values, beliefs, and practices that are contrary to the basic norms of society – they simply aim to allow all citizens to benefit from the same rights, no matter their cultural affiliation;
8. as a pluralist model, interculturalism concerns itself with the interests of the majority culture, whose desire to perpetuate and maintain itself is perfectly legitimate, as much as it does with the interests of minorities and immigrants – we thus find no reason to oppose either the defenders of the identity and traditions of the majority culture on one side, or the defenders of the rights of minorities and immigrants on the other; it is both possible and necessary to combine the majority's aspirations for identity with a pluralist mindset, making for a single process of belonging and development; and
9. except in extreme cases, radical solutions rarely meet the needs of the problems posed by ethnocultural diversity.

My presentation will use the description provided in the Bouchard-Taylor Report[5] as a point of departure but will also clarify and add a number of elements. I will also rely on the important contributions of a number of authors from Quebec who have a long history of reflecting on this topic[6]. Finally, I should note that the Aboriginal experience will not

5 Bouchard and Taylor, Report, *op. cit.*, pp. 116-118.

6 See especially Gagnon, Alain-G., "Plaidoyer pour l'interculturalisme", *Possibles*, vol. 24, nº 4, 2000, pp. 11-25; Gagnon, Alain-G. and Raffaele Iacovino, "Le projet interculturel québécois et l'élargissement des frontières de la citoyenneté" in Alain-G. Gagnon (ed.), *Québec: État et société*, tome II, Montréal, Québec Amérique, 2003, pp. 413-436; Rocher, *op. cit.*; Labelle, Micheline, "La politique de la citoyenneté et de l'interculturalisme au Québec: défis et enjeux" in Hélène Greven-Borde and Jean Tournon (eds.), *Les identités en débat: Intégration ou multiculturalisme?*, Paris, Montréal, L'Harmattan, 2000, pp. 269-293; McAndrew, Marie, "Multiculturalisme canadien et interculturalisme québécois: mythes et réalités" in Marie McAndrew *et al.*, *Pluralisme et éducation. Politiques et pratiques au Canada, en Europe et dans les pays du Sud. L'apport de l'éducation comparée*, Montréal, Paris, Les publications de la Faculté des sciences de l'éducation, Association francophone d'éducation comparée, 1995, pp. 33-51; McAndrew, Marie, "Quebec's Interculturalism Policy: An Alternative Vision. Commentary" in Keith Banting *et al.* (eds.), *Belonging? Diversity, Recognition and Shared Citizenship in Canada*, Montreal, Institute for Research on Public Policy, 2007, pp. 143-154; Juteau, Danielle, "Multiculturalisme, interculturalisme et production de la nation" in Martine Fourier and Geneviève Vermès (eds.), *Ethnicisation des rapports sociaux: Racismes, nationalismes, ethnicismes et culturalismes*, Paris, L'Harmattan, 1994, pp. 55-72; *A Pluralistic Quebec in the Light of an Intercultural Practice: Memorandum to the Consultative Commission on "Reasonable Accommodation" of Cultural Differences in Quebec*, Intercultural Institute of Montreal, 2007, unpublished, archived at [Online]: http://www.iim.qc.ca.

be taken into account here. This is because the government of Quebec, in accordance with demands made by Aboriginal peoples, has resolved that relations with these communities should be treated as "nation to nation"[7] affairs. From their perspective, the populations concerned do not wish to be seen as cultural minorities within the nation of Quebec. For the moment this issue would require a different line of thought than interculturalism as defined here, since our model aims at integration within a single nation.

1. Interculturalism: Some Basic Principles

First, interculturalism incorporates a number of elements that are not exclusive to it. For example, it endorses the rather widely accepted idea that an official language, legal framework, and territorial unity are not sufficient to make a cohesive nation – they must be combined with a symbolic element that helps foster identity, collective memory, and belonging[8]. What we term the principle of recognition (in the sense used by Charles Taylor and others) is also part of interculturalism[9]. It is also found at the heart of multiculturalism and in a few other models. Another element of interculturalism found in the majority of Western democracies is a pluralist mindset, meaning sensitivity to ethnocultural diversity and the rejection of all discrimination based on *difference*[10]. Inherited from the moral awakening following the two World Wars, fascism, totalitarian regimes, and decolonization, this mindset came into being in the 1950s and 1960s as a new sensitivity towards minorities of all kinds.

---

7 This is in accordance with the two resolutions passed by the National Assembly of Quebec, one on 20 March 1985 (see Quebec, National Assembly, *Motion for the recognition of aboriginal rights in Québec*, Journal Débats, 32nd Leg., 5th Sess., vol. 28, N° 39 (20 March 1985) at 2570, the other on 30 May 1989 (see Quebec, National Assembly, *Resolution of the Quebec National Assembly* on the recognition of the Maliseet nation, Journal Débats, 32nd Leg., 2nd Sess., vol. 30, N° 117 (30 May 1989) at 6079.

8 I will allow myself to insist on this point. Certain critics of interculturalism credit me with a strictly civic ("legalist") conception of nationhood, a conception that I have always rejected in my writing. See especially Bouchard, Gérard, *La Nation québécoise au futur et au passé*, Montréal, VLB, 1999, pp. 10-20 and 22-23. Identity and national memory are central elements of nationhood and must always be taken into account.

9 According to the current conception, the principle of recognition refers to the status or to the condition of minorities in a given society. It calls for the respect of different cultures, and the people or groups that embody them, in accordance with the dignity to which all people have a right. In effect, the principle postulates that any individual or group's sentiment of self-worth or dignity requires that, in the spirit of equality, its differences be recognized, especially by members of the majority culture. For an account and critical discussion of this topic, see Taylor, Charles, *Multiculturalism and "The Politics of Recognition"*, Princeton, Princeton University Press, 1992.

10 Pluralism should not be confused with plurality, which is synonymous with diversity. Pluralism advocates a specific attitude towards ethnocultural plurality, which is in itself a simple state of fact.

That said, it is important to note that these components (national symbols, recognition, and pluralism) are susceptible to a variety of interpretations and applications that open the door to a number of possible models. Thus, contrary to widespread perception, a pluralist mindset, as with all recognition principles, does not necessarily lead to multiculturalism.

Likewise, reasonable accommodation is a very widespread practice in the United States, anglophone Canada, Australia, and several European countries, including England. We can define these accommodations as adjustments made to the administration of certain norms or rules for certain individuals or groups (immigrants or not) possessing some sort of distinctive characteristic that places them outside of the mainstream culture. These adjustments aim to encourage the integration of these groups and to shield them from precisely the kind of discrimination that could result from their distinctive characteristics. Once again, and contrary to current perceptions, this does not mean awarding certain people exclusive rights or privileges. In the spirit of equity (or equality), the goal is always to more fully implement the fundamental rights granted to all citizens[11]. When referring to recognition, pluralism, or accommodations, it is important to distinguish between their founding principles and the specific criteria and methods of their administration.

Accommodation is not unique to interculturalism and can be enacted in accordance with a variety of philosophies, sensitivities, and policies. Consequently again, we must prevent ourselves from associating accommodation exclusively with multiculturalism. Certain adjustments can seem perfectly admissible in one society and cause problems in another, even if both adhere to pluralism.

In light of this discussion, we see that in the particular case of Quebec it is necessary to develop a form of pluralism that acknowledges that the francophone majority is itself a precarious minority that needs protection in order to ensure its survival and development in the North American environment and in the context of globalization.

2. Paradigms and Levels of Analysis

Before going further, and in order to properly distinguish interculturalism from the other models of management of ethnocultural diversity, it is useful to review the five major paradigms these models tend to follow. These paradigms are large schemas that will help situate

[11] For example, denying a young girl the right to wear a certain kind of bathing suit to a swimming class or a gymnastics class might deprive her of her right to learn. Refusing to allow a student to reproduce religious symbols in a drawing class could lead to a similar result.

the primary intention, or defining outlook, of each model. They structure the public debate of a nation, determine the parameters and the basic issues, inspire the policies and programs of the state and, finally, fuel the perceptions citizens hold of each other.

A first paradigm is that of diversity. In particular, we find this in English Canada, the United States, Sweden, Australia, and India. The guiding premise in these cases is that the nation is composed of a collection of individuals and ethnocultural groups placed on equal footing and protected by the same laws – there is no recognition of a majority culture and, in consequence, no minorities per se. Under the official banner of diversity, all assert themselves and express themselves as they see fit, within the limits prescribed by law. Secondly, we can speak of a paradigm of homogeneity (i.e., a unitary paradigm), which fundamentally asserts an ethnocultural similarity in public life and sometimes also in private life – included here are nations such as France (at least in the public space), Italy, Japan, and Russia. Thirdly, there is the paradigm I call bi- or multipolarity. This refers to societies composed of two or more national groups or subgroups, sometimes officially recognized as such and granted a kind of permanence. Nation-states such as Malaysia, Bolivia, Belgium, Switzerland, and Northern Ireland (i.e., all the pluri-national states that recognize themselves as such)[12] operate under this paradigm.

The fourth paradigm is that of duality. We see this where diversity is conceived and managed as a relationship between minorities from a recent or distant period of immigration, and a cultural majority that could be described as *foundational*. Let us pause for a moment to examine this last concept. I include as foundational any culture resulting from the history of a community that has occupied a single area for a long period (one century, several centuries, or several millennia); that has formed a territory or settlement (what certain geographers call "territoriality") with which it identifies; that has developed an identity and a collective imagination expressed through language, traditions, and institutions; that has developed solidarity and belonging; and that shares a sense of continuity based in memory. In such societies, long-established minorities can also hold the status of foundational cultures. In Quebec, examples include the Aboriginal communities, which were founded before the majority culture, in addition to the anglophone population[13].

---

12 See especially Gagnon, Alain-G., *The Case for Multinational Federalism: Beyond the All-Encompassing Nation*, London, New York, Routledge, 2010.

13 It should be noted that the qualifier "foundational" refers less to a moment of settlement or a founding act than to a process spread out over time. This process is inevitably accompanied by a structuring effect on the culture of a society.

With certain exceptions, majority cultures are foundational cultures, although they never stop incorporating important new contributions that blend with the existing cultural fabric and ultimately transform it. Through the effects of migration and intercultural relations, the reality underlying these concepts is fundamentally shifting and dynamic, even if the dominant discourse tends to erase this characteristic. As we will see later on, other factors make it so that the concept of a majority culture can accommodate diverse and malleable realities.

Parenthetically, it is worth noting that I avoid using the term "ethnic group" or "cultural community". These concepts presuppose a degree of structuring that seldom exists in reality. With this in mind, the idea of a minority must be understood, in a very general sense, to designate a cultural nexus or community life that carries on in coexistence with the majority culture and the borders of which are often quite fluid.

The majority/minorities duality thus acquires the status of a paradigm so that it can structure discussion and debates over diversity in a given nation. It appears as a dichotomy or an us/them divide that is more or less pronounced. I maintain that the duality paradigm does not create this divide – rather, this is its point of departure, its anchor. Rather than challenging the paradigm on this ground, one would be best advised to tackle the factors that have created the duality and contribute to perpetuate it. I will add that the vast majority of Western nations (including Quebec) currently seem to be operating under or shifting towards this paradigm.

The fifth paradigm is that of *mixité*. It is founded on the idea that, through miscegenation, the ethnocultural diversity of a nation will be progressively reduced, eventually creating a new culture separate from its constituent elements. We find this paradigm primarily in Latin America, notably in Brazil and Mexico.

I will add three further details on this subject. Paradigms are the first level of analysis for ethnocultural diversity. The different models associated with them (such as multiculturalism, interculturalism, the melting pot, hyphenation, republicanism, assimilationism, consociationalism, etc.)[14], are the second level. The third is the concrete ethnocultural structure of populations as revealed by empirical data (census statistics and monographs) on ethnic origin, language, religion, and spatialization (geographic concentrations, ghettos, and clustering).

14 I do not mention federalism because this notion seems to refer primarily to a method of distributing political power between diverse national or other entities rather than a model for managing or dealing with ethnocultural reality.

I will also point out that, as with all models, these paradigms are the result of a collective choice often codified in official documents. Thus, we see many examples of nations that have changed their paradigms over the last decades. Between 1960 and 1970, Canada and Australia moved from a homogeneity paradigm to a diversity paradigm while Quebec abandoned homogeneity for duality. Similarly, it seems that England is currently distancing itself from the diversity paradigm[15] and that we are currently witnessing in Quebec some attempts to introduce elements of republican-style non-differentiation (against accommodation and expression of religion in state institutions).

Finally, it is worth noting that a paradigm can accommodate more than one model – and sometimes very different models – as seen particularly in Canada and the United States (diversity), and France and Italy (homogeneity). The simplest example is that of a nation that adheres to a single paradigm (or to a predominant paradigm). However, we should not write off nations where public debate is more animated and might simultaneously subscribe to two or three competing paradigms. The United States comes to mind. The diversity paradigm is markedly dominant throughout, since the nation was (at least officially) founded on universal ideals capable of accommodating the greatest possible diversity. Yet we are currently seeing the manifestation of two other paradigms, namely duality ("*mainstream*" culture versus minorities perceived as resistant to integration) and assimilation (a radical version of the "*melting pot*"). In this vein, Brazil also deserves attention to the degree that the dominant schema of racial mixing (supported by the great myth of racial democracy) makes space for the diversity as well as the homogeneity paradigms. In this case, official discourse and public debate often reveal how this nation does not define itself by race, but at the same time remains very aware of ethnocultural diversity.

Furthermore, we should note that there is not a linear relationship between these three levels of analysis. One should not assume that what happens at one level is determined by what happens at the other two. Certainly it is difficult to imagine countries like Belgium or Switzerland adhering to the homogeneity paradigm. Nevertheless, there can sometimes be important disparities between the ethnocultural reality of a nation and the general schema it uses to imagine itself (the examples of France and Italy again come to mind).

---

15 Here, an important new strain of ideas is currently creating a dualist vision of the nation. See e.g. Goodhart, David, *Progressive Nationalism: Citizenship and the Left*, London, Demos, 2006. See also the journal *Prospect*, of which he is the founding director.

3. Characteristics of Interculturalism

I will mention seven main points that characterize interculturalism with respect to other models of management of diversity. But it should be mentioned in the first place that the model operates at two levels. One is the societal or macrosocial level where the challenge is to define principles and general guidelines for integration. The second level is interculturality. It refers to the microsocial scale of neighbourhoods, community relations, and the daily life of institutions (schools, hospitals, workplaces, etc.). However, focus will be given primarily to the first dimension, with priority placed on defining the principles and basic philosophy of the model.

A. Majority/Minorities Duality

First and foremost, as a global model for social integration, interculturalism takes shape principally within the duality paradigm[16]. One of the inherent traits of this paradigm is a keen awareness of the majority/minorities relationship and the tension associated with it. More precisely, I am referring to the anxiety that the majority culture can feel in the face of cultural minorities. Indeed, they can create a more or less acute sense of threat within the majority culture not only in terms of its rights, but also in terms of its values, traditions, language, memory, and identity (not to mention its security). This feeling can be fuelled by a number of different sources. For example, in England, the United States, and many other countries, terrorism is currently a major concern. In Quebec, a significant source of anxiety comes from the fact that the francophone cultural majority is a fragile minority in the North American environment (representing less than two percent of the total population). Also, this anxiety is often supplemented by the presence of a demographically significant ethnocultural minority perceived as hostile to the traditions and values of the majority group and resistant to integration (which can happen when this minority fears for its own values and culture). This unease can also occur in countries where the foundational culture is experiencing a period of instability or undergoing some kind of crisis. Be that as it may, it follows that the duality thus risks being experienced as the intersection of two sets of anxieties since minority groups often, and for obvious reasons, fuel their own feelings of uncertainty about their future. Finally, there are nations in which duality is the result of a sustainable agreement forged in the history between two groups, one a majority, the other a minority.

---

16 As indicated earlier, this model can also apply to the (bi)pluri-polarity paradigm. However, I will limit my discussion to the duality paradigm.

Regardless of its sources, this insecurity and the reciprocal mistrust it produces can help perpetuate the us/them duality. And yet, as mentioned previously, interculturalism seeks to care for the future of the majority culture as much as that of minority cultures. From this perspective, it is essentially a search for conciliation. Under the arbitration of the law, it seeks to articulate the tension between continuity and diversity, i.e., the continuity of the foundational culture and the diversity brought in by past or recent immigration[17]. In this sense, I would say that interculturalism intends to connect cultures as much through their roots as through encounters. That said, the tension underlying this duality can be corrosive and give birth to stereotypes, exclusionary or reactionary behaviour, and various forms of discrimination from the majority group. It can also be positive, experienced as a constant reminder for vigilance, dialogue, and necessary concerted adjustments. The central challenge of interculturalism is to smooth over and to alleviate the us/them relation rather than inflame it.

The preceding remarks require a few warnings:

1. We should avoid a reductive vision that represents the majority/minorities divide as an opposition between a homogeneous majority and heterogeneous minorities. When we look closely, we see that beyond a common language and shared symbols, important elements of diversity almost always extend to the very core of the majority (differences of morality and belief, ideological divisions, generation gaps, social divisions, regional identities, etc.). For this reason, it seems better to talk about a cleavage between two different kinds of diversity. The fact remains that, when faced with a perceived threat, the majority group is likely to erase important aspects of its own diversity. This phenomenon is apparent in debates in Quebec and elsewhere in the West.
2. We must also avoid conceiving of the majority/minorities duality as a fixed set. If this dual structure is durable, the contents of its two components, as well as the context and modalities of their connection, are in constant flux (hence the danger of too rigid a conception of the majority/minorities duality). Again, this dynamic character does not always come through in public debate. The majority culture can contract, expand, and reconstruct itself to meet the mood and challenges of the hour and as a function

[17] Note that this tension is found throughout all of Quebec's history, from the second half of the eighteenth century onwards beginning with the British regime. On one side, there was the reproduction of francophone culture and resistance to assimilation, on the other, the integration of immigrants who were nevertheless subject to various forms of ethnocultural exclusion (e.g., Aboriginal peoples, Jews, Blacks, etc.).

of its discursive strategies. If we refer to the current debate and perceptions in Quebec, we might say that the "cultural majority" covers a quite large territory. In its narrowest meaning, it coincides with the most militant fragment of the "old stock" French-speakers[18]. Yet in its widest acceptance, the majority includes all French-speakers and even the entire host society, especially when the core values held by most Quebecois (gender equality, separation of church and state, etc.) contrast with the values associated with some immigrants. In this last case, the cultural majority is larger than the francophone majority[19]. These considerations are a reminder of the need for vigilance when analyzing public debate in duality nations.

3. It can also happen that the "majority" evoked in debates is rather theoretical or even imaginary. Whatever the case, the duality paradigm remains with its majority/minorities dichotomy (at least until the public debate eventually shifts to embrace another paradigm).
4. The threat or insecurity felt by the majority in the face of minorities must always be considered with a critical eye. We know of too many examples of majorities who made their minorities into scapegoats because they saw themselves as powerless to act against the real causes of their adversity. For Western nations currently under attack on many fronts (the numerous uncertainties linked to globalization, the rise of a new individualism, the erosion of social bonds, deficits and the growing weakness of the state, aging populations, precarious employment, etc.), it can be tempting to blame immigrants or minorities for problems that actually stem from fundamental changes on a global scale.

   In the context of Quebec, feelings of insecurity are also fueled by the growing presence of immigrants and cultural minorities, largely concentrated in the area surrounding Montreal. This feeling is justified since it is an expression of the fragility of francophone Quebec in America, a condition accentuated by globalization and by uncertainty over the francization of immigrants. It is also justified to the extent that it affirms the importance of preserving fundamental values like gender equality and the separation of church and state. Finally, it is accentuated by the fact that the national question remains

[18] During the hearings of the Bouchard-Taylor commission, it was principally this group that expressed deep concern for the survival of what was termed "our culture" and "our values". That said, other groups also expressed unease, particularly in regard to reasonable accommodations.

[19] Think, for example, of Arab women who advocate in favour of secularism and male-female equality.

unresolved and even seems to be sliding towards an impasse. That said, it is undeniably conflated by some participants in the public debate with a desire to formally consecrate the dominant status of the foundational culture and to give legal recognition to this precedence. The (incontestable) fragility of francophone Quebec does not seem to me to justify measures so radical that they would institute a regime of a priori inequality between citizens[20].

5. Here again we see a potential risk associated with the duality paradigm. By recognizing the legitimate interests of a majority, this paradigm could exacerbate rather than smooth over us/them divisions because it allows space for the dominating trends of majority groups, the results of which are visible throughout the history of the West and other continents (xenophobia, exclusion, discrimination, etc.). Thus, it is important to instill a pluralist mindset and protective mechanisms at the highest levels of the duality paradigm in order to avoid falling into ethnicism (impingements on the rights of others for inadmissible reasons)[21]. In summary, interculturalism recognizes the status of the majority culture (its legitimacy, its right to perpetuate its traditions, its heritage, and its right to mobilize around developmental goals) within a framework designed to reduce the excesses that all majorities are capable of enacting on minorities – as ancient and recent history has taught us.

B. A Process of Interaction

The second original attribute of interculturalism is that, while fostering respect for diversity, the model favours interactions, exchanges, connections, and intercommunity initiatives. It thus privileges a path of negotiations and mutual adjustments, but with strict respect for the values of the host society as inscribed in law or constitutional texts and all while taking into account the so-called shared values of a common public culture. A spirit of conciliation, balance, and reciprocity presides over the process of interaction at the heart of interculturalism.

---

20 Advocates of this idea seem to forget, for example, that the francophone majority currently controls most large public and private institutions, which manifests most notably in a marked under-representation of other citizens in public or semi-public jobs. Furthermore, because Quebec is not politically sovereign, its capacity to act collectively remains limited, although it still has a large margin for manoeuvre when it comes to legislating on cultural matters.

21 See Bouchard, *La Nation québécoise au futur et au passé*, *op. cit.*, p. 30. On this subject, other authors speak of "ethnocracy" or of "majoritarianism". See respectively Yiftachel, Oren, "Ethnicity: The Politics of Judaizing Israel/Palestine", *Constellations*, vol. 6, 1999, pp. 364-391; Pathak, Pathik, "The Rise of the Majority", *The [Edinburgh] Journal*, 2 October 2008. The idea of "majoritarianism", which comes from political philosophy, is an old one – it traditionally refers to a system that grants majorities excessive privileges.

C. The Principles of Harmonization: A Civic Responsibility

The preceding makes a case for a culture of genuine interaction and mutual adjustments as a condition for integration. This is why interculturalism makes all citizens responsible for maintaining intercultural relations in daily life, especially when facing the inevitable incompatibilities that surface at the levels of institutions and communities. It is the duty of each citizen placed in an intercultural situation to contribute to mutual adjustments and accommodations. The courts obviously retain their indispensable function, though only as a last recourse after citizen action has failed to resolve disagreements. It also follows that beyond state policy, interculturalism encourages creative initiatives from individuals and groups working on a microsocial level. In total, we can identify four avenues for action corresponding with as many categories of actors: (a) the judicial system, (b) the state and its subsidiaries, (c) civil institutions and organizations, (d) individuals and groups in their living and work environments.

This view presupposes the existence of a culture or ethic of exchange and negotiation, which might seem idealistic. However, and this was an important finding of the Commission I co-chaired, such a culture already exists within a large part of the population of Quebec. We saw it in action in the daily life of institutions (notably in the spheres of education and healthcare), as well as in the hundreds of groups that have been formed primarily in metropolitan areas in the last few years to foster the socioeconomic integration of immigrants. Many municipal councils, even in rural areas, have also enacted policies designed to attract and integrate newcomers. In any case, these efforts must obviously be extended and expanded with support from the State, which should work to put in place a whole network of officials, locations, and communication channels that encourage connection, mutual recognition, and integration.

D. Integration and Identity

Contrary to the so-called communitarian mindset and for the sake of countering the risks of fragmentation ordinarily associated with multiculturalism, interculturalism aims for a strong integration of diverse coexisting traditions and cultures. According to the most commonly accepted sociological view, the term integration designates the totality of mechanisms and processes of insertion (or assimilation) that constitute the social bond, which is further cemented by its symbolic and functional foundations. These processes and mechanisms engage all citizens (new and long-standing), operate on many levels (individual, community, institutional, and state), and work in multiple dimensions (economic, social, cultural, and so forth). On a cultural level, the concept of integration is devoid of any assimilationist connotations. Nevertheless, during the recent controversies in Europe, it sometimes came to acquire this kind of connotation. To avoid any confusion, we could use the term "integrationism" to refer to those forms of integration that are not respectful of diversity.

In keeping with these ideas, interculturalism advocates a particular type of pluralism that I would define as integrationary. This is its third defining trait. A majority culture that feels threatened by its minorities will feel the need to either assimilate them (which predicts the end of duality) or to integrate them (the road that Quebec has thus far taken). It instinctively fears all kinds of fragmentation, ghettoization, or marginalization. This is even truer when this majority is a minority on the continental level, as is the case with francophone Quebec. This state of affairs becomes an imperative that frames the discussion on how to approach the intercultural reality of Quebec. It highlights the importance that must be given to the integration of minorities and immigrants in order to strengthen this *francophonie* and ensure its future. Measures that run counter to pluralism (such as those currently proposed by republican secularists) tend to increase the risk of marginalization and fragmentation – two phenomena precisely associated with multiculturalism that have contributed to its rejection. The central idea here is that francophone Quebec is itself in a difficult situation and must avoid fostering costly long-term divisions – it would do much better to create the allies it needs within immigrants and cultural minorities. All attempts at a general model must incorporate this basic concern[22].

Furthermore, when speaking about Quebec one cannot ignore its more than two centuries of struggle for survival in a context marked by an unfavourable population imbalance, unequal power relations, and by the various assimilation policies of the colonial authorities. Memories of this period naturally feed present-day anxieties. They also provide a constant reminder for vigilance. The current advocates of a francophone Quebecois identity (although sometimes in opposition to the supposed "excesses" of pluralism) are one manifestation of this. They cannot be ignored.

Interculturalism therefore advocates in favour of integration, thus emphasizing the need for interactions and connections. Boiled down to its essence, the argument is simple – the best way to counter the unease we sometimes feel towards foreigners is not to keep them at a distance, but to approach them in a way that breaks down stereotypes and facilitates their

[22] What do the opponents of interculturalism propose to do about this issue? How, for example, do they intend to resolve the antinomy that would result from the rejection of pluralism (as defined here) and the necessity for integration? What measures do they envision to ensure that immigrants and members of cultural minorities become allies, or even standard bearers, of francophone Quebec?

integration in the host society. In other words, exclusion is reprehensible not only on a moral or legal level, but from a sociological and pragmatic standpoint as well.

And yet interculturalism is not a straitjacket. It acknowledges the right of ethnoreligious groups to organize themselves in small communities that, while respecting the law, maintain a rather distant relationship from the rest of society. In the opposite direction, it gives great latitude to individuals who wish to identify themselves first and foremost as Quebecois by relegating their identification with their group or culture of origin to the background, or by renegotiating this belonging.

On another, often-neglected level, it is of course true that social and economic incorporation must accompany cultural integration. It may even be a necessary precondition[23]. Thus, it is through access to large social networks that interactions and cultural diffusion (values, norms, and so forth) can take place. For this reason and for others having to do with basic social justice, we must lament that current debates on integration do not give this fact the attention it deserves. In Quebec as elsewhere, access to employment is the area most likely to be affected by discriminatory practices. Prolonged negligence on this front has important social costs, as we have seen recently in various European countries.

E. Elements of Ad Hoc Precedence for the Majority Culture

Cultural integration contains a fifth characteristic that deserves greater attention. While seeking an equitable interaction between continuity and diversity, interculturalism allows for the recognition of certain elements of *ad hoc* (or contextual) precedence for the majority culture. I say *ad hoc* because it is out of the question to formalize or establish this idea as a general legal principle, which would lead to the creation of two classes of citizens. In this way, interculturalism distinguishes itself from radical republicanism that, whether directly or not, uses the pretext of universalism to bestow a systematic, a priori precedence on what I term the majority or foundational culture. This kind of arrangement, which establishes a formal hierarchy, opens the door to abuses of power. That said, I think that as long as the nature and the reach of *ad hoc* precedence are carefully circumscribed it can avoid the excesses of ethnicism while giving some advantages (or the needed protections) to the majority culture.

This principle is justified on several levels. The first stems from what I term the identity argument. In order for the majority group to preserve the cultural and symbolic heritage that serves as the foundation of its identity

[23] On this subject, which is worth further investigation, see Bouchard and Taylor, *op. cit.*, chapter XI. See also Weber, Serge, "Comprendre la mobilité, réinterroger l'intégration", *Projet*, nº 311, 2009, pp. 58-67.

and helps to ensure its continuity, it can legitimately claim some elements of contextual precedence based on its seniority or history. This claim is, as already mentioned, even more grounded when the cultural majority is itself a minority in the continental environment. As we will see, it is always difficult to establish in the abstract the full extent of this concept, which should take shape in specific situations conditioned by democratic debate and through negotiations mediated by the *Charter of Human Rights and Freedoms*[24]. In certain situations it could happen that elements of precedence are established as rights or laws, but then the reasoning must invoke higher motives – think of Bill 101 on the French language in Quebec[25], which was necessary for the survival of francophone culture and whose central objectives and measures were declared legitimate by the Supreme Court of Canada.

In any case, I maintain that to varying degrees, these elements of precedence are present in all societies, even the most liberal (or the most "civic-oriented") by virtue of forces that are difficult to control. This is a second argument, based on history and custom. Many intellectuals, liberal and otherwise, have in effect demonstrated or recognized that while the cultural neutrality of nation-states (or more precisely, the majorities that control them) is sought-after and proclaimed in principle, it does not exist in reality – some authors even maintain that it is impossible. They see the margin of non-neutrality as an unfortunate inevitability. For others, it proves even useful and necessary. For example, it allows for the consolidation of national identity, which is at once a source of solidarity and a foundation for responsible citizen participation and social justice[26].

24 RSQ c C-12 [*Quebec Charter*].

25 Charter of the French language, RSQ c C-11.

26 Of course this subject merits further development. I must, however, limit myself to giving the reader a few relevant references. See especially Dieckhoff, Alain, *La nation dans tous ses États: Les identités nationales en mouvement*, Paris, Flammarion, 2000, chapter 3; Young, Iris Marion, *Justice and the Politics of Difference*, Princeton, Princeton University Press, 1990; Kymlicka, Will, "Nation-Building and Minority Rights: Comparing West and East", *Journal of Ethnic and Migration Stuies*, vol. 26, nº 2, 2000, pp. 183-212; Lecours, André and Geneviève Nootens, "Comprendre le nationalisme majoritaire" in Alain-G. Gagnon, Geneviève Nootens and André Lecours (eds.), *Les Nationalismes majoritaires contemporains: identité, mémoire, pouvoir*, Montréal, Québec Amérique, 2007, pp. 19-45; Yack, Bernard, "The Myth of the Civil Nation" in Ronald Beiner (ed.), *Theorizing Nationalism*, Albany, State University of New York Press, 1999, pp. 103-118; Modood, Tariq, "Multiculturalism, Securalism and the State", *Critical Review of International Social and Political Philosophy*, vol. 1, nº 3, 1998, pp. 79-97; Miller, David, *On Nationality*, Oxford, Clarendon Press, 1995; Miller, David, "Reasonable Partiality Towards Compatriots", *Ethical Theory and Moral Practice*, vol. 8, nº 1, 2005, pp. 63-81; Van Parijs, Philippe (ed.), *Cultural Diversity versus Economic Solidarity*, Proceeding of the Seventh Francqui Colloquium, Brussels, 28 February – 1 March 2003, Brussels, De Boeck, 2004; Spencer, Vicki, "Language,

What is involved here are some initiatives or policies that aim to preserve a so-called national culture, which we know to be in large part the culture of the majority. These initiatives usually have the effect of supporting the religion of the majority, its language, and some of its institutions and traditions, all in the name of history, identity or continuity[27]. I include in this list the possibility that a majority culture might express a special sensitivity to one or a few universal values amongst those it endorses. Think of gender equality in Quebec, individual liberty in the United States, racial equality in places formerly rife with segregation, familial solidarity in Mediterranean societies, social equality in Scandinavian countries, and so forth. It was precisely in this spirit that the report of the Bouchard-Taylor Commission stated that "[i]n the health care sector as in all public services, [the gender equality value] disqualifies, in principle, all requests that have the effect of granting a woman an inferior status to that of a man"[28].

In fact, although it is never put in a theoretical, normative or even explicit form, the principle behind elements of *ad hoc* precedence occupies an important place in the functioning of democratic societies. Secular states in particular make for an eloquent example. Beyond their founding principles, values, norms, and laws, these states typically incorporate a number of contextual and historic elements as well as political and social choices befitting the majority. We could claim that all secular regimes are an arrangement of four constitutive principles or values: the freedom of conscience and religion, the moral equality of citizens, the separation of church and state, and the neutrality of the state in matters of belief, religion, or worldviews[29]. But another component could be added to these four, namely the traditional values and customs of the majority culture. Seldom formalized, this component is nevertheless powerful enough to sometimes take precedence over the others, which occurs notably when it is in conflict with the neutrality of the state and/or the moral freedom of individuals. For example, it is in the name of traditional values (and more precisely "historical heritage") that in May 2008 the National Assembly

History and the Nation: An Historical Approach to Evaluating Language and Cultural Claims", 2008, *Nations and Nationalism*, vol. 14, n° 2, 2008, pp. 241-259. See also Daniel Weinstock's remarks advocating for a state that is "as culturally neutral as possible" ("La neutralité de l'État en matière culturelle est-elle possible?" in Ronan Le Coadic (ed.), *Identités et démocratie. Diversité culturelle et mondialisation: repenser la démocratie*, Rennes, Presses universitaires de Rennes, 2003, pp. 365-380).

27 Remember that even Canada, which is held up as a model democratic and "civic" nation, celebrates the symbols of monarchy and included a reference to the supremacy of God in the 1982 preamble to its constitution.

28 Bouchard and Taylor, *op. cit.*, p. 21.

29 See *ibid.*, chapter VIII.

of Quebec unanimously declared itself in favour of keeping a crucifix above the chair of the President of the Assembly, in spite of the rule of religious neutrality on the part of the state and the rule of separation between church and state.

Actually, there is little new in my proposition. What I add is a willingness to acknowledge these forms of *ad hoc* precedence and to consider them head-on in order to clarify their status, reach, and limits, rather than pushing them to the margins as though they were accidental or non-existent. So, this second argument relies on a wisely institutionalized and unavoidable practice that is seen as useful, if not necessary, to even the most democratic of societies, even if it is dealt with as a blind spot[30].

From a general perspective, and this is the third argument, this practice can be considered a kind of accommodation that minorities accord to majorities, under certain conditions subject to debate. This is very much in the spirit of interculturalism, which seeks harmonization through mutual adjustments according to a principle of reciprocity. In this respect, an important lesson can be drawn from recent experience in Quebec. The principal criticism levelled against the Bouchard-Taylor Commission Report came from members of the francophone majority. According to them the Report granted a great deal to minorities and immigrants but very little to the majority – a forceful reminder that because francophone Quebec was also a minority, it too needed protections; so, there was a need for balance. The elements of *ad hoc* precedence are conceived in this spirit.

A fourth argument, which calls for closer examination, is a legal one. The law has always recognized the value of antecedence. Think of birth rights (primogeniture) and all the advantages conferred by virtue of seniority. The most eloquent example in this regard is the ancestral rights recognized for Aboriginal populations as first occupants. On what grounds and to what extent can this logic be transposed to the world of intercultural relations as the basis for an *ad hoc* precedence in favour

---

[30] For many (myself included) this was, however, an abusive use of the historic argument – that if the government of Quebec is secular, as we like to say it is, we should expect that this character would be reflected at the heart of the government itself. We can cite a number of other reasonable examples of this kind – national funerals of secular heads of state held in Catholic churches, symbols of Christian holidays (Christmas in particular) in public squares or buildings, the biased schedule of public holidays, the cross on the Quebec flag, the recitations of prayers before municipal council meetings, crosses erected along rural roads, and so forth. It is in this same spirit that in Italy a majority of citizens favour keeping crucifixes on the walls of public schools. For a more detailed analysis of this subject, see Gérard Bouchard, "Laïcité: la voie québécoise de l'interculturalisme" dans Jean-François Plamondon and Anne de Vaucher (ed.), *Les enjeux du pluralisme; l'actualité du modèle québécois*, Centro interuniversitario di studi quebecchesi, Bologna: Édizioni Pendragon, 2010.

of foundational majorities? First of all, we must avoid easy and abusive conclusions; the situation of francophone Quebec is obviously not the same as that of Aboriginal cultures. The idea does, however, deserve our attention, even if only to articulate the required nuances.

A fifth argument relates to the diversity of cultures and identities on a planetary level, which is celebrated by UNESCO as a source of innovation and creativity at the same level as biodiversity. In November 2001 the organization made diversity one of its chief priorities, receiving the support of 185 member states[31]. But if we agree to maintain cultural plurality on this scale, then will not majority groups – the main staples of national cultures – see themselves as invested with specific responsibility in the struggle against the powerful currents of uniformity brought about by globalization?

Contextual precedence justifies itself in a sixth way, this time from a sociological perspective. As I indicated above, all societies need a symbolic foundation (identity, memory, belonging, and so forth) to sustain their equilibrium, reproduction, and development, since the legal framework alone (or so-called civic principles) does not adequately fulfill this function. Especially in situations of tension, change, or crisis, only widely shared common reference points – that is to say, a culture or an identity – provide for the solidarity that forms the basis of any kind of collective mobilization towards the pursuit of a common good. This process is a prime engine in the struggle against inequalities, and this is where the ideal of liberal individualism reveals what is likely its greatest weakness.

All these conditions require a continuity that is guaranteed to a large extent by the majority culture and the values forged in its history[32]. In addition, this is not only about social cohesion. In order for a society to take hold of its destiny, it must devote itself to principles and ideals that encompass both its heritage and its future. If the former is the responsibility of all citizens, the latter is primarily the work of the foundational majority.

A final argument, this one more pragmatic, makes the case for this thesis. Ancient and recent history has taught us to fear minorities that are terrorized or fanaticized in some way. But it has also taught us to be equally, if not more, afraid of cultural majorities that take on aggressive behaviour when they feel profoundly humiliated, unjustly treated, and victimized. Wisdom demands that we take this into account. The principles behind

31 See the *Universal Declaration on Cultural Diversity*, UNESCOR, 31st Sess, 20th Plen. Mtg, 2001. The first article states that cultural diversity is "the common heritage of humanity".

32 This remark should reassure those who accuse interculturalism of neglecting the past and even erasing the memory of the majority culture.

ad hoc precedence can soothe majority anxieties that could easily turn into hostility – especially when there are social or political actors who readily stand to profit. However, the principle of contextual precedence might be unacceptable to advocates of an absolute legalism or liberalism. This is the place to remember that in aiming for the perfect society, we sometimes sow the opposite seeds.

To conclude this point, it would be an error to believe that all majority cultures are basically menacing or harmful. Some have a remarkable history of openness and generosity towards minorities, while others, despite difficult circumstances, have managed to maintain their liberal leanings. Often dominant cultures are helpful agents in advancing democracy and individual rights[33]. In this regard, Quebec of the 1960s and 1970s is an eloquent example – the period was marked by both intense neonationalism on the part of the francophone majority, and spectacular advances in liberal values culminating in the 1975 adoption of the *Quebec Charter*. Nineteenth-century Europe also provides a number of examples of national majorities that promoted democratic and liberal values.

Again, the above argument may in a certain light run counter to the principle of formal equality between individuals, groups, and cultures. In its defence, one can say that it does nothing more than reflect and conform to a state of universal reality, namely the impossibility of cultural neutrality of nation-states. Likewise, it somewhat detracts from the ideal and abstract vision of a society formed of a group of perfectly autonomous, rational, and self-made citizens. However, it brings us closer to the complex, shifting, unpredictable, and omnipresent reality of identity dynamics and the vagaries of political life. The argument for elements of contextual precedence thus proceeds from a more sociological and realist vision of liberalism.

It would be a grave mistake to underestimate the weight or deny the legitimacy of collective identities. It is often said, and rightly so, that they are arbitrarily constructed or even invented, but that does not prevent them from being lived as profoundly authentic by the large majority of individuals who need them to make sense of their life and to ground themselves. Finally, they come to acquire a level of substance that keeps them from being entirely arbitrary or artificial. Largely driven by emotion, they arouse suspicion in the consummate rationalists. And like all myths that they feed on[34], they partake in a universal mechanism that

---

33 On this topic, see Brown, David, "The Ethnic Majority: Benign or Malign?", *Nations and Nationalism*, vol. 14, n° 4, 2008, pp. 768-788.

34 I use this word in its non-normative, sociological sense to designate a particular kind of collective representation carrying values, ideals, and beliefs, which can be true or false, beneficial or harmful to a community, and which act similarly on all societies due to the

is acting in the history of all societies and weighs strongly on the direction of their future. Unpredictable and irrepressible, they can be linked both to the most noble and the most vile endeavours. In any case, they fulfill an essential function of unification, stabilization, and mobilization.

In this vein, democracies may have an important lesson to learn from what happened in Russia after the fall of the USSR. In short, during the transition liberal elites sought to instill new values and imprint a new direction on their society. However, out of either negligence or too much concern for rationalism, they failed at reshaping Russian identity – in other words, at inscribing their ideals into a new identity dynamic; drawing on a modern set of myths. For a variety of reasons, it was the ancient myths stemming from Russian tradition that prevailed and, because they were unsympathetic to democracy and freedom, contributed to the failure of the liberal agenda. This resulted in the regime we know today – an authoritarian government with minimal respect for individual rights and democracy[35]. In other words, advocacy for integrational pluralism and interculturalism must necessarily take into account the emotional aspect and the non-rational element that permeates all societies, more specifically the powerful myths[36] that support collective and national identities.

It would certainly take a lack of wisdom not to cultivate wariness towards identity dynamics that can give birth to "tyrannies of the majority", but it would be just as crucial an error to ignore their useful functions or to condemn them a priori. All of this speaks in favour of the effort to foster a conjunction of identity and pluralism. And this kind of alliance is possible, as Quebec has shown over the course of the last decades – there is no intrinsic incompatibility between the continuity and growth of majority cultures (or national cultures) and the law.

In the Quebec debate over ethnocultural relations in recent years, several interlocutors have tried to foster extreme polarization in order to discredit pluralism. According to their vision, on one side there are the defenders of the majority and on the other, the defenders of minority rights who give little thought to the majority's concerns. This harmful opposition is groundless and must be rejected. In the spirit of interculturalism, these

---

quasi-sacred quality with which they are imbued. On this subject see Bouchard, Gérard, "Le mythe: Essai de définition" in Gérard Bouchard and Bernard Andrès (eds.), *Mythes et sociétés des Amériques*, Montréal, Québec Amérique, 2007, pp. 409-426.

35 See Brudny, Ytzak, "Myths and National Identity Choices in Post-Communist Russia" in Gérard Bouchard (ed.), *National Myths: Constructed Pasts, Contested Presents*, 2013, pp. 133-156.

36 Again, I use the word "myth" in its sociological sense, stripped of its normative connotations. On this subject, see text accompanying note 34.

two imperatives are not competitive but complementary – it must be reminded that interculturalism does not operate only for the benefit of minorities and immigrants, but that it must also take into account the interests of the majority, whose desire for affirmation and development is perfectly legitimate.

That said, we realize that the criteria for *ad hoc* precedence must be carefully mapped out. Otherwise it may simply jeopardize the practice of accommodations designed, as outlined above, to protect minorities from the majority's often involuntary or unconscious excesses[37]. Here too, there is a delicate balance to be negotiated with prudence and moderation. In this respect, remember that important responsibilities fall to all majority groups because they largely control the institutions of the host society. They must embrace the general principle of equal rights for all citizens and fight all forms of discrimination. Due to the institutions under their control, it is also their duty to facilitate the integration of newcomers and minority groups into society. Except in extraordinary circumstances, contextual precedence must therefore operate within the limits of basic rights. If it must act against these rights, it can do so only to an extent that is proportional to the threat or peril incurred against the cultural majority – failing which it simply slips into ethnicism.

Minority groups are required to adapt to their host society, adhere to its basic values, and respect its institutions, but due to the double obligation just explained, the majority group must also sometimes amend its ways. That is why it is important to encourage the reasonable promotion of accommodations or concerted adjustments: (a) as a mechanism of inter-cultural harmonization that prevents or defuses tensions, (b) as a facilitating measure to encourage the integration of immigrants and reduce the risk of fragmentation, and (c) as a protection against the forms of discrimination that often arise from majorities. Contrary to the current perception, these adjustments are not privileges; they are arrangements that are at once useful (in favour of integration) and necessary (for the preservation of rights, including equality and dignity). This being said, it is well understood that their implementation must be subject to strict guidelines in order to prevent a slip into a laissez-faire mentality that would compromise the basic values of the host society[38].

---

37 Some examples of excesses are: (a) a single public holiday regime modelled on the dominant religion, (b) textbooks that ignore minority experiences, and (c) uniform menus in the cafeterias of public institutions, and so forth.

38 See the Bouchard-Taylor Commission Report for suggestions on the kind of counterweights necessary to discipline the implementation of accommodations (Bouchard and Taylor, *op. cit.* chapter VIII). It is regrettable that a few poorly thought-out high-level decisions have largely contributed to discredit this practice in the eyes of many Quebecois.

Finally, here too, the rule of reciprocity applies. For example, the report of the Bouchard-Taylor Commission clearly established that "[a]pplicants who are intransigent, reject negotiation and go against the rule of reciprocity will seriously compromise their approach"[39]. Courtrooms adopt the same rule for examining requests for accommodations.

As we may guess, it is difficult to precisely set up in the abstract the limits of *ad hoc* precedence and the terms of its application. But is it not the same with several basic values and rights, which creates the necessity of interactions, negotiations, and debate? In this context, and for the purpose of the present discussion, it can be useful to turn to a few examples, relevant to the Canadian and Quebec context. Some of them, as we will see, are rather superficial, while others strike at the heart of fundamental issues – but each illustrates an aspect of contextual precedence.

The following could, to my thinking, be considered legitimate according to the criteria for *ad hoc* precedence:

1. the institution of French as the common public language;
2. allocating a prominent place to the teaching of the francophone past in history courses, or in other words, a national memory that is inclusive but gives predominance to the majority narrative;
3. the current priority position given to the presentation of Christian religions in the new course on ethics and religious culture;
4. the official burials of heads of state in Catholic churches;
5. keeping the cross on the Quebec flag (which has already been subject to challenges)[40];
6. laying Christmas decorations in public squares or buildings; and
7. the sounding of bells in Catholic churches at various moments throughout the day[41].

On the other hand, I consider the following examples to be abusive extensions of the principle of *ad hoc* precedence:

1. keeping a cross on the wall of the National Assembly and in public courtrooms;
2. the recitation of prayers at municipal council meetings;

---

39 *Ibid.*, p. 21.

40 See e.g. Macpherson, Don, "A Symbol of France: If Quebec is Serious about Inclusiveness, it Should Adopt a New Flag", *The [Montreal] Gazette*, 7 August 2001, B3; Macpherson, Don, "Raising a Flag: Montreal and Quebec Flags are Outdated Symbols of the People They Are Supposed to Represent", *The [Montreal] Gazette*, 22 January 2002, B3.

41 Note that all of these examples contain elements of *ad hoc* or contextual precedence, including the protection of historic heritage or the identity of the cultural majority.

3. the funding of chaplain or Catholic pastoral care positions in public hospitals with state funds, to the exclusion of other religions[42];
4. the general prohibition against wearing religious signs for all employees in the public and semi-public sectors;
5. the reference to the supremacy of God in the preamble of the *Canadian Charter of Rights and Freedoms*[43];
6. including articles or clauses in a charter that establish a formal hierarchy between the cultural majority and minorities; and
7. the prohibition against wearing a burka in streets and public places (except for security or other compelling reasons).

F. A Common Culture

A sixth facet of interculturalism that stems from the preceding ones is the idea that beyond and separate from ethnocultural diversity, elements of a common culture (or a national culture) begin to take shape, giving birth to a belonging and an identity that grafts itself onto initial belongings and identities[44]. This is a logical, predictable, and welcome consequence of the goals of integration and the dynamic of interactions that are at the heart of interculturalism. In the long-term, both the majority culture and minority cultures will find themselves changed to varying degrees[45]. As indicated earlier, it is also inevitable that in the course of continued exchanges and informal transactions in daily life, the impact of the majority culture will be proportional to its demographic and sociological weight, giving it a de facto advantage in ensuring its continuity. On the other hand, the formation of a new, truly "pan-Quebecois" culture provides a guarantee to minorities and newcomers of full citizenship and protects them from exclusion. This outlook also offers cultural minorities an exit strategy from what some of their members can perceive as imprisonment in ethnic ghettos.

---

42 This example is becoming more and more theoretical as the law now stipulates that pastoral care providers, as givers of spiritual support, must serve all faiths.

43 Part I of the *Constitution Act, 1982*, being Schedule B to the *Canada Act 1982* (UK), 1982, c 11 [*Canadian Charter*].

44 This conception is similar to what many in Quebec refer to as common public culture. The two concepts, however, differ to the extent that I see no objection to the idea that the common culture should incorporate elements beyond laws, procedures, and citizenship *per se*.

45 The idea that interaction with immigrants and minority cultures inevitably leads to changes within the majority culture sometimes inspires reluctance. It is, however, one of the clearest lessons taught by social and historical sciences. As we are seeing currently, cultures change primarily through the effects of contact with each other. It would be easy to show that the history of Quebec is an eloquent example of this.

In other words, the cultural evolution of Quebec is already the result of three threads weaving together in subtle and complex ways, stemming from their sociological influence and their dynamism – the culture of the foundational majority, the culture of immigrants and minorities, and the culture resulting from the mixture of the two. It would certainly be quite difficult to disentangle the contributions of each, but what good would that do?

G. The Search for Equilibriums

Fundamentally, interculturalism is a search for balance and mediation between often-competing principles, values, and expectations. In this sense, it is a sustained effort aimed at connecting majorities and minorities, continuity and diversity, identity and rights, reminders of the past and visions of the future. It calls for new ways of coexisting within and beyond differences at all levels of collective life.

Furthermore, the majority/minorities dichotomy is not immutable. Through the prolonged dynamic of interactions, it is not unrealistic to think that it may one day dissolve. Here we see two possibilities – either the two basic components of the dynamic will melt together completely, or that one of them will disappear. Both scenarios would mean a departure from the interculturalist model and the duality paradigm. In the case of Quebec, however, this eventuality remains largely theoretical. It would require that immigration – which tends to renew the duality – diminish substantially, and that cultural minorities (or the majority itself) choose not to perpetuate themselves. This is at once a consequence and a paradox of a pluralist philosophy within a duality paradigm: to the extent that this presupposes a respect for diversity, it tends to diminish the us/them relationship and defuse the tension it fuels, but at the same time it contributes indirectly to perpetuating the duality.

Whatever the case may be, these scenarios remain unpredictable and somewhat arbitrary for another reason. As indicated earlier, paradigms and models are ultimately a matter of choice. There is not, therefore, necessarily a correspondence between the evolution of a nation's ethnocultural reality and the form or the voices that frame the public discourse.

The preceding paragraphs highlight the issue of common values, which are already (or are becoming) subject to a very large consensus, and the necessity for their protection under the law. On this front, we know that over the course of the last few years some judgments by the Supreme Court of Canada have been met with sharp objections in Quebec. Some clarification is needed here. If we get to a point where the Supreme Court repeatedly and systematically contradicts or threatens the basic and consensual values of Quebec, such as gender equality, the French language, or the institutional separation of church and state, then Quebec would be perfectly justified in resisting these judgments, either through recourse to the notwithstanding clause in the Canadian Constitution[46] or through other legal and political means.

4. Interculturalism and Multiculturalism

I am opening a parenthetical discussion to situate Quebec interculturalism in relation to Canadian multiculturalism. I will first remind that, for political reasons, all Quebec governments (federalist or not) have rejected multiculturalism since its adoption by the federal government in 1971. Since the middle of the nineteenth century, francophones in Quebec have fought to gain acceptance of the idea that Canada is composed of two nations (anglophone and francophone). This vision of the country was undermined by the introduction of multiculturalism, which made francophones in Quebec simply one ethnic group among many others throughout Canada. In this sense, multiculturalism weakened Quebec and for this reason it is the source of keen opposition from the francophone population.

On a more theoretical or sociological level, researchers have often extrapolated in order to bring to fore the difference between these two models. For many reasons, this question does not lend itself to an easy answer. One is that Canadian multiculturalism has evolved a great deal since 1971. This is an important fact that we do not always take into account. In the 1970s, for example, the promotion of a diversity of languages and cultures was a central element of the Canadian model. Beginning in the 1980s, a social dimension (the struggle against inequalities and exclusion) emerged at the same time as the rights dimension was primarily being heard through the struggle against discrimination. In the 1990s and over the course of the 2000s there was a growing concern for social cohesion, integration and common values, and for the formation (or consolidation) of a Canadian belonging and identity. More recently still, the model has made more room for ideas of interactions, cultural exchanges, Canadian values, and participation[47].

We therefore note with interest that, in so doing, Canadian multiculturalism has slowly grown closer to Quebec interculturalism and that this is a source of persistent confusion in Quebec. Indeed, a number of interlocutors in the public debate argue for the similarity of the two models, but for opposite reasons. One group, on behalf of Quebec nationalism,

---

46 *Canadian Charter*, *supra* note 43, art. 33.

47 If we add the increasingly vocal criticisms expressed by English-speaking Canadians against multiculturalism, we come to ask ourselves whether Canada is in the process of questioning its diversity paradigm.

aims to discredit interculturalism by associating it with Canadian multiculturalism and blaming it for the drawbacks usually associated with that model (fragmentation, relativism, and so forth), although in reality, one suspects that it is pluralism that is targeted. The other group, working from a Canadian or federalist perspective, downplays or denies the differences that exist between the two models by claiming that interculturalism is simply a variant of Canadian multiculturalism.

It seems to me, however, that these two models remain quite different for the following reasons:

1. The most defining and obvious difference is that interculturalism pertains to the nation of Quebec, the existence of which was officially recognized by the federal government itself (through a motion adopted by the House of Commons on 27 November 2006)[48].
2. The two models are rooted in opposite paradigms. The federal government still adheres to the idea that there is no majority culture in Canada, that diversity defines the country, and that this idea must guide all discussion of ethnocultural reality[49]. For its part, Quebec continues to embrace the duality paradigm, emphasizing the majority/minorities structure. This choice conforms to the minority status of this French-speaking people on the North American continent and the anxieties that it inevitably entails. The crucial point here is that there really is a majority culture within the nation of Quebec whose fragility is a permanent fact of life. This results in a specific vision of nationhood, identity, and national belonging.
3. Since francophone Quebecers constitute a minority, they instinctively fear all forms of socio-cultural fragmentation, marginalization, and ghettoization. This is where interculturalism draws its particular conception of integration, namely the emphasis on interactions, connections between cultures, the development of feelings of belonging, and the emergence of a common culture. Traditionally, multiculturalism does not cultivate these concerns to the same degree – it puts more emphasis on the validation and promotion of "ethnic" groups.
4. Paradoxically, an extension of these arguments reveals the strong collective dimension (unity, interaction, integration, and common

48 *House of Commons Debates*, 39th Parl, 1st Sess, vol. 141, n° 87 (27 November 2006).

49 I will not go into a critique of this premise and will limit myself to noting that in many regions of Canada the anglophone population retains the feeling that there is a genuine *Canadian* culture inherited from the past and that this culture does not have sufficient space to express itself within the framework of multiculturalism. According to some, this culture is threatened by the diversification brought by immigration.

culture) permeating interculturalism, which distances it from the liberal individualism that is also inherent in multiculturalism[50].

5. Another distinctive trait comes from the fact that Canadian multiculturalism has little to say on the issue of protecting languages. Sooner or later, immigrants to English-speaking Canada will inevitably want to learn the dominant language of the continent in order to eke out a decent living. The case is very different for the French language in Quebec, where there is a constant struggle to find new linguistic protections. This anxiety is obviously culturally motivated, but it also comes from the fact that language is an important factor in civic integration and collective cohesion. Multiculturalism does not echo this anxiety over a common language because English is in no way threatened.
6. In a more general sense, all the rights and accommodations granted to immigrants in Western democracies are accompanied by a preoccupation with the values and even the future of the host culture. This concern is understandably stronger in small nations that are anxious about their survival. Here, respect for diversity takes an additional dimension. In other words, the challenges linked to pluralism in small nations have an impact and spark a level of tension seldom experienced by more powerful nations. These pressures lie at the heart of interculturalism.
7. Another difference has to do with collective memory. Due to the battles that Quebec francophones have waged over the course of their history, an intense collective memory of their small, combative nation has taken hold. For many French-speakers, this memory carries a message of loyalty, or even duty, towards past and future generations. References to this past lie at the heart of the francophone culture, which can be another source of tension: how to transmit the memory of the majority without diluting its symbolic content in a context of increasing diversity, and all the while making room for minority narratives?[51] This line of questioning clearly does not have the same resonance from a multiculturalist perspective, where the issue of a majority culture is simply absent.

---

50 In this sense, some have seen in this collective bend a French and/or Republican influence on interculturalism. I rather see it as the result of a continuity strongly rooted in the past of a dominated minority that has learned to band together in order to better survive and grow.

51 I am referring to a tension, not an impasse. It would be wrong to believe that this problem, as difficult as it is, lacks any solution. See, for instance, a proposition I made on this issue: Bouchard, *La Nation québécoise au futur et au passé*, *op. cit.*, pp. 81-137; Bouchard, Gérard, "Promouvoir ce qu'il y a de plus universel dans notre passé", *Le Devoir*, 30 January 2003, A9.

8. The specific elements that have been noted here are concretely translated in different ways, particularly in the practice of recognition and of accommodations. In this last case, one expects that requests for accommodations in Quebec are often evaluated in terms of integration – that is, a request is more likely to be met if it can be positively connected to this issue. Thus, permitting the wearing of the hijab in class encourages Muslim students to continue attending public school and to open themselves up more easily to the values of Quebec society. The same is true for the offering of special menus in school cafeterias, a flexible policy towards certain pedagogical activities that do not interfere with the Education Act[52], and so forth.
9. As we have seen, interculturalism is on the whole very sensitive to the problems and needs of the majority culture, which multiculturalism cannot provide since, once again, it does not recognize the existence of such a culture.

These remarks bring to light the contrasting visions of these two models. Nevertheless, if we compare the policies relating to interethnic matters actually put in place by the Canadian and Quebec governments over the last several decades, we see numerous similarities[53]. How to explain this paradox? Besides the already discussed recent shift of multiculturalism towards interculturalism, I think that these similarities are due in part to the fact that both models share a pluralist orientation. But it mostly stems from the fact that the government of Quebec has not adequately aligned its policies with the interculturalist model. A gap has developed between the official philosophy and the policies actually in place. A much greater effort should be made on this ground. It is urgent to conceive of projects and policies that give real body to the spirit and objectives of interculturalism. It is also important to mobilize the Quebec society towards this end – not only the state, but also semi-public and private institutions, the business sector, the major unions, the media, and advocacy groups.

To give an example of one measure among many others that the state might put in place, why not give interculturalism a level of official recognition equivalent to what multiculturalism has received in Canada? By virtue of article 27 of the *Canadian Charter*, multiculturalism enjoys

---

52 RSQ c I-13.3.

53 See McAndrew, "Multiculturalisme canadien et interculturalisme québécois: mythes et réalités", *op. cit.*; Juteau, Danielle, Marie McAndrew and Linda Pietrantonio, "Multiculturalisme à la Canadian and Intégration à la Québécoise: Transcending their Limits" in Rainer Bauböck and John Rundell (eds.), *Blurred Boundaries: Migration, Ethnicity, Citizenship*, Aldershot, Ashgate, 1998, pp. 95-110.

the status of an interpretative clause. Why not do the same thing for interculturalism in the *Quebec Charter*?[54]

Conclusion: A Future for Interculturalism and French-speaking Quebec

Like all democracies worldwide currently questioning or even shaken in their cultural foundations, Quebec is confronted with a dilemma that it cannot overcome except through debates, negotiations, and the search for new ways of integration. These concerns lie at the very heart of the model proposed here. Needless to say, interculturalism calls for a complex dynamic made up of interactions, continuity, and change that is constantly negotiated and renegotiated on all levels of society, within a framework of respect for basic values and in a spirit that can be summarized in a single maxim – firmness in principles, flexibility in their application. This seems to be the best recipe for fostering integration as far as Quebec is concerned. Within the framework of Quebec, I maintain that radical solutions must be avoided – solutions that would, for example, lead to a total ban of religious symbols in public institutions. Republican models along the lines of France or Turkey are not well matched to the context of Quebec[55] and do not correspond to the objectives and philosophy of interculturalism. Total prohibition, which entails the violation of a basic right, does not seem justified, at least at present, by any of the arguments made in its favour. Some of them draw on erroneous principles (e.g., equality of rights precludes difference of treatment, and the ban of religious signs is dictated by the separation of state and church). Others rely on suppositions and hypotheses that have not been tested enough empirically (the existence of an Islamist threat in Montreal, the belief that state officials wearing religious signs are biased in the course of their duties, the idea that the hidjab is the sign of female oppression (true in many cases, but the generalization is certainly abusive)[56], and so forth.

The spirit of interculturalism invites us to recognize the diversity of situations in order to provide a diversity of solutions within a clear normative framework. In some cases, prohibition is in order – for instance

54 This proposition recently received the support of a jurist at the University of Laval in Quebec. See Lampron, Louis-Philippe, "Comment déroger à la Charte canadienne sans déroger à la liberté de religion", *Le Devoir*, 8 March 2010, A7.

55 A weak state, decentralized society, liberal tradition, long-standing and well established recognition of minority cultures, strong North American influence in institutions and in public culture, and so forth.

56 The hearings (public and private) of the Commission that Charles Taylor and I co-chaired in 2007-2008 clearly demonstrated this. And where there is oppression, are we sure that prohibition is the most effective way to help those women?

with officials who embody the neutrality of the state and its autonomy from religion; for officials endowed with coercive power; and in the case of the burka or niqab, which should be banned in state employment locations and even in public spaces if it can be shown to pose a security threat; and so forth[57].

Interculturalism is built on the basic wager of democracy, that is, a capacity to reach consensus on forms of peaceful coexistence that preserve basic values and make room for the future of all citizens, regardless of their origins or nationalities. This path is certainly not the easiest. For the Quebec majority culture, the simplest thing would be to try to protect the old francophone identity to the point of isolating it, to freeze it – as it were – and thus to impoverish it, which would be another way of putting it at risk. The more promising but also the more difficult option is the one which offers a wider horizon to this identity and to its underlying values by sharing them with immigrants and minority groups. This last option, contrary to what is sometimes said, does not involve withdrawal or self-renunciation, but real affirmation. It means the expansion and enrichment of heritage. It also includes the important advantage of providing inspiration for all Quebec's citizens.

Finally, it must be restated that these propositions befit the new realities of francophone Quebec, which has entered a phase of demographic decrease, of diversification due to immigration, and of globalization. As a minority, the French-speaking majority cannot afford to be weakened by creating lasting divisions. It needs all its strength. To a large extent, its future lies in the respectful integration of diversity.

For Quebec, the key is to rely on a model of integration that preserves the rich achievements of this nation, while expanding the sphere in which they can be unfurled and extended. Until there is proof to the contrary, interculturalism appears to be the best way for effectively combining these objectives. I have tried to show, in particular, that it can ensure a future for the majority as well as for minorities. Thus, it is wrong to claim that interculturalism (or integrational pluralism) forces the majority culture to "renounce" itself (that is to say, its memory, its identity, and its aspirations) and deprives it of the means for self-assertion[58].

---

[57] I tried to summarize my conception of a secular regime in terms of interculturalism (see Bouchard, "Laïcité: la voie québécoise de l'interculturalisme", *op. cit.*, which, following Jean Baubérot, we can call inter-cultural secularism (see Baubérot, Jean, *Une laïcité interculturelle: Le Québec, avenir de la France?*, La Tour D'Aigues, Éditions de l'Aube, 2008). In any case, I easily admit that the interculturalist model can welcome many different conceptions.

[58] It would be easy to show that the real obstacles to assertion and development in francophone Quebec are primarily political in nature and that, as with the national question, it is in this sphere especially that they must be addressed.

This brief presentation of the interculturalist model has devoted much space to the specifics of Quebec and, more particularly, to the minority and majority double-status of this French-speaking people. It also brought into light the potential of interculturalism for transposition and expansion to all nations, Western and otherwise, that have chosen to adopt the duality paradigm in their dealings with diversity and integration. There is proof of this in the results of a broad survey conducted by the Council of Europe among its forty-seven member states (following the Warsaw Summit in 2005)[59]. They were asked about the best model for managing interethnic or intercultural relations. All these countries arrived at a consensus on three points: (a) the rejection of multiculturalism, which was associated with fragmentation and seen as harmful to social cohesion; (b) the rejection of assimilation due to the violation of individual rights that it entails; and (c) the choice of interculturalism as a middle path, as a model of balance and equity. Interestingly, the survey also brought out that this model maintained the best parts of multiculturalism (sensitivity to diversity) and of republicanism (sensitivity to universal rights)[60].

Interculturalism thus opens a large horizon for thought and action, at the same time that it presents Quebec with the opportunity to make a significant contribution to one of the fundamental problems of our time.

59 Council of Europe, Committee of Ministers, 118th Sess., *Living Together as Equals in Dignity*, White Paper on Intercultural Dialogue, 2008.

60 See Battaini-Dragoni, Gabrielle, "La voie de l'avenir: Vivre ensemble dans le respect de la diversité", Speech presented as part of a workshop, in *Les droits de l'Homme dans des sociétés culturellement diverses: Défis et perspectives. Actes de la conférence de La Haye, 12-13 novembre 2008*, Strasbourg, Direction générale des droits de l'Homme et des affaires juridiques, Conseil de l'Europe, 2009, pp. 141-145.

CHAPTER 10

Multiculturalism and Legal Pluralism

European Perspectives[1]

Joxerramon BENGOETXEA

Professor of Philosophy of Law, University of the Basque Country, (San Sebastian)

Introduction: Analytical Remarks

Cultural plurality is a sociological fact concerning the (co-)existence of different cultures in one society[2]. It can adopt different expressions in politics, in the economy, in social relations, in symbolic universe, in the cultural products and references created, produced and consumed in our societies, and also in law. Pluri-culturality or multi-culturality, can also, although it need not, be related to a sociological or a political theory: multiculturalism or its more recent spin-offs like the more hybrid inter-culturalism or "management of cultural diversity". As a sociological fact, cultural plurality is always interpreted from a sociological theory (in a spectre that spans from monist to pluralist poles).

---

1 This work has been produced within the framework of (i) project DER2010-19715 of the juri subprogram of the Spanish Ministry of Science and (ii) the Consolidated Research Group (GIC07/86-IT-448-07) led by Prof Gurutz Jauregi, with the financial assistance of the Education, Universities and Research Department of the Basque Autonomous Government.

2 The definition of "society" is obviously problematic: I use an intuitive concept, where the social grouping – involving population, communities (not only individuals and families), institutions, social (inter)action, symbols, artifacts – is territorially and jurisdictionally circumscribed, yet still elastic. There is a Basque society but also a Spanish society, even a European society. Their features and components differ because the networks formed by individuals occur in different contexts. On the other hand, so-called "civil society", even "transnational civil society" is out with this intuitive or pre-interpretative notion of society. My view is largely influenced by Geertz, Clifford, *The Interpretation of Cultures*, New York, Basic Books, 1973.

Still, regardless of the interpretative framework, one can always ask how and in what manner the law, the institutional normative order[3] of a society, deals with this fact of cultural plurality especially as regards the normative expressions of such plurality: recognition, accommodation, regulation, avoidance, limitation, denial strategies. From the modern standpoint of Human Rights, this fact of plurality and diversity is often regarded as an asset. But this does not mean that in any given society or community where a dominant, majoritarian normative framework exists and impregnates the official law, the different identifiable cultures (or rather all cultural practices and their normative claims), commensurable or not, will be or even should be catered for, supported or accommodated (this claim of cultural pluralism or multiculturalism can be related to ethical relativism).

At the same time, there can be plurality within law, so-called legal pluralism or variants and versions of it. This can be a consequence of the sociological fact of cultural plurality or it can be a consequence of a diversity of recognised and co-official institutional normative systems within the same territory, a plurality of legal systems, which can also be related to constitutional plurality and integrated into a theory of constitutional pluralism[4] and law. This plurality of laws in the same territory can, again, be seen as a sociological or socio-legal fact – legal plurality or diversity – or as a theory of law and state where they translate into legal pluralism versus monism to incorporate useful categories from international law. Much will turn around the contemporary notion of the Nation-State as the dominant but no longer exclusive normative framework in the European context. Statist views stress the special, central and predominant place of the state in the definition of law, understood as positive law. According to the Parliamentary Assembly of the Council of Europe, "the general trend of the nation-state's evolution is towards its transformation depending on the case, from a purely ethnic or ethnocentric state into a civic state and from a purely civic state into a multicultural state where specific rights are recognised with regard not only to physical persons but also to cultural or national communities"[5]. But in this picture, the state and its official law

---

3 For the definition of law as institutional normative order see MacCormick, Neil, *Institutions of Law*, Oxford, Clarendon Press, 2007.

4 On constitutional pluralism see MacCormick, *ibid.*, and MacCormick, *Questioning Sovereignty*, Oxford, Oxford University Press, 1999. This concept was taken up by Neil Walker in *The Idea of Constitutional Pluralism*, and has since become the subject of heated debates in the European legal scholarship (Weiler, Kumm, Maduro, Baquero, Menéndez, Tuori, Komarek).

5 Resolution 1735 (2006) on the concept of nation, Assembly debate on 26 January 2006 (7th Sitting) (see Doc. 10762, report of the Committee on Legal Affairs and Human Rights, rapporteur: Mr Frunda).

is still the focal point of such recognition and legal plurality is brought under the general supervision of state law.

To the extent that state and law are thought to be conceptually connected, legal pluralism will be denied and some version or variant of monism will be adopted as the interpretative framework where plurality or diversity is explained away. This need not lead to a denial of cultural rights and indeed the aforementioned resolution in its point 16.4 invites the member states to bring into line their constitutions with the contemporary democratic European standards which call on each state to integrate all its citizens, irrespective of their ethno-cultural background, within a civic and multicultural entity, and to stop defining and organising themselves as exclusively ethnic or exclusively civic states. Indeed the risk in both extremes is to become ethnically exclusive (of those who do not share the same ethnic or religious identities) or civically exclusive (of those who do not have the nationality, the culture of *laïcité* or the national language).

When facing plurality, the major law-makers – the Constitution-makers, amendment-makers, constitution interpreters, and the legislators, but also lawyers and judges generally – develop different strategies. Democratic legislators, at the level of sources of law, tend to accept cultural plurality and diversity within the confines of democratic constitutions and Human Rights Bills and International Human Rights instruments. This cultural plurality can even become a major feature of modern constitution-states. However this acceptance of *cultural* plurality does not amount to recognition of *legal* plurality, of the normative claims made from the different cultures, at the more fundamental level of the rule of recognition of the sources of law.

Such plurality and diversity of laws, which is denied at the level of sources, might nevertheless be recognised in the interpretation and application of the law, through the mediation of cultural plurality. The contrast here is between universal norms adopted by the legislator and particular norms of judicial decisions. Judges and legislators can recognise some relevance and effect to cultural plurality, this recognition being facilitated by theories of Human Rights-conforming interpretations. Notions and theories concerning the cultural exceptions, or reasonable accommodation are then developed in the context of legal discourse – law-application, legal argumentation and judicial reasoning – in order to achieve results that reconcile cultural diversity and non-discrimination with the denial of legal pluralism at a more foundational, conceptual level. Human Rights-conforming application and interpretation can then take different forms; one of these is equity.

The theoretical claim of this paper is that reasonable accommodation or cultural sensitivity (exception), related to the concept of equity, has the potential to integrate normative claims that can be interpreted as coherent with the higher normative principles of a society – tolerance and equality, freedom and autonomy of the person comprising respect for (cultural) difference, and solidarity towards others. A key contention I would like to make in relation to legal pluralism in European societies is that such pluralism refers not to competing, not even co-existing legal orders but rather to specific norms and practices like those concerning family law, marriage and weddings. Family law is an area where such pluralistic norms and practices coexist and can be accommodated in some cases within the dominant normative framework, even by judges. Legal pluralism would then relate to the coexistence, in one jurisdiction, of different (individual) norms having their origin, their source in normative orders, that are different from official law. This is perhaps more workable a concept than the classical definition of legal pluralism as the existence of different *legal systems*, assuming one can isolate norms from the systems where they belong, as one does in private international law with choice of law[6], by treating the norm as a sociological normative fact or quasi-fact, but not as a *valid norm of the system* into which it is incorporated. The analogy with choice of law or collision norms also applies in that some of those "imported norms" might not satisfy the test of the public policy/ public order exception.

Family law, excluding those rules that would be considered against the basic principles of public order, like polygamy, is a proper area for the expression of plurality in contemporary European societies. Marriage is a social institution and a legal institution as well: it comprises social arrangements and prohibitions; it channels sexual taboos; it generates social relationships; it is the way to create a family and to ensure reproduction; it encompasses a property regime, an inheritance regime and a set of economic relationships; it is the locus for cultural transmission; it arranges relations between groups, sometimes in confrontation; and it generates loyalties and solidarities that go beyond the two spouses. Of course, in modern societies some or many of these social functions are only latent, and marriage is not the only institution serving those functions, but it is a crucial institution all the same.

These complex issues will be examined through two cases originating in the European context, in the EU and in the Council of Europe. The cases have to do with different forms of marriage, in one case, the wedding rites and customs followed by the Rom people that are not registered

6 An interesting application of choice of law techniques to multicultural challenges to the law in context of the feminist post-essentialist cultural debate can be found in Knop, Karen, Ralf Michaels and Annelise Riles, "From Multiculturalism to Technique: Feminism, Culture and the Conflict of Laws Style", *Stanford Law Review*, vol. 64, n° 3, 2012, pp. 589-656.

and therefore not recognised by official Spanish law. In the other case is the legal treatment given by the European Commission applying the EU Staff Regulations to special forms of union between two people who have adopted a "convention for living together", an institute recognised in Dutch family law and which could in theory be entered into by more than two people. The law does not prejudge or predetermine the social functions of the different forms of marriage, but it allows a normative framework for their expression, either through the legislation contemplating these different forms or through the reasonable accommodation expected from judges and law-applying authorities taking into account the different cultural and normative situations and frameworks of persons belonging to cultural minorities.

1. Two Cases from the European Context

1.1 Rom Marriage and the Spanish Civil Law: The Muñoz Díaz Case[7]

Spain refused to recognise the Applicant's widower's pension on the ground that she had not legally contracted marriage. The European Court of Human Rights found that Spain had breached Article 14 of the Convention in relation to Article 1 of Protocol N° 1 concerning the Right to Property. The Court ordered Spain to pay the Applicant 70 000 euros plus defence legal costs.

The Applicant and M.D. "married" in 1971 following the gypsy rite recognised by the Rom community. At the time the Spanish Civil Code (Art. 42) provided that when one of the spouses is Catholic, the wedding was to follow the Catholic rite and form. Civil wedding was recognised when neither of the spouses was Catholic. The only possibility for a Catholic to marry through the civil wedding was to abandon the Catholic faith by an act of apostasy performed before the local priest (Art. 245 of the Law regulating the Civil Registry).

The couple had six children. The children were registered in 1983 in the Civil Registry and, although Spanish law required a formally registered marriage, a Family Book was issued to them though the wedding was not officially recognised or registered. They were given recognition of the status of a large family (familia numerosa) in 1986. The new Civil Code was adopted in 1981 and provided for civil marriage. Spain has entered into agreements with several confessions providing for the civil

7 European Court of Human Rights (3rd Chamber), case *Muñoz Díaz v Kingdom of Spain*; N° 49151/07 (lodged 29-10-2007). Judgment of 8 December 2009. Amicus Curiae: Unión Romaní.

recognition of the weddings performed according to their own rites following the model of the Concordat with the Catholic Church. No such agreement has been entered into with the Rom community concerning the Rom wedding or marriage, which has no specific formality other than the mutual expression of the will to live together and set up a family.

M.D. died in 2000. He had worked and contributed to Social Security for over 19 years. The Applicant then applied for a widower's pension and this was refused by the INSS (Spanish Social Security Authority) on the ground that there was no formal marriage and the law regulating the INSS (law of 7 July 1981, 7th additional provision and legislative degree 1/1994 establishing the General Law of Social Security, article 174, requiring officially recognised marriage) did not apply. The Applicant appealed before the Labour Court of Madrid (Nº 12). This Court recognised civil effects of the marriage and ordered the INSS to award the pension. The judgment was based on several legal arguments drawn from the 1966 International Covenant of Civil and Political Rights prohibiting all forms of discrimination from, indirectly by analogy, Directive 2000/43/CE prohibiting all forms of discrimination outside the workplace, and from Art. 14 of the Spanish Constitution prohibiting ethnic discrimination, amongst other forms. The State could not forgo its duty of protection even if it did not recognise the gypsy marriage. This judgment is very important and indicates a special sensitivity developed by the Labour Court. Labour Courts are often more advanced in their interpretations[8].

However, on Appeal, the Higher Court of Justice of Madrid upheld the INSS decision giving priority to Art. 49 of the Civil Code, which provides for civil effects of religious marriages when the State has so provided. Gypsy marriage was not contemplated and could be considered, at best, as a custom that would only apply in the absence of a statutory norm (Art. 1.3 of the Civil Code). It would have no *erga omnes* effect. The concept of spouse used by the General Law of Social Security has to be interpreted strictly as excluding concubines and similar cases.

Amparo or special protection appeal before the Constitutional Court was denied by judgment of 16-04-2007, on the argument that there was no discrimination in the fact that the law restricted pensions to lawful marriages excluding other unions *more uxorio*. The legislator has discretion to make such choices, especially in the context of limited resources. The basis for the widower's pension is not the need of the widower but her legally recognised marriage with the deceased worker who had contributed to the Social Security pension fund. There would be no right of the Applicant to a differentiated treatment. A dissenting

---

8 See Pallín, José Antonio Martín and Jesús Peces Morate, *La Justicia en España,* Madrid, Ediciones Catarata, 2008.

vote was cast by judge Rz Zapata relying on a previous judgment of the Constitutional Court 199/2004 where a catholic marriage had not been civilly registered and yet had been considered valid for the purposes of awarding pension rights. It would be disproportionate for the State to grant a Family Book, to recognise the status of a large family and to receive over 19 years of contributions from the deceased partner but to refuse the pension.

The 40/2007 Law on measures of Social Security finally changed the law in Spain. The third additional provision provides for pension rights in cases of six years of concubine status (living together) and children in common. The Applicant, Muñoz Díaz, was awarded her widower's pension.

The Reasoning of the European Court of Human Rights

The Applicant invoked the violation of Art. 14 of the Convention prohibiting all forms of discrimination in relation to the enjoyment of any of the rights of the Convention or its Protocols, in this case the right to property protected by Art. 1 of Protocol 1 and the right to marriage and family life protected by Art. 12 of the Convention. The main argument of the Defendant State, Spain, is that there is no discrimination in this case since the pension was denied simply because there was no marriage at all, only a *more uxorio* relationship, with no legal effects. After the entry into force of the Spanish Constitution, the Applicant could have contracted a civil marriage, perfectly in line with the Convention[9]. The refusal to award a pension is clearly in prejudice of the Applicant's property interests and the main question for the Court is to decide whether the pension was refused because the Applicant is a member of the Rom minority, taking into consideration the decisions the defendant State has made in like situations such as the one mentioned in the dissenting vote of the Constitutional Court where a registered Catholic marriage was recognised for the purposes of pension rights.

The Applicant believed in good faith that her gypsy marriage was lawful and produced effects like an ordinary marriage. The State officials had awarded some form of recognition by granting the "Family Book" or the status of large family and had thus generated some expectations on the Applicant. The beliefs of the member of a well-defined cultural group cannot be ignored or neglected, and *cultural pluralism* is beneficial to the whole of society. It is true that belonging to a minority can afford no

[9] The Court did not find a violation of Article 12 since the State has the right to regulate marriage and the effects it recognises to marriages. In this case it could decide, as it did, that only marriages contemplated in special Conventions between the State and Religious Institutions or Confessions would be given *erga omnes* effect.

excuse not to respect the law but it can have an effect on the way the laws are applied. The Court is here relying on *Chapman v. UK*, paragraphs 61 and 96, a case concerning the right to a home of the Rom in the light of licensing and land management (caravan sites). Living in caravans is there identified with gypsy ethnic identity and measures limiting this right to dwell in caravans would also affect the right to privacy, private and family life. The decision of the UK authorities to refuse the right to camp in the particular site under the circumstances was however considered proportionate and thus compatible with the Convention.

In the current case the Applicant had legitimate expectation to be considered the lawful wife of M.D. The refusal of the pension by the State somehow contradicted the recognition that the very State had expressed towards the Applicant concerning her family condition. The State should have taken into account the Applicant's good faith and her cultural and social conditions, in line with the Framework Convention for the Protection of National Minorities[10], which Spain had ratified in 1995. There was therefore an unjustified different treatment.

Judge Myjer gave a dissenting vote on the ground that the precedents cited by the Court concerning the Rom (*Chapman v. UK*[11], *Buckley v. UK*[12], and *Connors v. UK*[13]) were in the field of land management and building or camping licenses, not family law. In the case of Connors, the statutory scheme which permitted the summary eviction placed "considerable obstacles in the way of gypsies pursuing an actively nomadic lifestyle while at the same time excluding from procedural protection those who decide to take up a more settled lifestyle" (para. 94); the delicate situation of gypsies required providing sites for parking the

10 For a summary of The Framework Convention for the Protection of National Minorities, refer to: http://www.ohchr.org/Documents/Publications/GuideMinorities8en.pdf. Page consulted on 12 February 2014.

11 Five cases were joined: besides Chapman, *Beard v. UK*, *Coster v. UK*, *Lee v. UK* and *Jane Smith v. UK*, see para. 96: "although the fact of being a member of a minority with a traditional lifestyle different from that of the majority of a society does not confer an immunity from general laws intended to safeguard assets common to the whole society such as the environment, it may have an incidence on the manner in which such laws are to be implemented. […] [t]he vulnerable position of gypsies as a minority means that some special consideration should be given to their needs and their different lifestyle both in the relevant regulatory planning framework and in arriving at decisions in particular cases. To this extent there is thus a positive obligation imposed on the Contracting States by virtue of Article 8 to facilitate the gypsy way of life". These judgments were very split, seven judges gave separate dissenting opinions considering there were very few realistic alternatives to carry out the gypsy lifestyle.

12 ECHR Eur Commission, 25 Sep 1995. See also *Turner v. UK*, Eur Commission 26 Feb 1997.

13 Judgment of 27 May 2004.

caravans. In a statement that came very close to the concept of reasonable accommodation the Court said, in paragraph 84:

> The vulnerable position of gypsies as a minority means that some special consideration should be given to their needs and their different lifestyle both in the relevant regulatory framework and in reaching decisions in particular cases (Buckley judgment cited above, at 1292-95, paras. 76, 80 and 84). To this extent, there is thus a positive obligation imposed on the Contracting States by virtue of Article 8 to facilitate the gypsy way of life (see *Chapman, op. cit.*, para. 96 and the authorities cited, *mutatis mutandis*, therein).

This case concerning the Rom has been chosen because of the special features of the Rom in Europe, suffering discrimination in many European countries (Italy, Hungary, Kosovo, Check Republic, Slovakia, Romania, Serbia; the UK and Spain are not amongst the least respectful) and deprived of basic rights like education, employment, home, and health. According to Joke Kusters, the Rom are the genuine European minority: they lack a country of their own; the 10 million Roms are scattered throughout Europe in lands that are not their own, often with nomadic practices or lifestyles. They cannot be considered a national minority, not even a linguistic minority, nor a religious minority[14]. Perhaps they are a true European minority[15].

The EU is now contemplating special action plans to combat discrimination against the Rom, following the steps of the Council of Europe[16]. If the initial approaches focused on integration as absorption into the dominant culture (e.g. seeing nomadic lifestyle and the lack of a permanent residence as an obstacle to e.g. education), the later developments have stressed the need to recognise and respect such nomadic culture and lifestyle as an essential part of their identity. Of

14 Kusters, Joke, "Criminalising Romani Culture through Law" in Marie-Claire Foblets and Alison Dudes Renteln (eds.), *Multicultural Jurisprudence*, Oxford, Hart, 2009, pp. 199-227.

15 Capotorti's definition is useful but still relates to the State as the stage where minorities operate: "A group inferior to the rest of the population of the State, in a non-dominant position, whose numbers – being nationals of the State – possess ethnic, religious or linguistic characteristics differing from those of the rest of the population and show, if only implicitly, a sense of solidarity, directed towards preserving their culture, traditions, religions or language" (*Study on the Rights of Persons Belonging to Ethnic, Religious and Linguistic Minorities*, United Nations, New York, 1991, para. 568.).

16 See Council of Europe Parliamentary Assembly Recommendations, "On the situation of Gypsies and other Travellers in Europe", n° 563, 1969; "On Gypsies in Europe", 1993, n° 1203; "Concerning the Plight of the Roma in Europe", n° 1557, 2002. The European Commission has adopted on 7 April 2010 a Communication on social and economic integration of the Rom in Europe. Also, Amnesty International has produced special reports on the issue (EUR 71/004/2009, EUR 30/001/2010 and EUR 39/001/2010, see at [Online]: www.amnesty.org/es/library). See also the European Committee on Migration: Report on the Situation of Gypsies and Other Travellers in Europe (1995).

course, this case is only a tiny example of the way cultural plurality can lead to situations resembling legal pluralism.

1.2 Different Forms of Marriage in Dutch Law and their Relevance in the EU Staff Regulations

Case T-58/08P *Commission v. AP Roodhuijzen*, Court of First Instance (now General Court) judgment of 5 October 2009, Court of Justice of the EC (Now of the EU) is a different type of case also concerning marriage but, apparently, devoid of ethnic or cultural minority components. The Staff Regulations of the EC provide for a general regime of social security coverage "RCAM" for the spouses of civil servants of the EU. The *un*married partners will be considered as *spouses* for the purposes of the Regulation if three conditions are met: (1) the partner produces a certificate given by the relevant Member State to the effect of a non-matrimonial partnership (2) the unmarried partners are not already married or linked to other persons by any other form of non-matrimonial partnerships, and (3) there is no close parenthood between the two partners.

Mr Roodhuijzen is a Dutch national working for Eurostat. He applied to the Commission to give social security coverage of the RCAM to his partner, with whom he has a *samenlevingsovereenkomst* or living-together convention recognised before a Notary Public. Dutch law recognises two types of union besides ordinary civil marriage: a registered partnership or *geregistreerd partnerschap* which has similar effects to marriage, and the convention for living together, *samenlevingsovereenkomst*, which has the effects the contracting parties wish to give it and can be entered into by more than two persons and also between close relatives. When registered before a Public Authority, it can give rise to pension rights and other social advantages. The Commission examined this institute and decided it was not comparable to the non-matrimonial partnership provided for by the Staff Regulations.

Mr Roodhuijen brought an action against this decision before the Civil Service Tribunal who proceeded to interpret this notion of non-matrimonial partnership in an autonomous manner. Autonomous interpretation, the view that concepts used by EU law have an autonomous meaning and not necessarily the meaning they have in the domestic legal orders, is of course one of the distinguishing features of EU law[17]. The problem is that the Tribunal further went on to analyse and compare the specific convention for living together entered into by the Applicant and his partner, considering that the conditions agreed by them were comparable to a marriage. The Commission appealed before the Court of

---

17 On these issues of interpretation in EU law I refer the reader to my *The Legal Reasoning of the European Court of Justice*, Oxford, Clarendon Press, 1993.

First Instance (now General Court), invoking, amongst other arguments, the case law of the European Court of Human Rights:

> un *samenlevingsovereenkomst* pourrait être conclu entre plusieurs personnes et entre parents proches. La Commission rappelle à cet égard que la Cour européenne des droits de l'homme a rejeté l'allégation de discrimination, en ce qui concerne les droits de succession, avancée par deux sœurs engagées dans une "relation stable, solide et mutuellement solidaire" (voir Cour eur. D.H., arrêt *Burden c. Royaume-Uni* du 29 avril 2008, para. 10), par rapport aux partenaires engagés dans un partenariat civil organisé par la loi du Royaume-Uni, notamment au motif que "l'une des caractéristiques définissant le mariage ou l'union fondée sur la loi sur le partenariat civil tient à ce que les formes d'union sont interdites aux personnes qui ont des liens proches de parenté" (para. 62 de l'arrêt)[18].

The General Court interpreted the notion of non-matrimonial partnership by stressing that it need not be equated with marriage nor regulated by law or subject to a registry condition. A stable partner is the term used by the exposition des motifs in the Staff Regulations. All that is required is that the three conditions be met. The Tribunal should not have looked into any comparison of the concrete convention for living together with any form of marriage:

> En effet, eu égard à la grande hétérogénéité des législations nationales en ce qui concerne la mise en place de régimes légaux accordant une reconnaissance juridique à diverses formes d'union autres que le mariage, la notion de "fonctionnaire enregistré comme partenaire stable non matrimonial", visée dans la première phrase de l'article 1er, paragraphe 2, sous c), de l'annexe VII du statut, ne saurait en tant que telle être interprétée comme se référant à un régime de "partenariat enregistré" clairement identifié dans l'ensemble des États membres, lequel correspondrait en l'occurrence, en droit néerlandais, au *geregistreerd partnerschap*. Sous cet aspect, et à ce stade de l'évolution des divers systèmes juridiques nationaux, la notion de "partenariat enregistré" se distingue ainsi de celle de "mariage", dont le contour est clairement déterminé dans l'ensemble des États membres, ce qui a permis au juge communautaire de définir la notion de mariage visée dans le statut comme désignant exclusivement un rapport fondé sur le mariage civil au sens traditionnel du terme (arrêt du Tribunal du 28 janvier 1999, D/Conseil, T-264/97, Rec. FP p. I-A-1 et II-1, point 26)[19].

This concept is found to be compatible with the notion developed by the ECHR in the mentioned *Burden* case because the Staff Regulations rule out any close parenthood between the partners. And it is telling in itself that the General Court should be aware of the need to reach an

18 Paragraph 55 of the judgment, not available in English yet.

19 Paragraph 75 of the judgment, not available in English at the time of writing.

interpretation cohering with that of the Strasbourg Court. It is true that the convention for living together can cover other forms of union which do not fulfil the three conditions of the Staff Regulations and that would not satisfy the *Burden* principle, but that is for the Commission to control in each case by looking not at the terms or definitions or qualifications given by the laws of the Member States but rather at the three conditions imposed by EU law. In other words, the law-applying and law-interpreting authority need not look beyond the notions and concepts used by the Staff Regulations which have expressly contemplated the plurality or diversity of forms of union or partnerships between persons. In other words, to paraphrase the view of the Court, formalism would be the correct approach for the judge when the legislator has already incorporated pluralism or reasonable recognition, but flexibility and accommodation can be an acceptable approach when the legislator has not thought of the diversity of forms of union.

Conclusion: Legal Pluralism vs. Reasonable Accommodation

While being fully aware of the impossibility to infer any, even provisional non-falsified statements from only two cases, I would still argue that the European approach to cultural diversity is systemic, combining the levels of legislation and application. The Courts do not, indeed cannot, impose any specific version of legal pluralism; that would be something, if at all, for the legislator to do at the level of the sources or of their recognition. The Strasbourg Court does not tell Spain that it should recognise gypsy marriages.

In the strict sense of the term, or the focal meaning, legal pluralism implies two claims: (1) the existence of different institutional normative orders applying simultaneously in the same territory or jurisdiction and to the same society and (2) possibly offering different normative solutions to the same type of problems[20]. The first claim is arguable and plausible within law. At most, it would involve different legal orders coordinated by shared, albeit permanently contested, meta-principles. It is hotly debated within internal legal culture – from constitutional scholars to judges and administrators – whether such situations of contested claims necessarily require a final answer and who should provide it. Constitutional pluralism of the type predicated of a post-national legal constellation like the EU would postulate the desirability of not deciding, once and for all, on

20 On legal pluralism see Wolkmer, Antonio Carlos, *Pluralismo Jurídico. Fundamentos de una nueva cultura del Derecho*, Sevilla, Mad-Eduforma, 2006, and the preliminary study by Sánchez Rubio, David, "Estudio preliminar".

the issue of ultimate authority, but rather leaving it open[21]. One can discuss whether these co-existing legal orders are then to be grouped and subjected into a higher legal system of EU law, itself perhaps part of the more universal system of international law, in Kelsenian vein, or whether it is the state legal systems that having created the supra-national and international legal orders that would retain original authority and sovereignty. This pluralist debate can be extended, perhaps even more convincingly, to the European Convention of Human Rights[22].

The debate is mostly academic. Rather than instances of this constitutional pluralism of co-ordinated legal orders competing for primacy and ultimate authority in practice one tends to find more concrete manifestations of pluralism in areas like family law, more generally in the law of persons and the law of things, or commercial law and other fields[23]. The second claim of legal pluralism seems to rule out any possibility of coordination between incompatible norms. Such coordination would require accepting different personal status depending on the fact of belonging to one ethnic, national, linguistic, religious, social minority or another. Many non-Western systems accept or recognise such pluralism[24]. But this pluralism of personal status will not be considered a valid concept of law in contemporary Western societies characterised by cultural plurality[25].

In my opinion, the interesting question for contemporary European socio-legal studies of Legal Pluralism is not so much to enquire what are the attitudes of the legal actors in the face of different legal orders competing in pluralism – an aspect which can be worth pursuing, if at all, from a constitutional point of view – but rather what are the attitudes to these concrete manifestations or expressions or pluralistic phenomena in a context where official state law still dominates the elaboration and application of law and the internal legal cultures. Such specific expressions

---

21 Thus, Aida Torres (*Conflicts of Rights in the European Union*, Oxford, Oxford University Press, 2009), passim, favours a constitutional pluralist framework of interdependent legal orders with no hierarchy between the foundational texts of national and supranational norms.

22 Cormac MacAmlaigh holds that domestic courts can claim that they are upholding the values of the Convention while disagreeing with the Strasbourg Court's interpretation thereof ("Questioning Constitutional Pluralism", *University of Edinburgh School of Law Working Paper Series*, nº 17, 2011, p. 30).

23 See Neil MacCormick's fantastic work *Institutions of Law*, *op. cit.*, for a modern definition of the law of persons, of things, of wrongs, etc.

24 Werner Menski, in his many interesting works, hints at this personal status pluralism as a viable solution for some multicultural conflicts. See e.g. "Flying Kites in a Global Sky: New Models of Jurisprudence", *Socio-Legal Review*, vol. 7, 2011, pp. 1-22

25 It was expressly ruled out by the ECHR in *Refah Partisi*, cases Nº 41340/98, 41342/98, 41343/98, Judgment of 13-02-2003.

of pluralistic phenomena are linked to cultural plurality or diversity and the results in the law deliver results such as accommodation formulae: e.g. when the EU legislator adopts the Staff Regulations recognising a variety of forms of partnerships or unions. But when the legislator fails or decides not to accommodate[26], then the interpreter will have a second chance to apply (reasonable) accommodation, cultural defences as developed in cultural jurisprudence, sensitivity, empathy, or equity. In either case, the accommodation is performed into or unto official law.

If Spanish authorities – Social Security officials, Madrid's Higher Court of Justice and Constitutional Court – had been coherent with or sensitive to the European Framework Convention for the Protection of Minorities[27] they would have taken into account applicant Muñoz Diaz's good faith and considered the importance of gypsy weddings in her community, as a social norm to which other authorities of that State – civil registry, social services – had given due consideration and effects for other legally relevant purposes like issuing the Family Book or recognising the large family status. Menski reports on a similar case in the UK[28] where an unregistered religious Sikh marriage in the UK in the 1950s created a legal status equivalent to marriage under English law entitling the widow to pension rights. For Menski, in this decision, the Court of Appeal "ultimately achieved a just and fair outcome by applying principles of equity, certainly not uniformising equality"[29].

---

26 "It is widely felt that a regime allowing specific religious/cultural minorities to follow their specific proper personal law, like family law, and on that basis to be recognized as married, divorced, etc. in the Dutch legal order on a par with the dominant family law should not be introduced in the Netherlands, partly for a host of practical reasons, but more fundamentally because then the state would have to define what groups qualify as religious/cultural communities which it is not the function of the secular state to determine. As is clear, in individual cases and within the boundaries of fundamental principles, legal pluralism is not principally rejected" (Van Rossum, Wibo, "Dutch Judges Deciding Multicultural Cases" in Fred Bruinsma and David Nelken (eds.), *Explorations in Legal Culture*, The Hague, Elsevier, 2007, p. 62).

27 See the article by the former Deputy President of the Framework Convention's Advisory Committee, Lidija R. Basta Fleiner, "Participation Rights under the Framework Convention for the Protection of National Minorities: towards a legal framework against social and economic discrimination" in *Institutional accommodation and the citizen: legal and political interaction in a pluralist society*, Strasburg, Council of Europe Publishing, 2009, pp. 67-83.

28 *Chief Adjudication Officer v. Bath* 2000 (1) FLR 8.

29 Menski, Werner, "Asking for the Moon: Legal Uniformity in India from a Kerala perspective", Paper presented at the Max Plank Institut in Halle on 13 September 2012. Cited by permission of the author.

Equity[30], empathy[31], sensitivity or reasonable accommodation[32] here require going beyond the formalism of State official law monism and to an awareness of legal pluralist phenomena that may have a bearing on equal treatment and the prohibition of discrimination. A certain attitude is expected from the law-interpreters and from officials to be able to modulate the formalism of legal decision-making in the making of administrative and judicial individual norms in order to take into account the particulars of the situation, especially in hard cases: respect for cultural norms; awareness to cultural, social and personal differences; and preserving the dignity and autonomy of the person throughout.

Similarly, all institutions of democratic states must ensure all persons take part in the life of the community (equal and active citizenship), while taking due account (recognition) of their diversity and difference. Equity in some way departs from equality because it involves sensitivity to difference. Religious, linguistic, cultural, ethnic, and social differences may sometimes require different treatment but it may not always be possible to identify those situations beforehand in the making of universal norms[33]. This is the

---

30 We cannot here develop this concept introduced by the Roman law pretors and authors (Cicero, "summum ius, summa iniuria", *De oficiis*, I. p. 33) and by the Middle Ages scholastics, cannonists and glosastors inspired by the rediscovery of Aristotle, and to some extent by the English Common lawyers to distinguish it from the Common Law, but not the way it later developed in the Chancery Courts. See Aquinas, Thomas, *Summa Theologiae*, 2a 2ae 60.5. See generally Kelly, John Maurice, *A Short History of Western Legal Theory*, Oxford, Clarendon Press, 1992, Chapter on "Greek Philosophy and Roman Equity".

31 When nominating Sonia Sotomayor to the Supreme Court, President Obama suggested that a sense of empathy might make for a better judge. See Stone, Geoffrey, "Our Fill-in-the-Blank Constitution", *The New York Times*, April 14 2010: "empathy helps judges understand the aspirations of the framers, who were themselves determined to protect the rights of political, religious, racial and other minorities. Second, it helps judges understand the effects of the law on the real world. Think of judicial decisions that have invalidated laws prohibiting interracial marriage, granted hearings to welfare recipients before their benefits could be terminated, forbidden forced sterilization of people accused of crime, protected the rights of political dissenters and members of minority religious faiths, guaranteed a right to counsel for indigent defendants and invalidated laws denying women equal rights under the law. In each of these situations, in order to give full and proper meaning to the Constitution it was necessary and appropriate for the justices to comprehend the effect that the laws under consideration had, or could have, on the lives of real people".

32 See the Bouchard-Taylor Commission (www.accommodements.qc.ca) and the first case *Ontario Commission of Human Rights and Theresa O'Malley (Vincent) v. Simpsons-Sears Ltd.*, [1985] 2. SCR 536 although similar developments had taken place in the USA in the field of labour relations.

33 Bossset, Pierre and Marie-Claire Foblets, "Accommodating diversity in Quebec and Europe: different legal concepts, similar results?" in *Institutional accommodation and the citizen: legal and political interaction in a pluralist society*, Strasburg, Council of Europe Publishing, 2009, pp. 37-65.

rationale behind equity: if the legislative were to face the particular situation, the hard case the judge is facing, it would have modulated the law in a special way to take account of the particulars. But the legislative has only given general norms and principles and general criteria for guidance. These general norms have to be applied in the instant cases by administrators and ultimately by judges. The judge would then become a sensitive, interstitial legislator and would modulate the rigid interpretation of the law.

This special accommodating attitude facilitates the adoption of a monist standpoint by the legal system and the respect for the cherished unity of the rule of recognition and the sources, while still striving to achieve equity and justice in the individual hard cases[34]. This seems to be the message sent by the Strasbourg Court in some, not all[35], of its judgments concerning cultural pluralism. In our discussed case, *Muñoz Díaz*, the Court did not require the recognition of gypsy weddings as a valid form of marriage in Spanish law. It imposed no legal pluralism on the legislator[36], but called special awareness to the attitudes of the actors in the legal field. This will require special practical argumentation, reasoning and specialised legal techniques but furthermore it requires a special attitude on the part of the judges[37]. As the former President of the Human Rights Court of Quebec, Michèle Rivet, has put it, courts must assume this idea of diversity and social change in their reasoning, seeking a balance between the values of autonomy, dignity, equality, and security and this requires the judge to cultivate the virtue of openness and readiness to listen[38].

---

34 "Even in the attenuated form of a simple dialogue between state and religious systems of rules, the issues raised by legal pluralism are quite distinct from those connected with the duty to accommodate, which in principle simply requires institutions' rules and practices to be adjusted in individual cases to redress established forms of discrimination. This does not imply the incorporation of the principles of religious law into the law of the land" (Bosset and Foblets, *op. cit*., p. 41).

35 Comp with, e.g. *Leyla Sahin v. Turkey*, 2005-XI ECtHR 173.

36 Indeed, the ECtHR is not keen on legal pluralism at all; see *Refah Partisi*, cases N° 41340/98, 41342/98, 41343/98, Judgment of 13-02-2003.

37 An idea also expressed by Tariq Ramadan: "[…] we also have to have a positive state of mind *vis-à-vis* pluralism in our societies: the same text read by a legal professional (a lawyer or judge, or even by a parliament) having a positive and confident view of diversity will tend to be interpreted in a receptive and inclusive way whereas if it is read through the prism of mistrust of the new citizens, their religion and/or their culture, it will be interpreted in a restrictive way as a means of protection, and on occasion exclusion. These phenomena […] are not always intentional" ("Accommodations for minorities or accommodations for all. Bringing about harmonious coexistence in pluralist societies" in *Institutional accommodation and the citizen: legal and political interaction in a pluralist society*, Strasburg, Council of Europe Publishing, 2009, p. 163).

38 Rivet, Michèle, "Introduction" in Myriam Jézéquiel (ed.), *La justice à l'épreuve de la diversité culturelle*, Cowansville, Éditions Yvon Blais, 2007, p. 15.

CHAPTER 11

Interculturalism and Republicanism

Is Dialogue Possible?[1]

María Isabel WENCES

Professor of Political Science, Carlos III University of Madrid

Introduction

The goal of this chapter is to explore possible paths toward convergence between a particular type of republicanism – inclusive pluralistic republicanism – and the Quebec model of integrating and managing cultural diversity known as interculturalism. The prospects for finding points of convergence through dialogue trace back, on the one hand, to characteristics such as liberty as non-domination or non-dependence, civic virtue, cooperative behavior, a commitment to the common good, and the vindication of politics and deliberative ideals, which are typical of republicanism; on the other hand, they may be found in characteristics such as pluralism and the resulting respect for diversity, integration based on reciprocity and deliberation, recognition of and respect for difference, the doctrine of reasonable accommodation and practice of intercultural reconciliation and the emphasis on social cohesion. In addition to this first level of analysis which attempts to make connections between two political theories, there is a secondary level that is of an empirical nature; this focuses on the consultation of citizens realized within the framework of the Bouchard-Taylor Commission[2], since it allows us to

1 This chapter was produced under the auspices of the I+D+i Research and Development Project, "The Law and Social Construction of Identity," financed by the Ministry of Science and Innovation within National Plan I+D, file number DER2009-12683. The author would like to thank Alain-G. Gagnon for assistance given during her Summer 2012 research residency at the Chaire de recherche du Canada en études québécoises et canadiennes (CREQC), Université du Québec in Montreal (UQAM).

2 The Bouchard-Taylor Commission was set up in 2007 by the Quebec government to examine how to accommodate requests for religious and cultural adjustments emanating from minority groups in the province.

observe, in a specific sociopolitical context, how a process of searching for ways to manage cultural diversity crystallizes into the proposal for an interculturalism that, from my point of view, carries implicit republican connotations.

1. What Republicanism? What Interculturalism?

Republicanism is a long-established tradition of political thought, developed in various cultural and political contexts with multiple interpretations. Considering the possible models of republicanism, the one that interests me here is the republicanism that is pluralistic, from the cultural point of view, and democratic, from the political perspective. These axes, cultural and political, shape different modalities of republicanism. According to Andrés de Francisco, regarding the cultural axis, republicanism ranges from pluralist to communitarian extremes. The political axis of republicanism situates oligarchy on one extreme and democracy on the other. On the oligarchic side, the citizenry is civically weak, while on the democratic side, it is robust and strong. De Francisco combines these two axes and obtains the following modalities: (a) pluralist oligarchic republicanism; (b) communitarian oligarchic republicanism; (c) communitarian democratic republicanism; and (d) pluralist democratic republicanism[3]. This last modality, with some nuances I will specify below, is the one that can, in my opinion, establish a productive dialogue with the interculturalism with which it will find special points of convergence, while maintaining difference in other arenas.

Pluralist republicanism feels "comfortable in culturally open societies"; it accept the plurality of conceptions about goodness and the good life, without that signifying that it advocates neutrality. It accepts difference and dissent without fear, which makes it inclusive. In other words, the republicanism that is of interest here, in addition to being pluralist, distances itself from assimilationism and opens its doors to diversity. In contrast, communitarian republicanism is static and clearly inclined toward a "more homogenous, culturally closed and self-referencing republic"[4]. Inclusive pluralist republicanism shares with its republican family the commitment to political equality, public deliberation, the

---

3 Republicanism is democratic, De Francisco affirms, when it attempts to fully incorporate the less powerful and more vulnerable in civil society with the goal of making them free; it is pluralist when it attempts "to incorporate the greatest number of ideas of the good society into the public sphere of political deliberation and to incorporate different forms of private life into a reasonably well integrated framework of social coexistence" (De Francisco, Andrés, *La mirada republicana*, Madrid, Catarata, 2012, p. 48).

4 *Ibid.*, p. 46.

need for virtue and the vindication of politics. But unlike some members of the family, it is dynamic, it recognizes that diversity is an inherent factor in our societies, and it does not resist cultural change. As a result, it places into question the model of the indivisible republic and endemic uniformity. Following this logic, the republicanism that is inclusive and pluralist does not believe there are justifiable reasons that some cultures, such as subnational or minority cultures, are more or less relevant than the national or majority culture, such as the culture of French republicanism[5].

Therefore, the republicanism I refer to in this chapter does not represent a singular, hegemonic vision; neither am I referring to the French model where "beneath the brilliant surface of the republican universalism of rights, the nationalist particularism of cultural assimilationism operated in the shadows"[6].

The term "Interculturalism", whether referring to a political project or a theoretical assumption, is being used here to signify a model for integrating and managing ethnocultural diversity based on the pluralist ideal. These two attributes, integration and diversity, are essential and converge through a dynamic of respectful interaction with the *Other* and a rejection of all discrimination based on difference. When we talk about integration, it is useful to have a very clear understanding of its meaning in order to avoid mistaken interpretations. The integration that interests us here has an inclusive dimension and is accompanied by two key points. On the one hand, it maintains that everyone must have equal conditions for debate in the public sphere, which means rejecting the idea that the majority group determines the playing field, establishes the rules of the game and adopts final decisions. On the other, integration should not be confused with providing all community members with identical points of reference, which would mark it as exclusive. Instead, it advocates for the recognition of minorities. This would mean that care must be taken when defending the supposed neutrality of the state since it conceals in most cases, beneath the umbrella of a series of policies, the hegemony of the majority group.

Both factors, integration and diversity, are found at the heart of the proposal for interculturalism in Quebec that "fosters the edification of a common identity through interaction between citizens of all origins"[7].

5 Laborde, Cécile, "The Culture(s) of the Republic. Nationalism and Multiculturalism in French Republican Thought", *Political Theory*, vol. 29, nº 5, 2001, pp. 716-735.

6 Máiz, Ramón, "Nacionalismo e inmigración en Francia: *La république une et indivisible* y el *affaire du foulard*," *Revista de estudios políticos (nueva época)*, nº 129, 2005, p. 25.

7 Bouchard, Gérard and Charles Taylor, *Building the Future: A Time for Reconciliation: Report*, Consultation Commission on Accommodation Practices Related to Cultural Differences, Les Publications du Québec, 2008, p. 88. The full report in English can be consulted at [Online]: http://collections.banq.qc.ca/ark:/52327/bs1565996.

For Gérard Bouchard and Charles Taylor, this interculturalism – also called integration through pluralism, since it supports the respect for diversity – cultivates a pluralistic focus that is deeply sensitive to the protection of rights. It preserves the tension between diversity, on the one hand, and the continuity of the French-speaking core and social cohesion on the other. It places particular emphasis on integration, celebrating interactive practices and encouraging the development of a feeling of belonging. To the extent that this process has been developing, cultural difference survives through respectful interaction with the Other and the recognition of diversity as a right that establishes a balance, which must always be dynamic, between integration, inclusion and diversity[8]. As a consequence of the interaction between distinct cultural groups, it is assumed that cultural identity will be transformed.

This model attempts to offer solutions to the challenge of reconciling an identity, with French as its linguistic base, while maintaining high respect for minorities and the diversity that comes from immigration. The ultimate goal is to develop a framework that assures social cohesion. In order to achieve this, common values should be promoted, individual liberties and respect for equality between men and women should be guaranteed, pluralism should be accepted, inclusion should be encouraged and the democratic mechanism of participation and public deliberation should be consolidated.

From the political point of view, interculturalism has not been officially adopted – by law or by constitutional recognition, for example – by the government of Quebec, which sometimes generates confusion as to its significance and scope[9]. However, we should not forget that Quebec has, with varied degrees of success, been equipping itself over time with policies to manage diversity, similar to the policies we have previously discussed. This distances them, in a normative fashion, from the traditional assimilationist model of the United States' familiar *melting-pot*, from Canadian multiculturalism, from ethnic communitarianism and from the French republican model. What we have here are the first steps toward inclusive pluralist republicanism.

---

8 Bouchard, Gérard and Charles Taylor, *Accommodation and Differences: Seeking Common Ground. Quebecers Speak Out*, Québec, Gouvernement du Québec, 2007, p. 21. See also Gérard Bouchard's chapter in this book.

9 See Rocher, François and Micheline Labelle, "L'interculturalisme comme modèle d'aménagement de la diversité: compréhension et incompréhension dans l'espace publique québécois" in Bernard Gagnon (ed.), *La diversité québécoise en débat. Bouchard, Taylor et les autres*, Montréal, Éditions Québec Amérique, 2010, pp. 179-203. Since Pauline Marois won the election on 4 September 2012, there could be a change in the previous position on officially adopting interculturalism.

This chapter focuses on what we believe could be three axes of convergence or points of encounter between inclusive pluralist republicanism and interculturalism. The first is the axis of liberty as non-dependence; the second, the axis of civic virtue and the commitment to the common good; the third, the axis of the deliberative ideal and participatory citizenship. To show the viability of this last connection or point of encounter for dialogue, reference is made to the process of citizen consultation carried out by the Bouchard-Taylor Commission.

2. Axis of Liberty as Non-dependence

In recent decades and after experiencing an unexpected resurgence, numerous neo-republican political theorists, even when they present differentiated profiles, have made the wise decision to once again place on the table the discussion about the political freedom of citizens, simultaneously emphasizing the rejection of any form of subjugation, not only from a historical perspective, but also as a fundamental philosophical project whose transcendence is not circumstantial[10].

Quentin Skinner, the well-known intellectual historian, an expert on early modern Europe's republican ideals, has delved deeply into the hegemony of the liberal paradigm and several of his works focus on presenting arguments in favor of a third concept of liberty or, more specifically, in favor of a non-conventional reading of negative liberty[11]. We are confronting schools of thought that discuss the same concept of liberty but have competing theories about what it means to be a free, autonomous agent.

In accordance with the neo-Roman theory of liberty that Skinner defends, our understanding of liberty can be different than the one

---

10 For contemporary republicans "the task is not simply one of excavation. History does not supply conceptions of political life that can be applied mechanically to current problems" (Sunstein, Cass R., "Beyond the Republican Revival", *Yale Law Journal*, vol. 97, 1988, p. 1539). However, Skinner successfully illustrated that only if we are capable of reconstructing the theories of the past on their own terms will we be able to discover the reasons why some traditions, e.g., liberalism, have become hegemonic while others, e.g., republicanism, have been neutralized.

11 The third concept references Isaiah Berlin's classic dichotomous taxonomy. Skinner believes this division, which was originally presented as a methodological approach, has led to a misrepresentation and weakening of the vision of liberty. In Skinner's words: "I agree with Berlin that there are two concepts of liberty, one positive and the other negative, I do not agree with his further assumption that, whenever we speak about negative liberty, we must be speaking about absence of interference. It seems to me that, as I have tried to show, we have inherited two rival and incommensurable theories of negative liberty, although in recent times we have generally contrived to ignore one of them" ("A Third Concept of Liberty", *Proceedings of the British Academy*, vol. 117, 2002, p. 237).

propagated by the liberal tradition, where liberty implied a lack of coercion of the individual by other individuals or groups. In contrast, for the older tradition, individuals are also deprived of liberty if they live in conditions where they depend on other people's good will. It is important to fully elucidate this detail in order to avoid mistaken interpretations. The conception of liberty that is defended by neo-Romans is characterized by the absence of constriction, but this constriction is caused not only by interference, but also by dependence. Therefore, individuals are free when they act without impediments and when they do not depend on other people's possible good will. There is the possibility that in certain circumstances some individuals or groups do not impose impediments on others, but those who have the potential, or a greater degree of potential, for being hindered will always confront the threat that those obstacles or certain coercive practices will appear. In the same way, a community cannot consider itself free to the extent that it finds itself in a situation of dependence on the will of a neighbor community when it comes to making decisions because that means it is unable to govern itself. In republican thinking, liberty is closely tied to self-government; it requires, in other words, the presence of a political community capable of controlling its own future.

Skinner believes that while, for liberalism, coercion or the threat of the use of coercion "constitute the only forms of constraint that interfere with individual liberty," for the authors he calls neo-Romans, "to live in a condition of dependence is in itself a source and a form of constraint"[12]. In this sense, liberty consists of people not feeling threatened by possible obstacles, impositions or the subjugation of others; in other words, they do not find themselves in a situation of dependence or subjection regarding an arbitrary volition. Following this logic, "the opposite of liberty is not *coercion*, but *dependence*. Being *free*, then, is not a *circumstance* (not being forced to do or not do something) but a *structural condition*: we stop being free as soon as we find ourselves in a position that makes us susceptible to being subjugated to someone else's control"[13].

In short, the republican political doctrine defends a compression of liberty as non-dependence (Quentin Skinner) or non-domination (Philip Pettit), which means a more reliable form of protection in the face of interference. Honohan provides a useful explanation by noting that it is not strictly a question of defying acts of interference, but combating the state of subordination that makes those acts possible. The political

12 Skinner, Quentin, *Liberty before Liberalism*, Cambridge, Cambridge University Press, 1988, p. 84.

13 Palti, Elías, "Ideas políticas e historia intelectual: Texto y contexto en la obra reciente de Quentin Skinner," *Prismas. Revista de historia intelectual*, nº 3, 1999, pp. 263-274.

implications of this conception of liberty are reflected in the demands for a collection of institutions that provide guarantees in the face of illegitimate interference, in such a way that citizens are not dominated and are able to act in an independent fashion[14]. This means that institutions should assure the independence of individuals and safeguard non-domination.

This republican principle is found among others at the heart of the defense of what are called reasonable accommodations. The point of encounter between republicanism and interculturalism is not the demand that citizens' individual identities should be recognized by the State; what has become important is that they not be dependent or dominated, either by members of their own community or by majority society. This requires, in turn, that equality be interpreted beyond its mere formal connotation.

Given the importance of this matter in our discourse, let us analyze it in more detail. It is possible to make a distinction between the legal norms that contain neutral and universal principles (for example, the equality of the sexes) and the norms and rules that reproduce the values and implicit norms of the majority culture (for example, the clothes women "should" wear). Regarding the first principle, both republicanism and interculturalism coincide in that they admit no possibility for exceptions or accommodation; while the second proposition is accompanied by a weaker type of normative force since it depends on a specific cultural context. This preoccupation with distinguishing between the universal and the particular – absent in other republicanisms – is found in inclusive pluralist republicanism; reasonable accommodations are compatible with a republicanism that knows that the public sphere is not culturally and religiously neutral and that we must adopt measures to express plurality. No one will claim, for example, that it makes sense to establish neutral policies regarding the language used for utilities, the courts, Parliament or schools. A political community cannot be completely neutral from the cultural point of view given that the norms of public life inevitably have a historic origin and emanate as a general rule from the cultural group that is in the majority. If the law is not neutral from the cultural and religious point of view[15], certain reasonable accommodations in favor of members of minorities could be considered demands for non-interference

---

14 Honohan, Iseult, *Civic Republicanism*, London and New York, Routledge, 2002.

15 If the norm of cultural neutrality is impossible to apply in practice, we should distinguish cultural neutrality from axiological neutrality: "The imperative of State neutrality requires that the State be neutral, not regarding public culture or language, but regarding citizens' axiological positions, regarding their profound beliefs of a religious, moral or philosophical nature" (Courtois, Stéphane, "Le Québec face au pluralisme: un plaidoyer pour l'interculturalisme", *Argument*, vol. 13, n° 1, 2010, pp. 101-113.

and the reestablishment of equality[16]. In order to better understand these affirmations, we must address the question of reasonable accommodations more in depth.

An essential characteristic of all democratic societies is establishing the conditions to eliminate all forms of discrimination and, in culturally diverse societies, this includes discriminations that stem from cultural differences. In the face of the doctrine that decrees uniform application of the law, there is an alternative doctrine that enables a type of flexibility, the flexibility of reasonable accommodations, meant to combat any type of discriminatory condition caused by the strict application of a norm whose effects, in some cases, can be to undermine citizens' rights to equality. The accommodation imperative is a particular modality of a legal obligation whose goal is to guarantee the exercise of the right to equality among individuals who belong to particular categories of citizens, often minority groups.

Reasonable accommodations are the legal consequence of understanding the principle of equality as a demand that allows differential treatment without it necessarily being interpreted as preferential. Gérard Bouchard, in his "What Is Interculturalism?"[17] which is reproduced in English in this book, emphasizes that accommodations are not privileges, they have not been conceived only for immigrants, and they do not give free rein to values, beliefs or practices that are contrary to a society's fundamental norms. The goal is that all citizens enjoy the same rights, regardless their cultural background.

This way of understanding equality also has its corollary in political theory, especially among the defenders of the paradigm of recognition; the proposal interprets recognition as a continuous dialogue. In an effort to reach agreement, the axis of reciprocity runs throughout the proposal. An ethics of recognizing minority cultures and difference constitutes not only a moral and political demand but also a matter of social justice[18].

16 Laborde, Cécile, *Critical Republicanism. The Hijab Controversy and Political Philosophy*, Oxford, Oxford University Press, 2008.

17 Bouchard, Gérard, "What is Interculturalism?", *McGill Law Journal*, vol. 56 nº 2, 2011, pp. 435-468 and reproduced in this volume.

18 Representative thinkers include Joseph Carens, Nancy Fraser, Bhikhu Parekh, Charles Taylor, James Tully and Iris Marion Young. See especially Carens, Joseph, *Culture, Citizenship, and Community*, Oxford, Oxford University Press, 2000; Fraser, Nancy, *Scales of Justice, Reimagining Political Space in a Globalizing World*, New York, Columbia University Press, 2009; Fraser, Nancy, "Identity, Exclusion and Critique. A Response to Four Critiques", *European Journal of Political Theory*, nº 6, 2007, pp. 305-338; Fraser, Nancy and Axel Honneth, *Redistribution or Recognition? A Political Philosophical Exchange*, London, Verso, 2003; Parekh, Bhikhu, *Rethinking Multiculturalism: Cultural Diversity and Political Theory*, Cambridge, Harvard University Press, 2002; Parekh, Bhikhu, *A New Politics of Identity: Political Principles*

One of the background debates in which these authors are immersed is the consideration that faithfulness to the principle of equality means contemplating it with a view to a principle of equalization between groups, cultures and territories. Numerous norms that are apparently neutral and universal reproduce visions of the world, values, implicit codes or informal rules that are not explicitly formulated, but are extended and applied. The same right can sometimes lead to two different responses when it is a question of correcting a failure in the application of a law or rule, and this should not be interpreted as assigning privileges. For that reason, we affirm that treatments can be differential without being preferential[19]. The footnoted authors believe the model of integration that is configured according to abstract principles of homogeneity and equality is outdated. They are looking for a model of equality that can be realized within recognized difference. To advance in the logic of equality, we must value differences. To assure individual liberties, we must respect cultural plurality. For that reason, Maclure asserts that accommodations and the corresponding public policies of cultural diversity that follow these same principles can be considered "morally just and politically judicious"[20]. It is worth emphasizing that in recent articles, some authors have noted that a politics of recognition is now a necessary condition for culturally diverse democracies, but it is insufficient for attempting to deepen democratic quality[21].

Reasonable accommodation is a formula the courts apply when they need to resolve conflicts stemming from religious practices concerning dress codes, vacation days, work schedules or places of worship, which has made it a very useful tool for managing diversity[22]. If the goal is to

---

for an Interdependent World, Basingstoke, Palgrave Macmillan, 2008; Taylor, Charles, *Sources of the Self: The Making of Modern Identity*, Harvard University Press, 1989; Taylor, Charles, "The Politics of Recognition" in Amy Gutmann (ed.), *Multiculturalism. Examining the Politics of Recognition*, Princeton, Princeton University Press, 1994; Tully, James, *Strange Multiplicity: Constitutionalism in an Age of Diversity*, Cambridge, Cambridge University Press, 1995; Tully, James, "Introduction" in Alain-G. Gagnon and James Tully (eds.), *Multinational Democracies*, Cambridge, Cambridge Universities Press, 2001, pp. 1-34; Young, Iris Marion, *Justice and the Politics of Difference*, Princeton, Princeton University Press, 1990; Young, Iris Marion, *Inclusion and Democracy*, Oxford, Oxford University Press, 2000.

19 Parekh, Bhikhu, *Rethinking Multiculturalism: Cultural Diversity and Political Theory*, Cambridge, Harvard University Press, 2002.

20 Maclure, Jocelyn, "Une défense du multiculturalisme comme principe de morale politique" in Myriam Jézéquel (ed.), *La justice à l'épreuve de la diversité culturelle*, Montreal, Éditions Yvon Blais, 2007, p. 77.

21 Gagnon, Alain-G., *L'Âge des incertitudes: essais sur le fédéralisme et la diversité nationale*, Québec, Presses de l'Université Laval, 2011.

22 Anctil, Pierre, "Quel accommodement raisonnable?" *Éthique Publique*, vol. 29, nº 1, 2007, pp. 186-191.

regulate discrepancies and arrive at resolutions founded on the principle of equality in difference, then we have an instrument that facilitates integration, even when its first vocation is to avoid discrimination[23]. Woehrling makes a similar point when he notes that the primary goal of the politics of accommodation is

> to favor the *inclusion* of minorities and immigrants in the host society, especially by freeing them from the norms that entail direct or indirect discrimination. The politics of accommodation and pluralism are sustained on the commitment that the recognition of difference and adaptations that are afforded minorities will facilitate, in the medium or long term, their harmonious integration into society[24].

Consequently, reasonable accommodations understood from the perspective of interculturalism have no place in a republicanism that defends coercive assimilationism as the route to social coexistence. They can, on the other hand, be a component of the inclusive pluralist republicanism that respects diverse differential characteristics with the goal of having different cultural groups enjoy the same opportunities as the citizens with whom they coexist, opportunities to live the type of life their culture establishes and to not be subject to legal demands that violate their convictions and way of life. Accommodations make sense and acquire legitimacy, Jézéquel affirms, if they are able to "maintain the balance between individual rights and the common good, if they manage to go beyond the commitment to reciprocal tolerance. The education of living together will depend as much on education about the value of accommodations as learning about reciprocal tolerance"[25].

This dialogue between interculturalism and inclusive pluralist republicanism, making use of the vocabulary of reasonable accommodations, is also appreciated by Cécile Laborde in her work "Républicanisme critique vs Républicanisme conservateur: repenser les 'accommodements raisonnables'" ["Critical Republicanism vs. Conservative Republicanism: Rethinking 'Reasonable Compromises'"][26]. In those cases where the law and the public sphere are not culturally and religiously neutral, certain

---

23 Jézéquel, Myriam (ed.), *Les accommodements raisonnables: quoi, comment, jusqu'où? Des outils pour tous*, Montréal, Éditions Yvon Blais, 2007.

24 Woehrling, José, "Neutralité de l'État et accommodements: convergence ou divergence?", *Options Politiques*, vol. 28, n° 8, 2007, p. 25.

25 Jézéquel, Myriam, "L'accommodement à l'épreuve des stratégies identitaires," in Myriam Jézéquel (ed.), *La justice à l'épreuve de la diversité culturelle*, Cowansville, Éditions Yvon Blais, 2006, p. 146.

26 Laborde, Cécile, "Républicanisme critique vs. Républicanisme conservateur: repenser les 'accommodements raisonnables'", *Critique Internationale*, n° 44, 2009, pp. 19-33. For a fuller discussion, see Laborde, *Critical Republicanism. The Hijab Controversy and Political Philosophy*, *op. cit.*, 2008.

reasonable accommodations in favor of minority members can be demands for what the author calls republican justice. Reasonable accommodations, to the extent they try to establish equality, are compatible with what Laborde considers republicanism properly understood; this republicanism comprehends that it is a good idea to take a critical look at its own cultural historical context. This type of critical approximation "has been absent from the republican debate in France," but we find it "at the heart of the redefinition of the doctrine of minority integration in North America, especially Québec"[27].

This approach leads to two questions that are important enough to demand attention. The first has to do with the deciding agent, the person who makes the decisions, regarding the practices of different cultural groups; the second alludes to the procedure, to how decisions are made. In other words, what is the procedure on the basis of which decisions will be adopted?[28] These two questions are present, both in the discussion about who decides which groups/practices are deserving of recognition and accommodation, as well as the identities that are unjustly imposed on members of a political community. The answers that interculturalism affords have a republican flavor. Let us look at the first of these assumptions. Although it is true that cultures should be understood as plural, open and dynamic, that does not mean that accommodations should be assumed in all cases; both the behavior of the host society and that of minority immigrant groups should be perceived as potentially mistaken or in need of alteration. It is unquestionable that cultures are made up of beliefs and principles and that we should not speak in terms of superiority or inferiority, but that does not mean that we have to assume that every component of a given culture has value and that we should try to accommodate any notion; both majority and minority cultures hold beliefs that are indefensible in a democracy and the way to confront them democratically should be criticism and deliberation[29]. The Quebec model of interculturalism insists that, faced with the eventuality of a conflict between individuals and groups, the procedure to resolve it should correspond to democratic norms and especially that "deliberative measures such as mediation, compromise and direct negotiation are preferred,

27 Laborde, *op. cit.*, 2009, p. 20.

28 Tuly, James, "La conception républicaine de la citoyenneté dans les sociétés multiculturelles et multinationales", *Politique et Sociétés*, vol. 20, nº 1, 2001, pp. 123-146.

29 Regarding the debate about the limits of a politics of recognition and the accommodations of cultural and religious diversity, see the arguments presented by Maclure, "Une défense du multiculturalisme comme principe de morale politique", *op. cit.*, pp. 66-90.

leaving as much initiative and autonomy to the parties in question"[30]. In a democratic society, dialogues between a plurality of actors should be carried out in the best possible conditions of non-domination[31].

Cultural identities that are worthy of recognition cannot be determined outside of the political process. There must be negotiation in order to construct agreement between citizens. The path is clearly political, and politics from a republican perspective "is action – the possibility of a shared, collective, deliberate, active intervention in our fate, in what would otherwise be the by-product of private decisions. Only in public life can we jointly, as a community, exercise the human capacity 'to think what we are doing' and take charge of the history in which we are all constantly engaged by drift and inadvertence"[32].

Inclusive pluralist republicanism believes that politics is a continuous activity that opens the door to citizens so they can develop their individual potential and their public vocation. In order to do that, it is necessary that a series of institutional conditions be established to allow the free exercise of civic capabilities, deliberation and responsibility. The reason for this is, in the first place, to let citizens control their representatives and keep watch over the agents in whom they place their confidence if a political task has to be delegated to experts or specialists. Secondly, this will afford citizens the means to demand accountability from those who govern them (recalling that the fundamental reason for this is not to maximize preferences for the majority, but to minimize the risks of tyrannical actions on the part of a government). Lastly, it allows citizens to become jointly responsible for decision making[33]. For the same reasons, Linda Cardinal and Marie-Joie Brady note that the conditions that should exist so that citizens can realize a multi-voiced dialogue in conditions of non-dominance include, in the first place, recognizing the freedom all citizens have to change the rules of the constitutional game of mutual recognition and association as identities are transformed. In the second place, everyone should be able to participate in decision making, since decisions affecting the community must be made, through just and reasonable deliberative measures, by

---

30 Gagnon, Alain-G. and Raffaele Iacovino, "Interculturalism: Expanding the Boundaries of Citizenship" in Ramón Maiz and Ferrán Requejo (eds.), *Democracy, Nationalism and Multiculturalism*, London, Frank Cass Publishers, Routledge, 2005, p. 32.

31 Tully, James, "Introduction" in Alain-G. Gagnon and James Tully (eds.), *Multinational Democracies*, Cambridge, Cambridge University Press, 2001, pp. 1-34.

32 Arendt, Hannah, *The Human Condition*, Chicago, University of Chicago Press, 1958, p. 28.

33 My analysis of this can be found in Wences, Isabel, "Cultura de la legalidad y rendición de cuentas," in Manuel Villoria and Isabel Wences (eds.), *Cultura de la legalidad. Instituciones, procesos y estructuras*, Madrid, Catarata, 2010, pp. 67-88.

all citizens, even when it is known that the opinion of a few may be excluded from the final decision. Nevertheless, "in the context of non-domination […] defeated citizens know that they can eventually restart the multilogue"[34].

The second of the two previously mentioned assumptions – namely, (1) who decides and (2) the procedures used to decide on the identities that are unjustly imposed on members of a political community – leads us to diverse terrain, but here we will briefly turn our attention to the area of national diversity, even though it is a side note to our main idea – which does not mean that it is a minor question. When the issue is how to find the best way to manage not only cultural but also national diversity, accommodation presents various dilemmas, especially if it is a question of the relationship between majority and minority nations, since the recipe of accommodation in this case could lead to the presence of a hierarchical point of view in power relationships that would raise questions about the legitimacy of the political actors. Faced with that possibility, some authors – and even politicians – propose strengthening cooperation in such a way that their life in common affords a relationship of equality where the minority nation is not perceived as a nuisance requesting accommodation, but as a partner with whom one can negotiate and whose relationship rests "on a set of principles that respect community pluralism, ideological pluralism and (why not) even legal pluralism"[35]. What is essential is finding a more harmonious balance among political forces so the inhabitants of minority nations are able to carry out their preferences in a way comparable to majority nations. Alain-G. Gagnon, from the Université du Québec à Montréal, states it clearly: "This quest for balance would contribute to renewed trust between communities as well as empower minority nations to achieve greater emancipation on the cultural, economic, institutional, legal, social and political levels"[36]. This is one of Gagnon's recent projects in political theory: going beyond a politics of recognition, which is limited to the accommodation of nations without altering the vertical dynamic, and imagining a politics of empowerment, allowing minority nations to acquire the instruments

---

[34] Cardinal, Linda and Marie-Joie Brady, "Citizenship and Federalism in Canada: A Difficult Relationship" in Alain-G. Gagnon (ed.), *Contemporary Canadian Federalism: Foundations, Traditions, Institutions*, Toronto, University of Toronto Press, 2009, p. 392.

[35] Gagnon, Alain-G., "Reconciling Autonomy, Community and Empowerment: The Difficult Birth of a Diversity School in the Western World" in Alain-G. Gagnon and Michael Keating (eds.), *Political Autonomy and Divided Societies*, Basingstoke, Palgrave Macmillan, 2012, p. 55.

[36] *Ibid.*, p. 57.

necessary to achieve their full potential, avoiding the loss of social references and the risk of political alienation[37].

We should now question whether this project is in line with a liberal notion of liberty or if it is more comfortable beneath the cloak of liberty in the republican sense that I have outlined here, where non-dependence tries to battle subordination and subjugation to the will of the other, whether they be individuals or communities. The question that Alain-G. Gagnon has posed about how to provide minority nations the guarantee of liberty and force majority nations to take into consideration their legitimate demands, whether it be the right to self-definition, the right to self-representation, the right to self-government or the right to self-determination[38], finds more resonance in the defense of an idea of liberty understood as the absence of dependence in agreement with which actions and decisions do not depend on the will of the other; they are not limited by them. This is confirmed in the following words: "A free state is one which is, in the first place, not subject to coercion, and that is, secondly, ruled by its own volition, understood as the general volition of all the members of the community"[39].

The legal dimension that accompanies reasonable accommodation is recognized in the final report of the Bouchard-Taylor Commission where it is noted that "the duty, under law, makes it the responsibility of the managers of public and private institutions to avoid all forms of discrimination by adopting relaxation or harmonization measures in the administration of certain statutes or regulations"[40]. Still, we must not forget that, when it comes to interculturalism, the indispensable role of the courts must be a last resort since what is essential is laying the foundation so that citizen action can be used in a friendly and informal manner to attempt to resolve disagreements that arise between the personnel of public or private institutions and other citizens.

This premise of interculturalism coincides with the idea of inclusive pluralist republicanism in constructing alternative systems of institutional design that, as Philip Pettit emphasizes, stimulate cooperative behavior by cultivating civic virtue, rather than simply inspiring repressive systems that punish behavior that deviates from the legal norm[41]. Reciprocity and

---

37 Gagnon, Alain-G., *L'Âge des incertitudes: essais sur le fédéralisme et la diversité nationale*, Québec, Les Presses de l'Université Laval, 2011.

38 Gagnon, "Reconciling Autonomy, Community and Empowerment: The Difficult Birth of a Diversity School in the Western World", *op. cit.*, pp. 57-58.

39 Ovejero, Félix, José Luis Martí and Roberto Gargarella, *Nuevas ideas republicanas*, Barcelona, Paidós, 2004, p. 20.

40 Bouchard and Taylor, *op. cit.*, p. 285.

41 Pettit, Philip, *Republicanism*, Oxford, Clarendon Press, 1997. See especially chapter VII.

a willingness to cooperate with others are attitudes and customs whose goal is to serve the common good[42].

3. Axis of Civic Virtue and Commitment to the Common Good

For inclusive pluralist republicanism, talking about civic virtue means talking about civic commitment, which is reflected in the relationship that good citizens maintain with their political community, where there is a strong disposition for preferring the common good over private interests. Civic virtue is the willingness and capacity of citizens to fulfill the responsibility of participating actively and responsibly in the achievement of the good of the entire political community, restricting their individual interests. Only when citizens find something more in the exercise of their civic virtue than a mere instrument to achieve their own private goals can they live worthy and autonomous lives, not as submissive, passive subjects who accept any government suggestion. If people are conscious of their role as creators of a history of public life and they take responsibility for their destiny, they will avoid letting common problems (the environment, security, allocation of resources, the management of diversity, mutual recognition) slip from their control. In this sense, republicans judge the rights and obligations of citizens, which the liberal tradition considers essential for public life, insufficient for living life in common. For republicans, virtues are essential; rights, on the other hand – which enjoy unassailable top-billing for liberals – are subordinated in the republican tradition to the needs of the community[43]. As Skinner rightly affirms, "there can be no individual liberty without civic virtue"[44]. In order to defend a robust idea of liberty – as non-domination, as non-dependence – we need virtuous citizens.

Civic virtue constitutes the cornerstone of public life. However, the list of civic virtues that have been and are exalted by republican thinkers throughout history is rather extensive. It includes prudence, responsibility, honesty, benevolence, moderation, hard work, love of justice, generosity, nobility, political activism and solidarity[45]. Clearly, current republican

42 Dagger, Richard, *Civic Virtues*, Oxford, Oxford University Press, 1997, p. 196.

43 Gargarella, Roberto, "La comunidad igualitaria y sus enemigos. Liberalismo, republicanismo e igualitarismo" in Andrés Hernández (ed.), *Republicanismo contemporáneo. Igualdad, democracia deliberativa y ciudadanía*, Bogotá, Siglo de Hombres Editores and Universidad de los Andes, 2002, p. 93.

44 Skinner, Quentin, "The Republican Ideal of Political Liberty", in Gisela Bock, Quentin Skinner and Maurizio Viroli (eds.), *Machiavelli and Republicanism*, Cambridge, Cambridge University Press, 1990, p. 305.

45 Gargarella, *op. cit.*, p. 91.

theorists do not herald a virtuous, engaged citizenry with all these attitudes and talents; what is important is not losing sight of the fact that "civic virtue has a permanent generic form – the commitment to the public good and the opposition to a particularist life view – but it is made manifest and realized (like any other virtue) according to the circumstances of the situation"[46]. In short, republicanism demands of its members an active commitment to public affairs, which presumes that citizens should direct their actions toward the attainment of the common good. Following this logic, civic virtue "is employed to denote the specter of capacities that each of us should possess as citizens: the capacities that allow us to serve the common good by our own volition"[47].

If we expect citizens, members of majority and minority ethnocultural groups, to act in ways that support civic virtue, it is necessary, from the stand-point of interculturalism, to make sure that institutions and society have established minimum political, economic and social conditions so citizens find ways for integration. But what does it mean to be integrated and, more specifically, to be integrated in an inclusive manner?

In his argument in favor of interculturalism, Alain-G. Gagnon contends that integration is one of the central objectives of interculturalism since it is seen as essential for the political affirmation of ethnocultural groups and for their full participation when a common public culture is being set in motion. Interculturalism is reflected in a particular type of integrating pluralism that is based on the principle of reciprocity and responsibility between new arrivals and those who make up the host society[48]. In this sense, interculturalism is respectful of diversity and cannot be accused of protecting assimilationist whims or of falling victim to the excesses of cultural relativism and the fragmentation of other models of multiculturalism[49]. Clearly, for this to be possible, it is necessary, as Saskia Sassen correctly points out, to pay attention to the demands for visibility made by minorities and the disadvantaged; in the tension between formal nationality and effective citizenry, we find subjects who "are authorized, but not recognized", in other words, full citizens who are not recognized as political actors[50].

46 Peña, Javier, "Ciudadanía republicana y virtud cívica," in María Julia Bertomeu, Antoni Doménech and Andrés de Francisco (eds.), *Republicanismo y democracia*, Buenos Aires, Miño y Dávila, 2005, p. 250.

47 Skinner, Quentin, "Las paradojas de la libertad política" in Félix Ovejero, Jose Luis Martí and Roberto Gargarella (eds.), *Nuevas ideas republicanas*, Barcelona, Paidós, 2004, p. 106.

48 See Gérard Bouchard's analysis in this book.

49 Gagnon, Alain-G., "Plaidoyer pour l'interculturalisme", *Possibles*, nº 24, 2000, pp. 11-25.

50 Sassen, Saskia, *Contrageografías de la globalización. Género y ciudadanía en los circuitos transfronterizos*, Madrid, Traficante de sueños, 2003, p. 88.

Inclusivity emphasizes the promotion and education of committed, participatory citizens and tries to avoid social fragmentation and retreat in search of personal interest, as well as the loss of self-government, scorn for the importance of public service and indifference to political participation. The political philosopher Charles Taylor claims that the identity of individuals constitutes a horizon of shared values. The social framework, ignored by atomism[51], shapes human beings, and their identification with the interests of the community in which they live is essential to maintaining a free society. This society is only possible if citizens make a commitment to the defense of liberty and act with solidarity for the joint endeavor. Politics that emerge from atomist approaches that present citizens as mutually disinterested are not striving for integration and their emphasis is placed on the advancement of citizens who are "indifferent to the global perspective and the impact of their actions on the community"[52].

Some authors might think that these affirmations reflect communitarian republicanism, but as we have tried to show here, inclusive pluralist republicanism promotes conditions so that virtue can be practiced and its action can focus on the public good, but unlike its communitarian counterpart, it does not attempt to defend dense cultural goods.

4. Axis of the Deliberative Ideal and Participatory Citizenship

In the republican family, there are notable differences regarding institutional proposals, but there is a consensus about the importance of the deliberative ideal[53].

The deliberative dimension in the republican sense is essential to the politics of inclusion because faced with the imposition of a uniform idea of equality or a closed and unquestionable version of the national majority culture, there is an institutionalization of the process. This allows us, first, to debate the features of majority and minority cultures and, secondly, to discuss and reach agreement about the conditions of coexistence, and finally, to find the means for coexistence between distinct and at times covert identities.

---

51 Taylor, Charles, "Atomism" in *Philosophy and the Human Sciences Philosophical Papers. Vol. 2*, Cambridge, Cambridge University Press, 1985, chapter VII.

52 Taylor, Charles, "Liberal Politics and the Public Sphere" in *Philosophical Arguments*, Cambridge, London, Harvard University Press, 1995, p. 282.

53 Pettit, Philip, *Republicanism*, Oxford, Clarendon Press, 1997; Sunstein, Cass, *Republica.com*, New Jersey, Princeton University Press; Skinner, *Liberty before Liberalism*, *op. cit.*

The ideal of open and public discussion, as befits the citizens of an inclusive pluralist republican citizenry, can, in modern culturally heterogeneous societies, find ways of connecting with the principles of difference. This presupposes, Ramón Máiz emphasizes, passing from a communitarian concept of the nation to a cultural political (or civic ethnic) concept. The pluralist and democratic nature of this concept should be accompanied by a principle of deliberation in whose public sphere the doors are open to the inclusion of distinct modes of life that are conflated in a political community where majorities and minorities coexist[54].

The Quebec model of interculturalism calls attention to the fact that, faced with the presence of a conflict, it is preferable to adopt deliberative measures such as mediation, compromise and direct negotiation, affording the involved parties as much initiative and autonomy as possible. This model "values deliberation, mutual understanding and, generally, dialogue as fundamental characteristics of democratic life, in the realm of civil society"[55].

However, it is useful to always bear in mind, as Seyla Benhabib does, that deliberation is accompanied by normative dimensions that cannot be renounced. First is "egalitarian reciprocity", which stipulates that majority groups will not discriminate against civil, political, economic or cultural rights on the basis of membership in a cultural, religious or linguistic minority. Secondly is "voluntary self-ascription", which means that an individual cannot be automatically assigned, on the basis of their birth, to a cultural, religious or linguistic group; they should be allowed, once they reach adulthood, to choose whether or not to continue being a member of that community. Thirdly is "freedom of exit and association", which means one should be able to exit a community without excessive sanctions and should enjoy a flexible right to association, which may require accommodation[56].

In this way, interculturalism believes it is essential to participate in the design of the management of demands that diverse cultural minorities carry out in order, first, to gain respect for their particularities, to assure themselves the right to recognition and, secondarily, to make their own preferences known. Alain-G. Gagnon presents it like this: "Interculturalism

---

54 See Máiz, Ramón, "Nation and Deliberation" in Ramón Máiz and Ferrán Requejo (eds.), *Democracy, Nationalism and Multiculturalism*, London, Routledge, 2005, pp. 58-80.

55 Gagnon, Alain-G. and Raffaele Iacovino, "Interculturalism: Expanding the Boundaries of Citizenship" in Ramón Maiz and Ferrán Requejo (eds.), *Democracy, Nationalism and Multiculturalism*, London, Frank Cass Publishers, Routledge, 2005, p. 32.

56 Benhabib, Seyla, *The Claims of Culture: Equality and Diversity in the Global Era*, Princeton, Princeton University Press, 2002, pp. 19-20.

affords special value to deliberation, to mutual understanding and dialogue, all of which are essential characteristics of democratic life, and help provide Quebec with a participatory citizenry"[57].

Inclusive pluralist republicanism understands participation in a different fashion than liberalism does, which views it mainly as a procedure meant to guarantee individual rights. Interculturalism champions the existence of a common ground that will allow every group to participate in democratic life with dignity and equality. Alain-G. Gagnon's explanation is helpful: "Interculturalism is viewed as a way to encourage every group to deliberate and participate in the public sphere, with the objective of achieving the greatest possible consensus in order to achieve greater social cohesion and the protection of individual rights"[58].

One example of this participation is seen in work performed by the autonomous and independent Commission charged with consulting the citizenry about the practice of reasonable accommodation between the different cultures that coexist in Quebec (Bouchard-Taylor Commission)[59].

Without a doubt, that consultation revealed the importance of creating an active public capable of discovering solutions to its problems on its own and conscious that democratic responses to the challenge of cultural diversity can only be achieved through a "genuine dialogue with the public"[60]. The consultative experience of the Bouchard-Taylor Commission generated a situation where "irreplaceable dialogue" allowed "participants to better articulate their respective positions and, perhaps, lay the foundations for a new language and a new shared identity"[61].

In a previously published study[62], we focused our attention on the consulting process and on citizen participation that came about within

57 Gagnon, "Plaidoyer pour l'interculturalisme", *op. cit.*, pp. 14-15. For a related analysis, see Gagnon and Iacovino, *op. cit.*

58 Gagnon, "Plaidoyer pour l'interculturalisme", *op. cit.*, p. 15.

59 *Décret numéro 95-2007, Concernant la constitution de la Commission de consultation sur les pratiques d'accommodement reliées aux différences culturelles (CCPARDDC)*, Québec, Gouvernement du Québec, 2007.

60 Bouchard, Gérard, and Charles Taylor, *Accommodation and Differences: Seeking Common Ground. Quebecers Speak Out*, Québec, Gouvernement du Québec, 2007, p. 6.

61 Laforest, Guy, "La Comisión Bouchard-Taylor y el lugar de Québec en la trayectoria del Estado Nación moderno", Proceedings from the *III* Congreso Internacional sobre Derechos Humanos: La gestión democrática de la diversidad cultural nacional, 10-13 June 2008, Bilbao, Vitoria-Gasteiz, Servicio Central de Publicaciones del Gobierno Vasco, 2009, p. 83.

62 Sauca, José María and María Isabel Wences, "Participación ciudadana y diversidad cultural: la Comisión Bouchard-Taylor", *Andamios. Revista de investigación social*, nº 10, 2009, pp. 9-37.

the framework of the Bouchard-Taylor Commission study. We analyzed it in the light of the crisis in representative democracy and the literature regarding participative and deliberative democracies, but we did not focus on a discussion of the results and the impact of the final report since that has received ample attention through the years. For the present study, what interests us is to revisit this process as an illustration of the belief, shared by inclusive pluralist republicanism and interculturalism, that involving citizens in the search and adoption of mechanisms and policies of intercultural harmonization is what allows the construction and/or consolidation of a common civic reality fostering understanding between cultures.

It is true that the citizen consultation led by the sociologist Gérard Bouchard and the philosopher Charles Taylor has sparked numerous criticisms. These include poor planning of the hearings, responding to purely political interests, becoming a circus of citizen complaints, propagating – with the help of the media – negative perceptions about the cultural values of "the Other" and leading to the retreat of certain communities. In contrast, I believe it was an exceptional participatory exercise whose lessons for the outside world should not be minimized[63].

Some of the lessons we can draw from this citizen consultation through public debate are the following[64]: in the first place, we have witnessed one of the modalities of the institutionalization of participatory practice in which the inhabitants of this nation, individually or through their associations, had an equal opportunity to make their opinions known, as well as diverse and ample occasions to express themselves. The opinions of citizens were heard in this exercise, and many of those citizens heard other people in turn. This means that members of this culturally diverse community have a voice when it comes to trying to come to an agreement about how to integrate difference in a civic fashion. In this way, we not only have participating actors, but also an institutional context that has designed consultative instruments and also creates some of the resources necessary for the political production of preferences, including attention to other people's positions, learning about other people's cultural

63 Some public officials, however, believe we cannot affirm that there was a "true debate about interculturalism in the public sphere"; they note that criticisms were expressed and concerns shared but that this did not lead to true deliberation (Rocher and Labelle, *op. cit.*).

64 I address some of these questions in greater detail in Wences, Isabel, "Cuatro lecciones de la Comisión Bouchard-Taylor: Acomodos razonables, pluralismo integrador, laicidad abierta y participación ciudadana" in Pedro Chaves and Carlos Prieto (eds.), *Forma Estado, Plurinacionalidad y Transiciones Constituyentes*, Madrid, Traficante de sueños, 2012, pp. 371-411.

values and more about our own preferences[65]. For republicanism, it is essential to design institutions that assure the independence of citizens and encourage public discussion of the common good. Arguing about the common good is perceived as a way to contribute to self-government and to afford citizens a voice regarding the way they want to organize community life[66].

In the second place, even when it is difficult to guarantee that the opinions that were shared were taken into account in political agreements, the quality of democracy is strengthened with the contribution of direct and local knowledge of problems because it allows us to obtain more and better information and, consequently, to have more information when it comes time to make a decision.

In the third place, the whole consulting process has revealed a society that has transitioned from merely tolerating difference to a society that opens doors to recognition. Tolerance "of the different ways of conceiving of oneself as a person leads to mutual recognition"[67].

In fourth and last place, it is important to note that norms and decisions must be legitimized in a democratic system. Any process of legitimation requires deliberation and debate; it is, therefore, necessary that there be open channels for citizens to express their opinions. The hearings carried out in Quebec during the fall of 2007 to know what citizens think about how to harmonize cultural differences between everyone who lives in this common space are also particularly relevant for understanding the model of interculturalism, as well as the open secularism that the presidents of the Commission propose in their final report. This is important since, on the one hand, it is a proposal that attempts to help improve the political and social management of cultural diversity and legitimize the potential public policies that come from the Bouchard-Taylor Commission recommendations. On the other, it is since it is a way for citizens to understand and accept the reasons for interculturalism and for the value of recognizing difference and its reflection in the creation of reasonable accommodations. And finally, it is important because it offers new elements that can help bring out the theoretical configuration of both interculturalism and a determined model of the State and society.

---

65 Máiz, Ramón, "Deliberación e inclusión en la democracia republicana", *Revista española de investigaciones sociológicas*, nº 113, 2006, pp. 11-49.

66 Gargarella, Roberto, "El carácter igualitario del republicanismo", *Isegoría*, nº 33, 2005, pp. 175-189.

67 Seymour, Michel, *De la tolérance à la reconnaissance. Une théorie libérale des droits collectifs* Montréal, Boréal, 2008, p. 21.

Final Reflections

If we want to continue viewing current Western societies as organic, objective wholes that are culturally homogeneous, heirs to a historical process of development and distanced from transformative processes, then internal diversity and the plurality of interpretations could simply be set aside. This would do nothing but exacerbate an uncritical discourse that is expressed in terms of ours versus theirs and that promotes the implementation of socializing guidelines established in the passive acceptance of tradition. The belief that minorities put the supposed purity of majority culture at risk leads us to a vision of the culture that is not only conservative, but isolationist and closed to any aspiration of free participation of everyone in the public sphere.

We were recently afforded the opportunity to observe a dialogue between inclusive pluralist republicanism, which is critical of monism and assimilationism, and an interculturalism that recognizes diversity and reciprocal integration and is critical of cultural relativism and fragmentation. This dialogue does not represent a conservative, communitarian model; it is an attempt to find ways of articulating the demands for recognition as well as political dimensions that emphasize non-dependence, equality, pluralism, participatory citizenry and the deliberative ideal. This requires, on the one hand, adopting an open attitude toward the demands of distinct identities and being able to distinguish between fundamental and trivial cultural features, accepting as a starting point the belief that there is no room for oppressive or humiliating practices. On the other hand, it means being inclusive, which signifies reaching consensus about the changes and transformations that accompany diversity for both majority as well as minority groups, for new arrivals as well as for members of the host society. Finally, it requires that the authorities establish a manner of guaranteeing that everyone, whether part of a minority or majority group, has access to full participation in the public sphere. If interculturalism and republicanism agree on all that, the doors for dialogue remain open.

N° 14 – Victor ARMONY y Stéphanie ROUSSEAU (eds.), *Diversidad cultural, desigualdades y democratización en América Latina*, 281 p., 2012

N° 15 – Chantal MAILLÉ, Greg M. NIELSEN & Daniel SALÉE (eds.), *Revealing Democracy. Secularism and Religion in Liberal Democratic States*, 176 p., 2013

N° 16 – Eduardo J. RUIZ-VIEYTEZ, *United in Diversity? On Cultural Diversity, Democracy and Human Rights,* 131 p., 2014

N° 17 – Bernard GAGNON et Jackie F. STEELE (dir.), *Concilier démocratie et diversité. Essais de théorie politique*, 222 p., 2014

N° 18 – Alain-G. GAGNON & José María SAUCA (eds.), *Negotiating Diversity. Identity, Pluralism and Democracy,* 260 p. 2014

Series Titles

N° 1 – François Charbonneau et Martin Nadeau (dir.), *L'histoire à l'épreuve de la diversité culturelle*, 173 p., 2008

N°.2 – Hugo Cyr, *Canadian Federalism and Treaty Powers. Organic Constitutionalism at Work*, 305 p., 2009

N°.3 – Ricard Zapata-Barrero (ed.), *Immigration and Self-government of Minority Nations*, 177 p., 2009

N° 4 – Ferran Requejo, *Fédéralisme multinational et pluralisme de valeurs. Le cas espagnol*, 199 p., 2009

N° 5 – Charles Gaucher et Stéphane Vibert, *Les Sourds : aux origines d'une identité plurielle*, 228 p., 2010

N° 6 – Christophe Parent, *Le concept d'État fédéral multinational. Essai sur l'union des peuples*, 495 p., 2011

N° 7 – Daniel Innerarity, *The Transformation of Politics. Governing in the Age of Complex Societies*, 154 p., 2010

N° 8 – Jacques Beauchemin (dir.), *Mémoire et démocratie en occident. Concurrence des mémoires ou concurrence victimaire*, 136 p., 2011

N° 9 – Alain-G. Gagnon et Ferran Requejo (dir.), *Nations en quête de reconnaissance. Regards croisés Québec-Catalogne*, 241 p., 2011

N° 10 – Michel Seymour et Guy Laforest (dir.), *Le fédéralisme multinational. Un modèle viable ?*, 343 p., 2011

N° 11 – Ramón Máiz, *The Inner Frontier*, 223 p., 2012

N° 12 – Louis-Philippe Lampron, *La hiérarchie des droits. Convictions religieuses et droits fondamentaux au Canada*, 396 p., 2012

N° 13 – Min Reuchamps, *L'avenir du fédéralisme en Belgique et au Canada. Quand les citoyens en parlent*, 264 p., 2011

Diversitas

The aim of this series is to study diversity by privileging an interdisciplinary approach, through political, legal, cultural and social frameworks. The proposed method of inquiry will be to appeal, at once, to the fields of political philosophy, law, political science, history and sociology. In a period characterized by the increasing diversity of contemporary societies, the authors published in this series will explore avenues for the accommodation and management of pluralism and identity. Such studies will not be limited to assessments of federal states, but will include states that are on the path to federalization as well as non-federal states. Serious efforts will be undertaken to enrich our comprehension of so-called 'nations without states', most notably Catalonia, Scotland, Flanders and Quebec. A point of emphasis will also be placed on extracting lessons from experiences with civil law relative to those cases marked by the common law tradition. Monist and competing models will be compared in order to assess the relative capacity of each model to provide responses to the question of political instability, while pursuing the quest for justice in minority societies. The series also addresses the place of cities in the management of diversity, as well as the question of migration more generally and the issue of communities characterized by overlapping and hybrid identities. A profound sensitivity to historical narratives is also expected to enrich the proposed scientific approach. Finally, the works published in this series will reveal a common aspiration to advance social and political debates without privileging any particular school of thought.

Series editor: Alain-G. Gagnon, Canada Research Chair in Quebec and Canadian Studies (CRÉQC) and Director of the *Centre de recherche interdisciplinaire sur la diversité et la démocratie* (CRIDAQ).